M000105409

SAY GOODBYE TO AMERICA

This book is dedicated to my sister, Jean

Say GOODBYE to America

The Sensational and Untold Story behind the Assassination of John F. Kennedy

Matthew Smith

EDINBURGH AND LONDON

First published in Great Britain in 2001 by
MAINSTREAM PUBLISHING COMPANY (EDINBURGH) LTD
7 Albany Street
Edinburgh EH1 3UG

ISBN 1 84018 502 3

A catalogue record for this book is available from the British Library

Typeset in Bembo and Gill
Printed and bound in Great Britain by
Butler & Tanner Ltd, Frome and London

Contents

Foreword

by Jim Marrs

Author of *Crossfire* (source for Oliver Stone's *JFK*), *Alien Agenda* and *Rule By Secrecy*.

ONE THING IS CERTAIN: President John F. Kennedy was shot to death on the streets of Dallas, Texas, on 22 November 1963.

Another thing is certain: America has never been the same since that fateful day.

Prior to the Kennedy assassination, the two biggest scandals in the twentieth century were Teapot Dome and the CIA's use of student organisations as cover for its espionage activities. Today, as I see it, with superpower America continuing to bomb small third-world nations, school children slaughtering each other and the government-ordained murders at Ruby Ridge and Waco, these past scandals appear tame by comparison.

In 1996, then Vice-President Al Gore oversaw the largest sale of public land in US history, much of which went as drilling rights to Occidental Petroleum, a company which had long provided financial benefits to the Gore family. This was the same basic scenario as the Teapot Dome scandal in which a government official leased public land to oil companies in exchange for money. Yet, unlike the muckraking press of the 1920s, today's corporate-owned news media failed to take much notice, much less exception, to this cosy business deal. No scandal here, just business as usual.

And as for the CIA, the use of foreign exchange students as spies pales beside the ongoing well-documented charge that the Company continues to import hard drugs into the United States to fund covert operations, much of it coming through Mena, Arkansas, the home state of Bill Clinton.

The 2000 national elections provided yet another example of America's decline. In almost any other country in the world, if a national leader was named by a Supreme Court made up primarily of that candidate's political party following an obviously skewed election process involving a state controlled by the winning candidate's brother, there would have been widespread demonstrations and much hand-wringing by the national media. But not in Corporate America, not in the Land of the Free and the Home of the Brave, not in a nation where just about three major corporations control the bulk of the mass communications media, where all but two of the major publishers are controlled by a German corporation.

How did the United States, with its exemplary Constitution and Bill of Rights, arrive in such a state of meek submissiveness? When did this greatest, most prosperous modern state become a nation of wage slaves, many of whom must suffer the humiliation of urinating in a bottle to maintain their job security? When did the free and self-reliant Americans who built the Arsenal of Democracy become a population of victims competing with each other for government subsidies and handouts? No one argues that the degradation of America began with the assassination of President Kennedy, for, not only was a man slain that day in Dallas, so too the hopes and aspirations of millions of Americans.

The millions who voted for JFK in hope of a better world were disenfranchised in a single moment by an assassin's bullet. And today, nearly half a century after the act, it is still unacknowledged exactly who shot Kennedy or what their motivation might have been. But British author Matthew Smith is on their trail. In past work Mr Smith has laid to rest the discredited 'Lone Assassin' theory of the assassination and even tied the deed to other American tragedies such as the assassination of Robert Kennedy and the political hijacking of Edward Kennedy.

In his latest book, Mr Smith provides compelling evidence for the innocence of the accused assassin, Lee Harvey Oswald, as well as disturbing new evidence for government complicity in the crime. He also delves into the power behind the American throne, the corporations and banking institutions that determine policies then implemented by subservient government bureaucrats.

He presents the names of the men surrounding the assassination and its aftermath, men tied to the secret societies that covertly set American national and international policy. It is now clear John F. Kennedy was an obstructionist to these policies of globalism and expansionism. President Kennedy opposed the

New World Order, as described by former President George H.W. Bush. He took on Big Oil, Big Steel, Big Banking, the Mafia, the military and the CIA. He took steps to bring America into a new era of peace and prosperity for all citizens.

And he died young.

Read on as Matthew Smith lucidly describes the background, the shooting and the cover-up which opened a bleeding sore in the American body politic. He also incorporates details of the many new developments into the live investigation into the ongoing Crime of the Century, which has caused so many of our people – and in the world – to say goodbye to the America they knew.

Jim Marrs
Texas, USA
April 2001

Introduction

THIS IS A BOOK ABOUT PEOPLE. It is about some who have been robbed of their most precious possession, life, and others who have dictated that those lives should be taken. It is about politics, for that is about life and living, and, in this case, the manipulation of government. It is about power and it is also about what drives people to murder, about the rich getting richer and who cares about the rest.

When John F. Kennedy was gunned down in Dallas in 1963 a groan might have been heard all around the world, for this was more than one man dying. He did not die of old age or of disease: he was not the victim of an accident, either. He died because a group of people sat together and planned that he should die in order that they might reap benefits from his removal from the Presidency of the United States. The people of America know this and privately, no doubt, members of the government know it also. Officially, however, the United States government stubbornly clings to the results of the long-since discredited Warren Commission, set up to investigate why and by whom President Kennedy was killed. The government of the United States does not, it appears, at any price, wish the truth of the Kennedy assassination to be discovered and acknowledged.

In the last few years they have released a very large volume of 'relevant' documents, most of which contribute nothing to our understanding of what happened in Elm Street on 22 November 1963. Those which do provide little which is of value, though these have been seized upon and the contents in total take us that bit further. This, of course, is paying lip service to the idea of identifying the murderers and their motives. It is the private researcher who propels the investigation and obtains the gains which are to be made from this messy and protracted investigation. And gains have been made. The last ten years have seen a great deal happening which takes the investigation further and contributes to our understanding. But the action so far having come from the grass-roots, the individual, it is patently obvious that the time has now arrived when the government should, at last, be taking the initiative to provide the truth for history, and justice, not only for John Fitzgerald Kennedy and those many others who have lost their lives in this bloody affair, but for the people of the United States and of the world.

The history of the United States and, indeed, the world was changed when Kennedy was killed. For the better, the conspirators would brazenly say. Better for whom? would be the response from the people. We have been hijacked, railroaded, robbed. There are many expressions which would fit what has happened here. The will of the people has been thwarted. The country is being run by those with the muscle to get their way by force. A hidden government, a government born of secrecy, of conspiracy.

I have written before on this subject and I am able to say that there is nothing of any consequence to change in my past books. There is, however, a substantial volume of new material to be added, and this I present in the following pages. I am mindful of the fact that there are many who require the background to the assassination to be included so that they may appreciate the advancements made in the investigation. It is my intention that if this is the first book the reader has obtained on this subject he or she will find it a satisfying, rewarding read and, hopefully, an inspiration to read further. Those who have followed the investigation via other literature and are abreast of the subject will find much here to take them a whole stage further in their understanding of what happened, why, how and by whom.

Having read the previous paragraph the reader will appreciate the desirability of including photographs and copies of documents which have been seen before. There are those which are different, however, and some which are new. They are all intended to illustrate the aspects in hand.

Finally, I am reassured that my many friends in the United States will not regard my forthrightness in this book as meddling in their affairs. They are mature enough to know that the murder of President Kennedy was neither a local nor a national crime. It was a crime of universal proportions. They also know of my desire to make whatever contribution I can to its solution.

Matthew Smith
Sheffield

Acknowledgements

CHAPTER ELEVEN DESCRIBES the work carried out over a period of four years by Joachim Markus, with the backing and facilities of his company, Vidit, and myself. We could not have achieved what we did without the help of a great many people. I was the one who was deemed to be the greatest beneficiary since I had the task of providing the carefully selected data for the insatiable computer. I turned to my many friends and contacts and they did not fail me. I particularly want to thank Colin McSween who, in Canada, has become the most knowledgeable person I know on the Lincoln automobile used by President Kennedy. After several attempts at providing the required accuracy, it was only when I obtained data from Colin that Joachim was completely satisfied.

Canover Hunt at the Sixth Floor Center at Dallas provided data and pointed me towards Jeff Flasch, a member of Oliver Stone's *JFK* team, when I was searching for accuracy in 'reconstructing' the Dealey Plaza as it was on 22 November 1963. I am grateful for Jeff's advice and assistance. R.B. Cutler sent me a map, the basics of which were useful, and Dr Walt Brown contributed two excellent prints of autopsy photographs. Dr Charles Crenshaw was kind enough to allow me to consult him on an important issue and his advice was appreciated. And the consistent accuracy of our work was underpinned by the work of Landmark Surveys, Dallas, who made a survey of the Dealey Plaza to Joachim's detailed instructions. Our thanks to them.

I have appreciated the ongoing help of Debra Conway and Tom Jones of *Lancer* who have seen that the most recent pertinent documents have been available to me, and the cooperation of National Archives at Washington and

Maryland has earned my appreciation, also. I particularly appreciated the fact that when they provided me with copies of the large volume of documents passed by President Boris Yeltsin to President Bill Clinton in 1999 they also sent translations. (Phew.)

Jim Marrs has been a good friend and has advised me and contributed valuable information. I am, of course, also indebted to him for writing a foreword to this book.

I feel I should particularly express my appreciation to Hank Gordon for selecting me to hear his 'Cuban pilot' evidence after thirty years of silence, and Mary Ferrell and Wayne January for helping me to authenticate this vital new evidence. My thanks also go to Donald Thomas, who conducted the new and updated analysis of the dictabelt recordings published while this book was in preparation, and who was kind enough to discuss certain aspects of his study with me.

I do not overlook my friends at home who willingly support me with their help. Ian Griggs and Steve Temich have earned my particular thanks and appreciation.

Finally, my warmest appreciation must go, as always, to my wife, Margaret, my mainstay, Stephen for proofreading with me, and to the other members of my family for their unfailing support in my work.

CHAPTER ONE

The Riddle of a Lifetime

IN THE YEARS WHICH HAVE ELAPSED since President John F. Kennedy was murdered on Elm Street at the Dealey Plaza in Dallas, our ideas about why and how he was killed have greatly changed. Notions about the Soviets taking revenge for Kennedy's dominance at the sweaty time of the Cuban Missile Crisis have generally disappeared and, for the most part, accusations relating to Fidel Castro having him killed in retaliation for the attempts made on his life by the CIA have also gone. The Mafia were front-runners as the President's killers to some, in view of the relentless – and very successful – campaign waged against them by JFK's Attorney General brother, Robert Kennedy, and also because President Kennedy had not used force to remove Castro and allow them to recover their lucrative gambling interests in Havana. But there is so much which does not fit this scenario that few serious researchers would now give it any credence.

Lesser speculations involving such flights of fancy as Bill Greer, the President's respected driver, turning round and shooting him have cut about as much ice as the tale which once circulated that JFK had survived and was living a cabbage-like existence in Canada. The more recent idea that a Secret Service man shot the President by accident has, thankfully, made little gain and, along with a number of other untenable conclusions, has been consigned by most to that small mountain of outworn conspiracy theories.

The fact remains, however, that the President of the United States was ruthlessly killed on his campaigning visit to Dallas, Texas, and the authorities have done relatively little to identify those responsible, let alone bring them to justice. The Warren Commission served only the purpose of going through the motions and muddying the waters. The fantastic notion that Lee Harvey Oswald was a nutcase who shot and killed the President without any aid whatever has also been consigned by most to the aforementioned small mountain, along with the idea that Jack Ruby was yet another nutcase who just happened to shoot and kill Oswald. What I postulated on Oswald in my first book on the assassination of President Kennedy, *JFK: The Second Plot*, has led to the attribution by an important British newspaper that I was the first to clear Oswald of any knowing participation in the murder of the President, and I am more than ever convinced of this.

This still leaves us with the tormenting question, however, who did kill President Kennedy and why? Kennedy, as I describe in more detail further on in this book, worked for the best interests of ordinary people, for the poor, and for the freedom and betterment of the negro population also. Among the many endeavours crammed into such a short space of time, he worked also for improvement in living standards for the Latin American countries, he advanced the cause of peace in the world, he signed the first international nuclear test ban treaty, and resolved the Cuban Missile Crisis without sending in the troops and bombers, as those around him advised him to do. He also made decisions about American involvement in Vietnam, which was in its early stages and undeveloped during his Presidency, showing his hand by recalling personnel from that country and planning to make further withdrawals with, it appeared, the intention of terminating altogether the policy which had taken a US presence there.

But the question remains, who killed this young man who displayed his fighting spirit, not by bombs and bullets, but by battling to make the United States a better place in which to live for all Americans, whilst having due regard to the needs of those in other lands? He courageously took on the task of breathing new life into the government of his great country and was succeeding in changing its direction.

Having dismissed so many of the conspiracy theories, we are left asking which was the real one, the one lost in the rush to blame the Communists or the others we mentioned above? Which was the plot which succeeded in removing the crusading Kennedy from the Presidency, changing the history of America and, indeed, the world? The immediate consequence of this supreme folly was a so-called investigation which has never satisfied those throughout the world who greatly respected President Kennedy, let alone the vast majority of the American people themselves. It appears the Warren Report only succeeded in undermining the confidence of the people in politicians and inspiring a deep suspicion of government.

The more recent attempt on the part of the American government to investigate the assassination – the House Select Committee on Assassinations which reported in 1979 – worked largely to shore up the discredited Warren Report, though in its dying days it found itself obliged to accept compelling evidence that a conspiracy had taken place. It is true it carried out some useful work but did little to restore the confidence of the people. Most of the progress obtained in investigating the assassination has been through the efforts of private individuals who, in spite of the government, have made considerable gains in unravelling the facts surrounding the murder of the President. Frustratingly, however, much time has had to be spent on penetrating the cover-up about what really happened and trying to see through the murky waters.

What was the sequence of events which led to President Kennedy's death? What did the cover-up do and how did it do it? How have the researchers stripped all of this down and what have they discovered? What is it that gives us a new perspective on the perplexing riddle of the murder of President Kennedy? It becomes necessary to carefully examine all of these things, which we do in the following chapters, before returning to the question of why President Kennedy was killed, and who was behind the conspiracy to murder him!

CHAPTER TWO

A Busy Day in Dallas

THURSDAY, 21 NOVEMBER 1963, was a busy day in Dallas. Tomorrow the President of the United States was paying a visit as part of his tour of Texas, and some Dallas citizens were excited because they belonged to the enthusiastic minority of local residents who supported John F. Kennedy. Preparations were made and the details of the motorcade route were examined so that the best location could be worked out for seeing the President and his wife Jackie. The children were making banners, 'Hoorah for JFK' and 'We Love Jack'. Not all were enthusiastic, however. Some who had decided to find a place on the motorcade route were merely curious, and looked forward simply to seeing the President. There were those, also, who were hostile to the President and some of these made banners, too, carrying messages such as, 'Help Kennedy Stamp Out Democracy' and 'Yankee Go Home'. The opposition would be well represented. Others, though, had no interest at all in what would happen tomorrow, for Kennedy was not a popular man here.

A sinister few were preoccupied in a different way: they looked forward to seeing the President in the cross-hairs of their rifle sights as they finally put into action a well-ordered, well-rehearsed, military-type plan to assassinate the President of the United States. They were not the conspirators: they were the tools of the conspirators, expert marksmen, ruthless killers, supported by a team of communications and security people brought to Dallas for this one purpose only: to rid the country of the 'young upstart' who had sneaked into the Presidency by a tiny margin at the last election and was now making huge gains in popularity. A dreadful mistake, they reasoned: the Presidency would have been safely in Richard Nixon's hands save for the unbelievable few who had wrenched it away in favour of the son of millionaire Joe Kennedy, hated among businessmen and politicians. And feared, too.

The conspirators themselves would no doubt be communicating with one another, running over the plans for the next day, some, perhaps, with the priority of making sure nothing had been left to chance, others, perhaps, with the priority of making sure that there was no way a trail could be laid which would lead back to them. Conspirators should not be confused with brave people.

Jack Kennedy had increasing support among the people of the country and it seemed on the cards that he was set to occupy the White House for a second term. There was no room for complacency, however, and he was not neglecting his chances in the south, particularly in Texas, where the party was being rent asunder by internal warring, primarily between those two principals, Governor John Connally and Senator Ralph Yarborough. Kennedy judged it time to sort out the problems between the two, and it was largely for this reason he planned a visit to the state.

Of all the places designated to receive a visit, Kennedy had been warned by a number of people not to go to Dallas. One of these was Billy Graham, the evangelist, and another Adlai Stevenson, the US Representative to the United Nations. Closer to the scene of things, National Committeeman Byron Skelton of Temple, Texas, was another who expressed his misgivings about the visit in conversation with the President's brother, Robert. And the feeling of apprehension was not confined to a wary few, it seems. A presidential assistant, Fred Holborn, sensed impending trouble and phoned London to his friend, Henry Brandon of the *Sunday Times*, telling him to get out to Texas. But Kennedy, anxious to stake a claim to the 25 electoral votes Texas held, was determined to undertake the major tour, and Dallas was not to be excluded.

By Thursday, 21 November, the President had successful visits to San Antonio and Houston behind him, and he was taking the opportunity for a little gentle knocking of heads together in his dealings with Connally and Yarborough. All was going well as he settled into the Hotel Texas in Fort Worth, where he would deliver a breakfast address next morning before going on to Dallas. Meanwhile, however, circulating in Dallas that Thursday was a cheap handbill designed in the manner of a police 'wanted' poster. 'WANTED FOR TREASON' it announced, displaying front and side view photographs of the President's face, and listing examples of his 'treachery'. The anti-Kennedy right wing was pulling no punches.

In Dallas that night a party was being thrown by Clint Murchison. Exactly why oil-baron Murchison should choose this particular night for a celebration is not known, but there has been a great deal of speculation about the event. The guest list was impressive. John Tower was there and H.L. Hunt, the oil billionaire, and so was Chase-Manhattan Bank's John McCloy (who would later become a Warren Commissioner). Richard Nixon, on business in Dallas that day, was there, and so was FBI boss, J. Edgar Hoover, I am told. Madeleine Brown, who was Lyndon B. Johnson's mistress, assures me that Johnson travelled from Houston and she saw him at the party. She told me a small group, including Nixon, Hoover and Johnson, went off for a private meeting, and that Johnson and she left when the meeting ended.

Madeleine Brown told me that Johnson, in an unguarded remark made in a telephone call to her next morning, betrayed, clearly, that he knew what was going to happen when the President reached Dallas. '*Those damned Kennedys will not be poking fun at me after today*,' he said. And from the way he had behaved the night before, she is convinced that he knew when he left the meeting at the Murchison party. If that is true it begs the question who also knew? And who told them? The most likely candidate was J. Edgar Hoover, who, by this time, had received a clear warning[1] that there was a plan to kill the President. (See Figure 1.) This warning even gave him the date and the city: 22 November, Dallas. But it was well known that Hoover was no friend of Jack Kennedy, who was seeking to oust him from his post as head of the FBI.

But if this is true, and there is strong evidence it is so, there is here an extraordinary situation in which two future Presidents together with the head of the federal internal security organisation were guilty of treason.

---

[1] Ex-FBI man, William S. Walter, on duty as night clerk at New Orleans office of the FBI received a telex which began: THREAT TO ASSASSINATE PRESIDENT KENNEDY IN DALLAS TEXAS NOVEMBER 22 DASH TWENTY THREE NINETEEN SIXTY THREE . . . (Full story page 222) The telex was from FBI Director J Edgar Hoover. The date of the telex was 17 November 1963, five days before the assassination, but no action was taken by anyone.

FIGURE 1

URGENT 1:45 AM EST 11-17-63 HLP 1PAGE

TO ALL SACS

FROM DIRECTOR

THREAT TO ASSISINATE PRESIDENT KENNEDY IN DALLAS TEXAS NOVEMBER TWENTYTWO DASH TWENTYTHREE NINETEEN SIXTYTHREE. MISC INFORMATION CONCERNING.

INFO HAS BEEN RECEIVED BY THE BUREAU
BUREAU HAS XXXXXXXXXXXXXXXXXXXXX DETERMINED THAT A MILITANT REVOLUTIONARY GROUP MAY ATTEMPT TO ASSINATED PRESIDENT KENNEDY ON HIS PROPOSED TRIP TO DALLAS TEXAS XXXXXXXXXX XXXXXXXXX NOVEMBER TWENTYTWO DASH TWENTYTHREE NINETEEN SICTYTHREE.

ALL RECEIVING OFFICE SHOULS IMMIDIATELY CONTACT ALL CI'S; PCIS LOGICAL RACIAL AND HATE GROPUP INFORMANTS AND DETERMINE IF ANY BASIS FOR THREAT. BHRGEU SHOULS BE KEPT ADVISED OF ALL DEVELOPEMENTS BY TELETYPE .

SUBMIT FD THREE ZERO TWOS AND LHM

OTHER HOFFICE HAVE BEEN ADVISED

END AND ACK PLS

MO....
DL.....

NO.....

KT TI TU CLR..@

This is a copy of a telex made by FBIman, William S. Walter. He was on duty as night clerk at the New Orleans office of the FBI when the telex was received. The date of the message was 17 November 1963, five days before the assassination, but no action was taken by Hoover or anyone else.

CHAPTER THREE

Mayhem

THE MORNING OF FRIDAY, 22 NOVEMBER, was inclined to be wet, though the President declined a raincoat when standing up on the back of a truck to speak to the crowd who had defied the rain to hear him.

There had been no problems the evening before or during the night, so it might have been somewhat surprising that the President had, that morning, passed the comment as though with some sixth sense, 'You know, last night would have been a hell of a night to assassinate a president.' What he did not know was that nine of the White House detail, including four agents whose job it was to protect the President, had been out carousing the previous evening, and the last of the group had not got back to the hotel until 5 a.m. Periodically they were joined by three agents who were assigned the night shift and who should have been guarding the President's door. Also, their boss, the man in charge of security arrangements, duty officer General Godfrey McHugh, was as lax as his men. He had left the hotel to pay a visit to friends around midnight. The President, without knowing it, got it exactly right. He was seriously exposed to the danger of assassination on the night of Thursday, 21 November. As he expressed it himself, 'last night would have been a hell of a night to have assassinated a president'.

The main speech he was to make in Fort Worth was an after-breakfast speech in the hotel's Grand Ballroom. He delighted his audience with his easy, informal style. His now famous words in what was to be his last speech beguiled those present. 'A few years ago in Paris I introduced myself by saying that I was the man who accompanied Mrs Kennedy to Paris . . . (laughter) I'm getting something of that same sensation as I travel around Texas. (More laughter, pause.)

FIGURE 2

WELCOME MR. KENNEDY

TO DALLAS...

... A CITY so disgraced by a recent Liberal smear attempt that its citizens have just elected two more Conservative Americans to public office.

... A CITY that is an economic "boom town," not because of Federal handouts, but through conservative economic and business practices.

... A CITY that will continue to grow and prosper despite efforts by you and your administration to penalize it for its non-conformity to "New Frontierism."

... A CITY that rejected your philosophy and policies in 1960 and will do so again in 1964—even more emphatically than before.

MR. KENNEDY, despite contentions on the part of your administration, the State Department, the Mayor of Dallas, the Dallas City Council, and members of your party, we free-thinking and America-thinking citizens of Dallas still have, through a Constitution largely ignored by you, the right to address our grievances, to question you, to disagree with you, and to criticize you.

In asserting this constitutional right, we wish to ask you publicly the following questions—indeed, questions of paramount importance and interest to all free peoples everywhere—which we trust you will answer... in public, without sophistry. These questions are:

WHY is Latin America turning either anti-American or Communistic, or both, despite increased U. S. foreign aid, State Department policy, and your own Ivy-Tower pronouncements?

WHY do you say we have built a "wall of freedom" around Cuba when there is no freedom in Cuba today? Because of your policy, thousands of Cubans have been imprisoned, are starving and being persecuted—with thousands already murdered and thousands more awaiting execution and, in addition, the entire population of almost 7,000,000 Cubans are living in slavery.

WHY have you approved the sale of wheat and corn to our enemies when you know the Communist soldiers "travel on their stomachs" just as ours do? Communist soldiers are daily wounding and/or killing American soldiers in South Viet Nam.

WHY did you host, salute and entertain Tito — Moscow's Trojan Horse — just a short time after our sworn enemy, Khrushchev, embraced the Yugoslav dictator as a great hero and leader of Communism?

WHY have you urged greater aid, comfort, recognition, and understanding for Yugoslavia, Poland, Hungary, and other Communist countries, while turning your back on the pleas of Hungarian, East German, Cuban and other anti-Communist freedom fighters?

WHY did Cambodia kick the U.S. out of its country after we poured nearly 400 Million Dollars of aid into its ultra-leftist government?

WHY has Gus Hall, head of the U.S. Communist Party praised almost every one of your policies and announced that the party will endorse and support your re-election in 1964?

WHY have you banned the showing at U.S. military bases of the film "Operation Abolition"—the movie by the House Committee on Un-American Activities exposing Communism in America?

WHY have you ordered or permitted your brother Bobby, the Attorney General, to go soft on Communists, fellow-travelers, and ultra-leftists in America, while permitting him to persecute loyal Americans who criticize you, your administration, and your leadership?

WHY are you in favor of the U.S. continuing to give economic aid to Argentina, in spite of that fact that Argentina has just seized almost 400 Million Dollars of American private property?

WHY has the Foreign Policy of the United States degenerated to the point that the C.I.A. is arranging coups and having staunch Anti-Communist Allies of the U.S. bloodily exterminated.

WHY have you scrapped the Monroe Doctrine in favor of the "Spirit of Moscow"?

MR. KENNEDY, as citizens of these United States of America, we DEMAND answers to these questions, and we want them NOW.

THE AMERICAN FACT-FINDING COMMITTEE

"An unaffiliated and non-partisan group of citizens who wish truth"

BERNARD WEISSMAN,
Chairman

P.O. Box 1792 — Dallas 21, Texas

A full page 'advertisement' in the *Dallas Morning News* that appeared on the morning of the President's visit. It was full of anti-Kennedy propaganda. (Courtesy National Archives)

Nobody wonders what Lyndon and I wear . . .' His audience roared with delight, and continued to hang on the words which the President hoped would win for him a part of Texas at the next election.

But then it was on to a luncheon engagement at the Trade Mart at Dallas. Dallas was an easy car drive from Fort Worth but it had been considered best to fly the short distance in order to obtain the benefit of an official reception at Love Field airport. The reception was outwardly cordial, with Governor Connally breaking protocol to greet the representatives of Dallas ahead of the President. Vice-President Johnson officiated once more in the welcoming party as he was designated to do at every city the President visited on this tour, Texas being his home state.

The motorcade began to assemble. By now Kennedy realised his gentle knocking of heads together was having no effect at all on Connally and Yarborough. If anything, the war was fiercer than ever. Senator Yarborough, who saw Lyndon Johnson as allied to Governor Connally, since Connally had once been his protégé, had refused to sit next to the Vice-President in a car at Fort Worth. The President had sent word to him then that he sat next to Johnson or else he walked. Here in Dallas the Senator was making as though to find a different car in defiance of the President when spotted by a Kennedy aide who hustled him into the Vice-President's car. In spite of this, Kennedy was not without sympathy for Yarborough, as Connally was losing no opportunity to demonstrate hostility to the Senator. In the arrangements for the tour the Governor downgraded Yarborough whenever he could, relegating him to the lowest designation possible. In the case of the dinner planned for Austin that night, in a snub to the Senator his wife had not been invited, and as for the reception planned for afterwards in the Governor's mansion, Yarborough himself had not been invited. 'I've had many telephone calls and letters from friends because Mrs Yarborough and I were not invited to the mansion,' the Senator had told reporter Jim Matthias. When Matthias tactlessly replied with the question, 'How does it feel to be slapped in the face?' the needled Yarborough had retorted, 'Well, I'm not surprised. Governor Connally is so terribly uneducated governmentally, how could you expect anything else?' And so the war between the two senior politicians had moved into the public domain. The President had his hands full with those who should have provided the greatest support for him in his bid to win the hearts – and the votes – of Texans. But for now it sufficed that Yarborough was sitting next to Johnson as the cars prepared for the drive to the luncheon venue.

The motorcade made its way through the streets of Dallas. The Kennedy supporters, although in the minority, were out in remarkable strength. But so were the merely curious and so, indeed, were the hostile. 'YOUR A TRAITER' (sic) proclaimed one poster, and there were others, also. Nor were the posters the only evidence of the hostility to Kennedy in Dallas. The *Dallas Morning News*

FIGURE 3

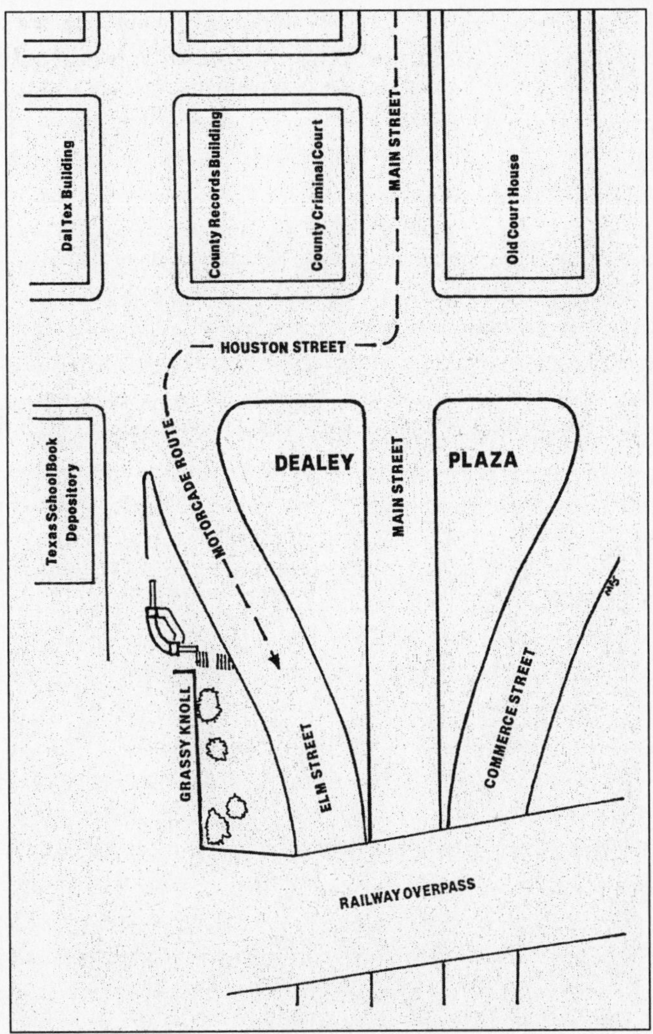

The Dealey Plaza. A right turn to Houston and an acute left to Elm slowed the motorcade exactly where the ambush took place.

had carried a full page 'advertisement' filled with anti-Kennedy propaganda paid for by Dallas businessmen. (See Figure 2.) The city was certainly living up to its reputation as the 'Southwest Hate Capital of Dixie'.

When the motorcade turned into Main Street, the President was but a few minutes from his destination. Main Street ran straight down to an underpass, below which three roads, Main Street, Commerce Street, and Elm Street, converged to pass below the rail tracks in what was called the Dealey Plaza. A right turn from Main would have led to the Stemmons Freeway and quickly to the glistening new Trade Mart. But the route was changed to include a right turn from Main to Houston Street, followed by an acute left turn on to Elm Street. It was on Elm Street that the shooting broke out.

The number of bullets fired has been the subject of argument ever since the day it all happened. Some said three shots, some four, some said as many as six. The Warren Commission, the official investigative body set up by President Lyndon B. Johnson, claimed three shots only had been fired. Interestingly, the FBI at first accounted for four shots, though the Bureau quickly revised this lest they scupper the Warren Commission, since the latter's entire findings were based on the claim that only three shots had been fired.

The shooting lasted for about six seconds at the point where Kennedy's limousine had reached a position consistent with a classic ambush location. The presidential car then abandoned the sedate pace it had adopted for the motorcade and raced off to the nearest hospital, where a team of doctors and nurses fought to save the President's life. The President had, alas, effectively been killed on Elm Street, and there was nothing the doctors could do. John F. Kennedy was pronounced dead at 1 p.m. and the announcement sent shock waves round the world. In the Dealey Plaza, people were in shock, and confusion reigned. Those who had thrown themselves to the ground when the shooting started had brushed themselves off and were trying to piece events together.

Where had the shots come from? The area behind the President's car, some said, in the direction of the Texas School Book Depository, while others pointed to the railroad bridge and some the grassy knoll, an area in front and to the right of the President's car. They were sure, they said, that shots had come from there. But no one knew for certain. The Dealey Plaza being a natural echo chamber, the reverberations complicated matters, both the number of shots and the direction from which they had come. At Parkland Hospital, where the President had been taken, women sobbed, and a stunned crowd tried to grasp the implications of what had happened, just as others would across the entire world. It would not be long before conspiracy became the prime topic of conversation, while the United States government adopted the position that nothing of the sort had taken place.

FIGURE 4

FD-302 (Rev. 3-3-59) FEDERAL BUREAU OF INVESTIGATION

Date 11/29/63

1

SA JOHN JOE HOWLETT, U. S. Secret Service, Dallas, advised that with the aid of a surveyor and through the use of 8 millimeter movie films depicting President JOHN F. KENNEDY being struck by assassin's bullets on November 22, 1963, HOWLETT was able to ascertain that the distance from the window ledge of the farthest window to the east in the sixth floor of the Texas School Book Depository Building, 411 Elm Street, to where the President was struck the first time in the neck was approximately 170 feet. He stated this distance would be accurate within two or three feet. The distance from the same window ledge to the spot where President KENNEDY was struck in the head by the assassin's bullet was approximately 260 feet. Mr. HOWLETT stated that Secret Service Agents, using the 8 millimeter film had been unable to ascertain the exact location where Governor JOHN B. CONNALLY was struck.

SA HOWLETT advised that it had been ascertained from the movies that President KENNEDY was struck with the first and third shots fired by the assassin, while Gov. CONNALLY was struck with the second shot. SA HOWLETT stated the window referred to above was the one from which the shots were fired and faces south.

on 11/29/63 at Dallas, Texas File # Dallas 89-43

The FBI report that said three 'hits' had occurred, two shots to the President and one to Governor Connally. Adding to this the shot that missed and hit the kerb, the FBI were saying *four* shots had been fired. This was quickly revised in deference to the Warren Commission, who could only account for three shots being fired if they wanted to blame Oswald.

CHAPTER FOUR

Inexpert Witness

WHILE THE DOCTORS AT PARKLAND HOSPITAL were fighting to save the life of the President, the police back in the Dealey Plaza were turning their attention to where the shots had come from and who had fired them. Within fifteen minutes of the shooting an 'all points bulletin' was broadcast giving details of a young man answering to the description of Lee Harvey Oswald, a worker at the Texas School Book Depository. Shortly after 2 p.m. Oswald was arrested in the Texas Theatre and he was later charged with the murder of President Kennedy.

What at first appeared to be a smart piece of police work later gave rise to a great deal of suspicion and disbelief. How was it the police had put out an APB on Oswald, who had already been questioned in the second-floor lunchroom by the first policeman to enter the School Book Depository, and who had strolled out of the building without hindrance not ten minutes before the broadcast had been made? It was certainly not Marrion Baker, the policeman who had spoken to Oswald, who had asked for his arrest. Police Chief Jesse Curry did not sound very sure about what had happened when he was asked why Lee Harvey Oswald had been described in the APB. One reason given for his arrest was that a roll-call of staff was taken at the School Book Depository and Oswald was the only one missing. But did all this happen within fifteen minutes of the shooting, when the staff were scattered, some having gone outside to watch the motorcade? Enquiries made later revealed that a number of employees had not returned to work after the assassination of the President. This, then, blew holes in the police's 'reason'.

There was only one eyewitness whose testimony could be linked to Oswald.

A man named Howard L. Brennan claimed he saw a man answering to Oswald's description at a sixth-floor window of the Texas School Book Depository firing a rifle and pausing for a moment as though to make sure his bullets had found their mark, before smirking and disappearing. Discrepancies began to arise, however, when Brennan's testimony was examined by the Warren Commission. He said the sniper was standing up, which he could not have been, as the sills are extremely low in the School Book Depository building and this would have meant he was firing through the glass of the lifted window. In an extraordinary example of how the Warren Commission 'adjusted' their evidence to suit whatever they wanted to prove, they said the man Brennan saw was either sitting or kneeling, thereby contradicting their witness. This would not have been allowed in a courtroom. Neither would the rest of Brennan's testimony have been acceptable. He estimated the sniper's height and weight based on his claim to have seen the man standing up. The Warren Commission, however, said, 'Brennan could have seen enough of the body of a kneeling or squatting person to estimate his height.' There was no doubt that Brennan's 'evidence' was extremely desirable to the Commission. When it came to Brennan's estimation of weight, however, they ignored it. This may have been because Lee Harvey Oswald's weight was a significant twenty-five to thirty pounds lower than Brennan's estimate. Neither did the Commission's report make reference to the fact that Brennan's estimate of age was six years out, also. In other words Brennan could have been describing one of scores of 'slightly built' men milling around the Book Depository that day. As a specific description of Oswald it left a lot to be desired.

Howard L. Brennan faced Lee Harvey Oswald in a police line-up later on during the day of the assassination and, in spite of the fact that he had seen Oswald's photograph on television, he still did not pick him out with confidence. In a book he wrote with J. Edward Cherryholmes, *Eyewitness To History*, he claimed he was embarrassed to be facing Oswald after having seen him on television and said so. He indicated it was because he feared his identity as a witness was becoming generally known – and he had been promised anonymity – that he refused to identify Oswald with certainty. The fact is, however, that in the months following, he changed his testimony again and again. In December he told the FBI '. . . I am sure the person firing the rifle was Oswald.' In January he was again uncertain about making a positive identification. In March he became sure again, and the record shows '. . . Howard L Brennan made a positive identification of Oswald being the person at the window.' It is plain, however, that in a court of law Howard Brennan's testimony would have been worthless. His assertions would quickly have been demolished by a defending counsel. Nevertheless the Warren Commission saw fit to accept his uncertain testimony because it suited its scenario.

Allowing that Brennan saw someone at the sixth-floor window, and said he gave the information to a Secret Service agent named Sorrels within minutes of the shooting, it might be thought that the Warren Commission was right in attributing this information as the 'probable' source of the description broadcast by the police in their APB. Sorrels, however, had followed the White House detail into Parkland Hospital after the shooting, making his way back to the Dealey Plaza, where Brennan was, some twenty to twenty-five minutes later. It must, then, have been about 1 p.m. before Brennan had the opportunity of speaking to him, and the APB had gone out fifteen minutes before. In his book Brennan said he gave his information first to a police officer and that this led to the APB going out. It is unlikely that an APB would be broadcast on the strength of details given by someone who had approached a police officer on the street, however, and in view of this it was hardly likely that Brennan's evidence solved the mystery of why the police broadcast Oswald's description.

Jim Marrs, in his excellent book *Crossfire*, quotes Brennan's boss, Sandy Speaker, as telling him, 'They took [Brennan] off for about three weeks. I don't know if they were Secret Service or FBI, but they were Federal people. He came back a nervous wreck and within a year his hair had turned snow white. He wouldn't talk about [the assassination] after that. He was scared to death. They made him say what they wanted him to say.' In his book, Brennan made no mention of these three weeks spent with the authorities. The book did reflect, however, his extreme nervousness, and gave the impression he had been warned sternly not, at any price, to speak to the media. He recalled inviting William Manchester, doing research for his book, *Death of a President*, to his house. Manchester arrived with the written request of the slain President's brother, Robert, for him to be granted an interview, and Brennan was aware of this. But in spite of the author having travelled a long distance, when he arrived Brennan refused to be interviewed. Something very similar happened on another occasion when he agreed to a leading CBS reporter travelling from New York to meet him. This time he gave the interview then called in a neighbour to witness he was now forbidding her to quote anything she had heard. During the rest of his life he appeared on television only once to talk about the assassination.

That Brennan had seen someone firing from the sixth-floor window of the School Book Depository is not doubted, for another man and a fifteen-year-old boy also claimed seeing a rifle at the window. They also heard shots. The difference is that Brennan was so sure of whom he had seen pulling the trigger while the others could not identify who they had seen. But then there were forces at work, exerting influences which ran counter to any attempt to establish the truth. A witness named Richard Randolph Carr identified a man wearing a tan jacket, a hat and horn-rimmed spectacles at a sixth-floor window. He was watching from a building site on the seventh floor of the new courthouse at Commerce and Houston and had a grandstand view. When he was interviewed by the FBI he was told, 'If you didn't see Lee Harvey Oswald in the School Book Depository with a rifle, you didn't witness it.' Carr protested that the man he had seen on television, whom they said was Lee Harvey Oswald, was not the man he saw. The FBI man then said he had better keep his mouth shut. Not only was the Warren Commission picking and choosing its evidence, it appears the FBI were filtering out information they didn't want Warren to get.

When it came to the crunch, Brennan's identification of Oswald left a trail of uncertainty in its wake. The tailpiece to it all came from the Police Chief, no less. Two days after the assassination, on 24 November, Jesse Curry was being interviewed for KRLD-TV. 'Chief Curry, do you have an eyewitness who saw someone shoot the President?' asked the interviewer. 'No, sir, we do not,' replied Curry.

CHAPTER FIVE

Ambush in Elm Street

THE LEAD CAR, in which sat Police Chief Jesse Curry, had turned into Elm Street, followed at a slow pace by the presidential Lincoln. Behind the Lincoln, a car carried Secret Servicemen, some of whom were standing on the running boards, and the rest of the motorcade straggled back through Houston Street and back into Main Street. Almost immediately the President's car had straightened into Elm Street the shooting started. President Kennedy's hands flew to his throat as his car passed the Stemmons Freeway sign and he was pushed forward a moment later by the force of another bullet. Seconds later, another bullet hit his head, blowing fragments of skull away, and it was here that, to all intents and purposes, the President died. The fact that he lived long enough for the Lincoln to be driven to Parkland Hospital, where he was examined by a team of doctors, gave hope that he might live, but he could not survive the hail of bullets on Elm Street.

When the Warren Commission convened to investigate the assassination of President Kennedy the following January, one of its prime tasks was to account for the wounds the President had sustained and thus to analyse in detail the shooting which had taken place in Elm Street on the day he died. The Commissioners had the benefit of the findings of the autopsy team at the Bethesda Naval Hospital near Washington, who had examined the body within a few hours of the shooting, as well as a great many witnesses, some of whom were direct eyewitnesses to the various shots. In addition to this, they had the film record of Abraham Zapruder, a dressmaker who had left his work to watch the motorcade, and who had filmed the entire shooting on his home movie camera in a long, unbroken sequence. Other movie film and many still photographs were also available.

In summary, the Warren Commission decided that only three shots had been fired, one of which had missed. The other two, the Commission said, had hit the President, the first in his upper back, exiting his throat, and the second his head. The second hit, it said, was the shot which killed the President. This created problems, since if only three shots had been fired, one of which missed, and the other two had hit the President, how could the various wounds sustained by Governor Connally be accounted for? To accommodate this, the Commission's Assistant Counsel, Arlen Specter, devised a scenario in which the bullet to the President's upper back exited his throat and entered Connally's back, exiting again to pass through the Governor's wrist and come to rest in his left thigh. For all this to be achieved in one shot became known as the 'single bullet theory', and the bullet which achieved all was not surprisingly nicknamed 'the magic bullet'. The Commission insisted, however, that all the wounds were accounted for in two shots.

The Commission also decided that all the shots had been fired from one gun from the sixth-floor window of the Texas School Book Depository building, which was located on Elm Street at the top of the Dealey Plaza. It was saying that all the shots came from behind the presidential car, and that there was only one gunman. No conspiracy had taken place, the Commissioners decided. The one gunman, it said, was Lee Harvey Oswald, a 'lone nut' who had acted without assistance from anyone else. Consequently, the entire Report issued the following November by the Commission, left no room for argument. There was no conspiracy and the only, unaided shooter was Lee Harvey Oswald. The ten-million-word report based itself four-square on three bullets being fired, only two of which hit their target, and all fired by Lee Harvey Oswald from the sixth-floor window of the Texas School Book Depository.

On the sixth floor of the Texas School Book Depository building a rifle found by Deputy Sheriff Eugene Boone was identified as a German 7.6 Mauser. Boone called Deputy Constable Seymour Weitzman to act as a witness to the discovery of the gun and both drew up affidavits testifying to the find. In addition, another Deputy Sheriff, Roger Craig, saw the Mauser, and he was also required to draw up an affidavit. Police Captain Will Fritz was present when the find was made and he, also, is claimed to have identified the make of the rifle in question. Rifles seemed to be everywhere, however. Another was filmed being brought down by a police officer from the roof. He held it aloft for all to see when he reached the ground and, although it clearly had no telescopic sight, it was nonetheless referred to, in the print of the film, as the assassin's rifle. But the rifle collected as evidence from the School Book Depository by Lieutenant J.C. Day and taken to Police Headquarters was entirely different from either of these. It was a 6.5 Mannlicher-Carcano Italian carbine. This rifle, it was claimed, belonged to Lee Harvey Oswald. The officers who had found the Mauser were pressed to reconsider their identification of it and Boone and Weitzman yielded. Roger Craig, to his credit, did not, and till his death stuck to his identification of the weapon he witnessed being found. He was ignored, however, in spite of the fact that District Attorney Henry M. Wade, in a television interview, had announced to the world that the rifle found was a Mauser. It is hardly to be wondered that confusion of this sort is regarded as highly suspicious. After all, a 7.6 Mauser had 'Mauser' stamped on the barrel whilst the Mannlicher-Carcano had the legend 'Made in Italy' stamped on the butt! What the other one was is anybody's guess. And where it went to is another mystery. Probably the same place as the disappeared Mauser.

Disappearing rifles came to the foreground again, however, when, early in the year 2001, a study by Donald B. Thomas was published by the US Forensic Science Society. Among other important claims, it showed that an analysis of the acoustics relating to the shots fired at the President revealed that the particular shot which actually killed JFK, the last one fired, was consistent with a weapon of .30 calibre having been used. This is the first time a .30 has been identified as the murder weapon and it is of vital importance. The sound of gunshots had hardly died away in the Dealey Plaza before Police Inspector Herbert Sawyer, on duty there, radioed in a description of a man as follows:

> The wanted person in this is a slender white male about thirty, five feet ten, one sixty five, carrying what looked to be a 30–30 or some type of Winchester.

Inspector Sawyer said he received the information from one of his officers. The man sought, however, was never identified, and the rifle was never found. The pile of missing rifles grows bigger. The one rifle which *was* found, as we said earlier, was the 6.5 Mannlicher-Carcano of extremely elderly design, which they said belonged to Lee Harvey Oswald.

As the expression goes, the Commission found itself between a rock and a hard place when it came to the question of how many shots had been fired. The overriding factor was that it was ascertained that the Mannlicher-Carcano could only be fired three times in the period of shooting, which was calculated from the continuous film sequence made by Abraham Zapruder. At a pinch, the wounds sustained could have been satisfactorily accounted for by three shots and it appears the Commission was set to ignore reports that a bystander, James Tague, had been injured by a fragment of concrete thrown up by a bullet which missed. The kerbstone damaged by the stray bullet was examined by the FBI who said, at first, they could find no sign of a bullet mark. Later, they found scars which, when examined, were found to contain traces of lead and antimony. The Commissioners were obliged to revise their ideas, however, when an assistant US attorney, Martha Jo Stroud, sent them a photograph taken by a *Dallas Morning News* photographer showing the damaged kerbstone. Their three available shots had now been reduced to two without the option.

The squeeze was now on to explain how so many wounds could have been accounted for by two shots. The only alternative was to say that more shots had been fired, but more than three shots in total would have indicated more than one shooter, and more than one shooter constituted a conspiracy. In the Commission's book this was to be avoided at all costs. As was mentioned earlier, the FBI originally accounted for three shots having found their mark and, allowing that one shot had missed, this made a total of four. In the circumstances, however, they quickly revised their report so as not to conflict with the Commissioners. (See Figure 4.)

When it was examined, no legible fingerprints were found on the Mannlicher-Carcano, though a palmprint belatedly reported found was said to belong to Lee Harvey Oswald. It had not been found when the rifle was at first 'dusted' at Dallas Police Headquarters. According to the Warren Report, Lieutenant J.C. Day 'lifted' the palmprint from the underside of the gun barrel, using adhesive material to lift off the dusting powder and the print. For some reason Day did not release this print until four days after the assassination, when the Dallas police were obliged to send to the FBI in Washington everything they had. Day sent photographs of two useless scraps of prints taken from the rifle trigger but did not include the palmprint. It is interesting that the Warren Report notes that the FBI in Washington found that 'the lifting had been so complete in this case that there was no trace of the print on the rifle itself.' The Warren Commission had doubts about the authenticity of the palmprint and asked Lt. Day to sign a statement that it was genuinely lifted from the rifle barrel. He refused.

CHAPTER SIX

Oswald and Tippit

THE WARREN REPORT GAVE A DESCRIPTION of Oswald's movements from the time the assassination occurred. He left the Depository building at about 12.33 p.m., they said, and went to get a bus. The bus, however, got bogged down in the snarled-up traffic in the wake of the shooting, so Oswald left the bus and looked for a taxi. He found a taxi and it took him close to where he was living. When he arrived at his lodgings he changed his jacket and quickly left again, taking a handgun with him. He walked some distance to the junction of tenth Street and Patton Avenue where a police car was waiting. The policeman, Police Officer J.D. Tippit, lowered his window and Oswald engaged him in conversation. Tippit then got out of the car, whereupon, said Warren, Oswald shot him and ran away, soon to be arrested in the nearby Texas Theatre. He was first charged with the murder of the police officer and later charged with the murder of President Kennedy.

There is a great deal to question about what the Warren Commission had to say about Oswald's movements. They got the time of his leaving the School Book Depository right, though it beggared belief that he became the most wanted man in America just a few minutes after simply strolling out of the building – and having already been questioned by a police officer, at that. And could this high-profile assassin be crass enough to attempt his escape by bus? When he switched to looking for a taxi, he actually stood back from the first cab to come in favour of a lady who was waiting. The action of a desperate criminal? When his taxi neared the place in which he lived he alighted some little distance from his lodgings. This was curious behaviour for someone apparently on the run and in a great hurry. While Oswald was in his lodgings, his landlady, Mrs Earlene Roberts, reported that a police car pulled up at the door and sounded its horn twice – pip, pip – as though giving a signal. Oswald left at once. When questioned by the Commission about this incident, Mrs Roberts said she glimpsed the car, which had two police officers in it, and a number which might have had a '1' and might have had a '0' in it. Tippit's car number was 10.

When it came to the shooting of Officer Tippit, the Warren Commission relied heavily upon the evidence of a Mrs Helen Markham. To say that Mrs Markham's evidence was unreliable is a gross understatement. Mrs Markham said she was standing on the sidewalk and saw the police officer gunned down. The Warren Report records the following:

> Ball: Where was the police car when you first saw it?
> Markham: He was driving real slow, almost up to this man, well, say this man, and he kept, this man kept walking, you know, and the police car was going real slow now, real slow, and they just kept coming in to the curb, and finally the [sic] got a little way up there a little ways up, well, it stopped.
> Ball: The police car stopped?
> Markham: Yes sir.
> Ball: What about the man? Was he still walking?
> Markham: The man stopped . . . I saw the man come over to the car very slow, leaned and put his arms just like this, he leaned over in this window and looked in this window . . . The window was down . . . Well, I didn't think nothing about it; you know, the police are nice and friendly and I thought friendly conversation. Well, I looked, and there were cars coming so I had to wait . . . This man, like I told you, put his arms up, leaned over, he – just a minute, and he drew back and he stepped back about two steps . . . The policeman calmly opened the door, very slowly, wasn't angry or nothing, he calmly crawled out of this car, and I just thought a friendly conversation . . .

Mrs Markham then described how the young man fired his gun four times and killed the police officer. She admitted that, by that time, she was in hysterics and somehow managed to place her shoes on top of Tippit's car. She was later taken to Police Headquarters to an identity parade, but not before she had taken a sedative. At the identity parade Mrs Markham first picked out a police officer but later very uncertainly identified Oswald. In her account to the Warren Commission she required prompting by her interviewer . . .

> Ball: Did you recognise anyone in the line-up?
> Markham: No, sir.
> Ball: You did not? Did you see anybody – I have asked you that question before – did you recognise anybody from their face?
> Markham: From their face, no.
> Ball: Did you identify anybody in these four people?
> Markham: I didn't know nobody . . . I had never seen none of them, none of these men.
> Ball: No one of the four?
> Markham: No one of them.
> Ball: No one of all four?
> Markham: No, sir.
> Ball: Was there a number two man in there?
> Markham: Number two is the one I picked . . . Number two was the man I saw shoot the policeman . . . I looked at him. When I saw this man I wasn't sure, but I had cold chills just run all over me . . .

So much for her shaky identification. She spoke of Officer Tippit trying to speak to her over a period of some twenty minutes before he died, but other witnesses said he died immediately after the shooting. Mrs Markham was, in any case, suffering from hysteria during this period, according to her own statement, and this went on during the afternoon. Her first description of Tippit's attacker, given to Police Officer J.M. Poe, was that he was about twenty-five years old, five feet eight inches tall, had brown hair and wore a white jacket. In this she was supported by a Mrs Barbara Jeanette Davis. Later on, however, in another description given to an FBI agent named Odum, she said Tippit's assailant was about eighteen, had black hair and a red complexion, wore tan shoes, a tan jacket and dark trousers. And Mrs Markham was to contradict herself yet again in an interview with writer Mark Lane, which he recorded, when she said the killer was short, on the heavy side and with bushy hair. Later, at a Warren Commission hearing when the recording of her interview was replayed, she denied it was her voice. One Commission lawyer was later, uncharitably, to dismiss her as an 'utter screwball', but Warren sorely needed Mrs Markham's testimony to make a case against Lee Harvey Oswald for the shooting of Officer Tippit. In turn this would bolster his case against him for the shooting of the President.

Warren needed Helen Markham's testimony because the only other witness claiming that Oswald was Tippit's killer was a taxi driver, William Scoggins. Unfortunately, he did not actually see the shooting because a bush obscured his vision, neither did he see the fleeing assailant because he ducked out of sight as he passed. Remarkably, Scoggins's evidence was also accepted by the Warren Commission. Scoggins, like Mrs Markham, was required to attend an identity parade. He went with a taxi driver friend, William Whaley, who was the one who had picked up Oswald in his cab after he left the School Depository building and driven him home. According to Whaley, the line-ups were a farce. He told the Warren Commission:

> . . . you could have picked [Oswald] out without identifying him by just listening to him because he was bawling out the policemen, telling them it wasn't right to put him in line with these teenagers . . . he told them what he thought about them . . . they were trying to railroad him and he wanted his lawyer . . .

Furthermore, Scoggins was to admit to the Warren Commission that he had seen a photograph of Lee Harvey Oswald in a newspaper before attending the identity parade, and he also admitted that on an occasion when an agent showed him photographs, he picked out another man, not Oswald.

Others had given varying descriptions of the man said to have killed Officer Tippit. Officer R.W. Walker phoned in a description very soon after the shooting. He said the suspect was white with slender build, black hair, in his thirties, five feet eight inches tall, wearing a white shirt and black slacks. Officer H.W. Summers called in with '. . . white male, twenty-seven, five feet eleven inches, 165 [lbs], black wavy hair, fair complected, wearing a light grey Eisenhower-type jacket, dark trousers and a white shirt,' while witness Mrs Acquilla Clemons described him as 'kind of a short guy', and 'kind of heavy'. Frank Wright, who, from his front door, saw Officer Tippit fall to the ground, said the killer was of medium height and wore a long coat. He said he saw the killer get into a grey car, maybe a Plymouth, either a 1950 or a 1951 model and drive off at speed. Said Wright: 'I've seen what came out on television and in the newspaper, but I know that's not what happened.'

But perhaps the witness who saw most, and most clearly, was Domingo Benavides. He was driving a pick-up truck on Tenth Street approaching from the opposite direction to Tippit's car when the shooting took place. His truck was quite close to the police car and he quickly pulled up and ducked. He clearly saw the gunman emptying his gun of spent shells before leaving the scene. Benavides then went to see if he could help the police officer. He wanted to use Tippit's radio to phone in details of what had happened but did not know how, but another man, T.F. Bowley, who joined him, obliged and the dispatcher received the news, Bowley said, at 1.10 p.m., a few minutes after the shooting.

Domingo Benavides resolutely refused to identify the killer as Lee Harvey Oswald and was, perhaps significantly, not asked to attend a line-up. It was only much later, after his brother had been murdered – in mistake for him, he thought – that, believing his life was in danger, he went along with the Oswald identification. Looking at all the descriptions offered by witnesses, however, the only real consensus which fitted Oswald was that the assailant was white.

The timing of the radioed report of the shooting was critical to establishing any part Lee Harvey Oswald may have played in the incident. Did he, in fact, have time to sprint the mile from his lodgings to the junction of 10th and Patton? Oswald's landlady said he left her house at three or four minutes after 1.00 p.m. Helen Markham, asked about the time she saw the shooting, answered, 'I wouldn't be afraid to bet it wasn't six or seven minutes after one.' Mrs Markham, for all her unreliability in other respects, would have a fair idea of the timing because she was at 10th and Patton to catch a bus to work which was scheduled to leave at 1.12 p.m. If T.F. Bowley radioed the news of the shooting to Police Headquarters at 1.10 p.m., that would seem to corroborate the timing of events and, that being the case, it would have been impossible for Oswald to have been there.

Lee Harvey Oswald was arrested in the Texas Theater about forty minutes after the murder of Officer Tippit. On the face of it, the police were called because a young man had entered the theatre without paying, but this would hardly account for a posse of policemen, with an assistant district attorney and an FBI agent turning up in squad cars and entering the theatre with guns drawn. This is just what happened, however, and Lee Harvey Oswald was soon identified in the auditorium. When approached, he raised his hands and cried, 'I am not resisting arrest,' which raises the question of whether he thought he was going to be gunned down on the spot, rather than arrested. It would have been difficult for officers of the law to have fired at a man who had called out he was not resisting arrest, especially with other people in the audience as witnesses. A scuffle did take place, however, and the arresting policeman, Officer M.N. McDonald, received a blow to his face as he tried to wrestle Oswald's gun from him. The hammer of the gun was heard to click, but there was no bullet fired.

The manner of the arrest of Oswald in the Texas Theater added a further mystery to the many surrounding the murders of President Kennedy and Officer Tippit. The police, who turned up in strength ostensibly to arrest a man who had entered a cinema without paying, seemed to know exactly who they were looking for when they arrived. To add a little more to the mystery, one report said that police officers had lain in wait for Oswald in an alley behind the Texas Theater. But then mystery may be added to mystery. A local shopkeeper,

Bernard J. Haire, witnessed a pale young man wearing a pullover being escorted from the rear exit of the theatre to a police car by officers who drove him away. He always believed he had seen Lee Harvey Oswald being taken away, only to discover many years later that Oswald had been brought out from the main entrance of the theatre and driven away. Were there two arrests made in the theatre at the same time? If so, who was the second man?

Regardless of the considerable uncertainty relating to the description of the killer of Officer Tippit, and notwithstanding that Mrs Helen Markham and William Scoggins were unreliable witnesses, the Warren Commission declared that the shooting occurred at 'approximately 1.15 or 1.16 p.m., and that Lee Harvey Oswald shot Officer Tippit four times, killing him instantly'.

The cartridge cases seen at the scene of the shooting created another problem for the authorities which was not advertised. They indicated that an automatic had been used to kill Tippit. Automatics spew out the used cases, which was what obviously happened here. Oswald carried a revolver, however, and revolvers retain their spent cases. When the bullets themselves were recovered from Tippit's body – four of them – three were copper-coated Winchester Westerns, while the other was a lead bullet made by Remington-Peters. This should have raised the likelihood that two gunmen shot Officer Tippit. Dallas police were obliged to send the recovered bullets to the FBI laboratory at Washington. In fact they sent only one, indicating that this was the only one recovered. Not surprisingly, the FBI reported the bullet had not come from Oswald's gun.

The Warren Commission pressed the FBI to look for other bullets, and the other three were discovered in the files at Dallas Police Headquarters. These were then sent to Washington but, again, the lab could not say that any one had come from Oswald's gun. Almost a week after the single recovered bullet had been sent to the FBI lab, Dallas Homicide produced four cartridge cases which they said had been found at the scene of the shooting. These were sent to the lab where the FBI confirmed they had come from Oswald's revolver. Further problems still lay in store for Dallas Homicide, however. It is normal procedure for an officer recovering spent shells to scratch his initials into the casings in order that the chain of evidence be unbroken. The two police officers involved in scratching their initials on casings, Officer J.M. Poe and Sergeant W.E. Barnes, were later required to identify their marks on the exhibits introduced before the Warren Commission. Embarrassingly, they could not find their marks, no matter how hard they looked. Dallas Homicide was left with egg on its face. Casings normally produced immediately had taken six days to appear and when they did, there was nothing to link them to the scene of the crime. There was clearly a smell of something rotten coming from Dallas Police Headquarters. In a court of law, a prosecution depending on this so-called evidence would have been thrown out.

It would appear that dirty work was not confined to one crossroads, however. In 1977, when the House Select Committee on Assassinations was in session, a document then released revealed that J. Edgar Hoover, Director of the FBI, had, within two hours of the assassination of President Kennedy, been in touch with Attorney General Robert F. Kennedy to tell him he thought he had apprehended the man who had killed his brother. He described him as an ex-Marine named Oswald who had defected to Russia and who was pro-Communist. He added that he was a 'nut' who was a mean-minded individual. At the exact time Hoover said he spoke to the Attorney General, Lee Harvey Oswald was being interrogated at Police Headquarters by Captain Will Fritz, who had not yet satisfactorily ascertained Oswald's identity, let alone obtained any background on the man.

CHAPTER SEVEN

Enter Jack Ruby

THE DIFFICULTY IN IDENTIFYING LEE HARVEY OSWALD arose from the fact that the prisoner was not inclined to be helpful. Having discovered that he was Lee Harvey Oswald, officers began questioning which was to extend to a total of twelve hours of the time Oswald was in custody. The story which circulated was that on Oswald's person were two identity cards, one for Lee Harvey Oswald and the other for an A.J. Hidell. In fact the Hidell identity card was not mentioned as found in his belongings until the day after his arrest, in circumstances which suggested it had been planted. It was to become very important, however, for Captain Fritz would later discover that the Mannlicher-Carcano rifle said to have been the murder weapon in the assassination of the President was ordered from a mail order company by an A.J. Hidell and delivered, it was claimed, to the mail box of Lee Harvey Oswald. There was no doubt that to a police officer investigating the most important case of his career, this represented solid evidence.

What Captain Fritz did not know was that when Lieutenant Colonel Robert Jones, operations officer for the 112th Military Intelligence Group, sought to establish what was happening in Dallas on the day of the assassination, he naturally contacted some of his own men who were in Dallas that day. They told him that A.J. Hidell had been arrested, which was curious, to say the least, since no mention of that name was made by anyone on that day, and certainly not in the press. It was later learnt that Colonel Jones checked the files at Military Intelligence and found one marked 'A.J. HIDELL'. Examining the file's contents he discovered Hidell was an alias for Lee Harvey Oswald, and he also observed that the file was quite updated on his background. The Warren Commission was never told about this file but the House Select Committee on Assassinations, in 1977, learned of it and asked to see it. They were informed that in 1973 it had been 'routinely' destroyed. Here was an enormous indication that Lee Harvey Oswald's true background was that of an intelligence agent; an enormous indication carefully concealed by Military Intelligence.

Although he was being held in custody at Police Headquarters, the press was allowed to question Oswald, while pronouncement after pronouncement was made by various law officers to satisfy the demand for information from across the world. During this time Oswald's mother, Marguerite, was not allowed to visit her son, however, and although he asked for a lawyer, one had not been assigned by Sunday, two days after his arrest. It had been decided that, on that Sunday, Oswald would be transferred to the county jail, and protection arrangements for the prisoner included adjusting transfer time by an hour and sending off an armoured car decoy. At the revised hour, Lee Harvey Oswald was brought down in the elevator to the basement car park where another car awaited him. The time was 11.20 a.m. and the area he was brought into was thronged with members of the press, radio and television. For the world to see by the means of television, a man stepped forward into the path of the prisoner and shot him in the stomach. That man was Jack Ruby.

Jack Ruby, born Jacob Rubenstein in Chicago in 1911, ran errands for Al Capone as a child. His parents had separated when he was ten years old, and 'Sparky', as he was nicknamed, was a street-wise kid who made a buck where he could. In 1937 he began working for the Scrap Iron and Junk Handlers' Union, suspected by the State of Illinois of being 'a front for organised crime'. It appears Rubenstein served a term in jail for involvement when the union's financial secretary, Leon R. Cooke, was shot and killed by its president, John Martin, in 1939. Martin served no time for the murder, claiming he acted in self-defence; altogether strange when Cooke was shot in the back. Reorganised as the Waste Material Handlers' Union, the Scrap Iron and Junk Handlers' organisation was eventually drafted into the Teamsters Union, a Senate Committee later confirming the State of Illinois worst fears when it declared it a link between Mafia boss Jimmy Hoffa and the criminal underworld.

Jacob Rubenstein went to war in 1943, and it was after his discharge in 1946 that he changed his name to Jack Leon Ruby. Ruby became one of twenty-five Chicago thugs and hoodlums to move down to Dallas at the Mob's behest to take over the pinball, slot machine and jukebox business in Texas, Louisiana and Arkansas. He was appointed as the manager of the Sovereign Club, which became the Carousel Club in 1960. Known for his involvement in gambling, prostitution and drugs, he was also suspected of gun-running to Cuba. It seems he was just a grown-up version

FIGURE 5A

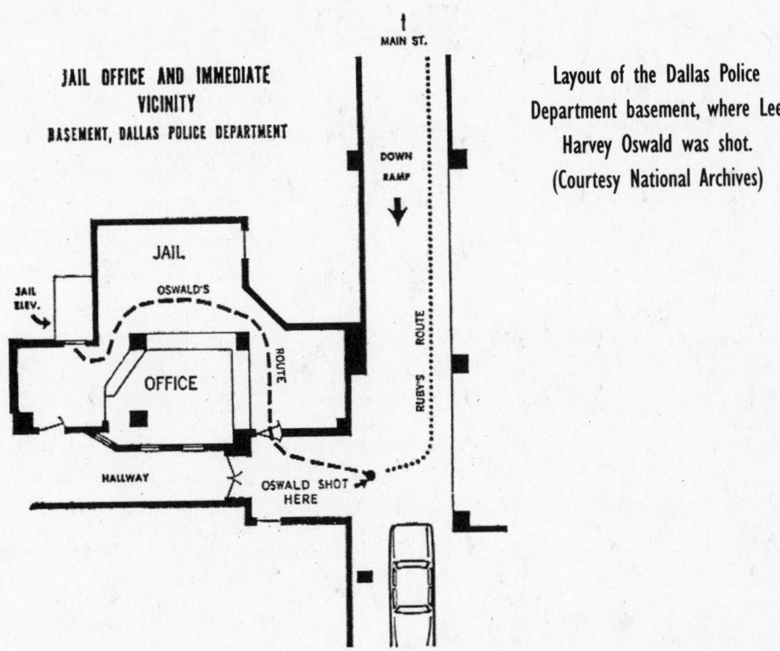

Layout of the Dallas Police Department basement, where Lee Harvey Oswald was shot. (Courtesy National Archives)

of the Chicago kid who made a buck where he could, and wasn't particular where it was. He would have been proud of being called 'one of our boys' by mobster Johnny Roselli, Sam Giancana's sidekick, when, much later, Roselli discussed Ruby with a reporter. This was Jack Ruby's preoccupation. He was a little guy trying to be a big guy. Someone once called him a 'small time peanut'. If he ever became bigger in his orbit, he became only a bigger peanut.

Several strange events are recorded in relation to the shooting of Lee Harvey Oswald. Seth Kantor, author of the book *Who Was Jack Ruby?* claimed that Ruby's flatmate, George Senator, telephoned a Dallas lawyer, Jim Martin, and asked him to represent Ruby for killing Oswald. On the face of it there was nothing exceptional in this. It was the timing of the call which made it incredible: Senator called the lawyer before the event took place. Ruby was, in fact, first represented by lawyer Tom Howard, who turned up in the Police Headquarters basement in time to see Lee Harvey Oswald appear from the elevator. He left saying, 'That's all I wanted to see.' Immediately afterward the sound of Ruby's shot rang out. The sequence of the shooting was recorded and researchers noted that a car horn sounded the instant Oswald appeared from the

FIGURE 5B

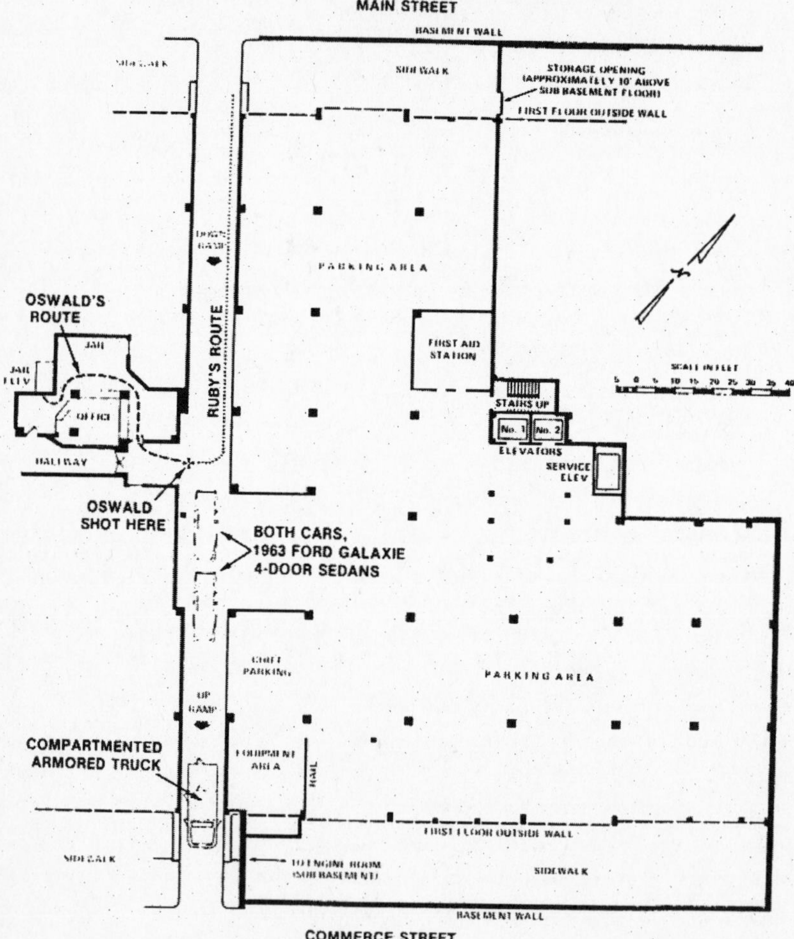

Layout of the Dallas Police Department basement,
where Lee Harvey Oswald was shot. (Courtesy National Archives)

elevator, and a second car horn sounded when Oswald came into line with Ruby's gun. Coincidence or signals?

The Warren Commission recorded that . . .

> . . . between 2.30 and 3 a.m., the local office of the FBI and the sheriff's office received telephone calls from an unidentified man who warned that a committee had decided 'to kill the man that killed the President'.

Sheriff's Officer Perry McCoy submitted a report to his superior saying:

> At approximately 2.15 a.m. I received a call from a person that . . . stated that he was a member of a group of one hundred and he wanted the sheriff's office to know that they had voted one hundred per cent to kill Oswald while he was in the process of being transferred to the county jail and that he wanted this department to have the information so that none of the deputies would get hurt. The voice was deep and course [sic] and sounded very sincere and talked with ease. The person did not seem excited . . . he seemed very calm about the whole matter.

He also said, later in his statement:

> I received one other call regarding the transfer of Oswald and when I answered the telephone a male voice asked if this is the sheriff's office and I said it was, he said just a minute and then another male voice stated that Oswald would never make the trip to the county jail. I could not determine whether or not this was the same voice that had called earlier.

The Commission said that details of the threats were passed to the Police Department and eventually to Chief Jesse Curry. The Chief's own department also received a call announcing that Lee Harvey Oswald was about to be killed, Lieutenant Billy R. Grammer taking the call. The caller, said Grammer, accurately outlined the plans for moving Oswald to the county jail, including details of the decoy car, and he told the lieutenant those plans had better be changed if Oswald was to survive. The voice was familiar but the caller would not give a name. Once again, a report was written up for Chief Curry.

Later on this Sunday morning, Grammer's wife woke him with the news that Oswald had been shot by Ruby in the basement car park at Police Headquarters. It was then that it clicked. The voice on the telephone had been that of Jack Ruby. He knew Ruby and had been speaking to him but a few days earlier.

There are quite a number of questions raised by Jack Ruby telephoning the Sheriff's office, the office of the FBI, and the Police Department, with the message that Oswald was to be killed. The key question was, of course, if Ruby had been chosen to be Oswald's executioner, as most researchers believe, why was he alerting the authorities? If Ruby was the murderer, he was obviously acting to the dictate of another. The other would have to be one of the conspirators or his representative, and it is almost certain that he was able to coerce Ruby, probably by blackmail, into carrying out the shooting. It is unlikely Ruby would relish the risk of the electric chair or a very long prison sentence, and it may be assumed, therefore, that he was an unwilling participant in the affair. If he was being blackmailed it may well have been a case of do this and we will see you are not electrocuted, and obtain for you a fairly early release (together with inducements of a number of kinds), or else go to jail for a long time as a consequence of being exposed (in some heinous crime) to the authorities. It was likely to have been a 'heads you win, tails I lose' situation. Spreading the word that Oswald was to be killed when being transferred to the county jail would constitute his only hope for getting off the hook. If Oswald was incredibly well protected to the degree that it became impossible for Ruby to reach him to carry out the murder, he would not be blamed because the plan had failed. Who was the representative of the conspirators likely to be? The Mafia are the least likely candidates on the grounds that they would not be able to offer the guarantees needed to persuade Ruby. On analysis it would seem to lie equally between a very powerful and influential citizen, or a well-placed CIA agent.

Speaking of powerful and influential citizens, one such person despatched his lawyer on the Saturday, the day after the assassination, to Police Headquarters to make an assessment of how securely Oswald was being protected. The lawyer returned saying how lax everything was: he had stepped into the elevator and found himself standing next to Oswald handcuffed to an officer! The lawyer was John W. Curington, and the man who sent him oil billionaire H.L. Hunt. Hunt was said to be elated when he heard this news. Details were confirmed as true by John W. Curington who was Hunt's assistant for twelve years. The story perhaps did not quite finish here, however. In a version I heard twenty years ago a powerful and infuential citizen sent for Jack Ruby that night.

Ruby had been in and out of Police Headquarters all weekend, no doubt keeping tabs on developments and, it would appear, calculating how to kill Oswald. He was outside the homicide office in which Oswald was being interviewed on the evening of Friday, 22 November, the very day of the assassination. Victor Robertson Jnr, a reporter for Dallas WFAA radio and television, told the FBI, and eventually the Warren Commission, that Ruby turned the knob of the homicide office door, and was about to enter when police officers stopped him, saying, 'You can't go in there, Jack.' Later that night, after he had been to the synagogue, he went back to Headquarters with sandwiches for the officers. Later still, after midnight, he went to the press conference held by District Attorney Henry Wade. When Wade, in error, referred to Oswald's association with the Free Cuba Committee, Ruby called out, 'Henry, that's the Fair Play for Cuba Committee.' This came as quite a surprise to those who knew Ruby and his general lack of interest in things political.

Next day, he was again at Headquarters asking reporters for information about the transfer of Oswald to the county jail. The earliest time, they thought, would be about 4 p.m. and Jack was back at that time. Chief Curry told the assembled reporters that if they came back at 10 a.m. on Sunday morning they would not have missed anything. On Sunday morning Ruby was at Police Headquarters early. At 8 a.m. he was seen by a cameraman for WBAP-TV, Warren Richey, whose colleagues corroborated his sighting. At about 9.30 a.m. he was seen again by a minister who travelled in the same elevator with him. He said Ruby got out at the floor on which Oswald was being held. Again at 10 a.m. he was seen by newsmen. We know he was back at his apartment by 10.30 a.m. for one of his strippers telephoned him there, asking him to help her out with her rent. By 11.17 a.m. Ruby was at Western Union, close to Police Headquarters, sending the girl $25, and at 11.21 a.m., four minutes later, he shot Lee Harvey Oswald. Taken to hospital, Oswald died at 1.07 p.m.

CHAPTER EIGHT

The House that Jack Built

JACK RUBY AND THE CAROUSEL CLUB were investigated by the Warren Commission. Warren was anxious to show that Ruby was not connected to Oswald and that they were not 'in this together', lest a conspiracy should be identified. For similar reasons he wanted to show that Ruby was connected neither to the police nor the Mafia. Earl Warren had his work cut out here, for there is much evidence that Jack Ruby and Lee Harvey Oswald had met each other. Jack was great buddies with many police officers (including those he specially cultivated), and as well-known mobster Johnny Roselli later acknowledged, Ruby was 'one of our boys'. Not that any of these connections drew him into the conspiracy to kill President Kennedy. Jack Ruby was not conspirator material. He was not trustworthy and placed his own interests first.

The Warren Commission listened to much talk about Ruby-Oswald connections but simply dismissed it all as untrue: 'All such allegations have been investigated, but the Commission has found none which merits credence.'

When it came to Ruby's police connections, much the same happened. In spite of evidence pointing clearly to a pronounced relationship between Ruby and the Dallas police, Warren recorded that the contrary was the case. An example may be found in the examination of witness Nancy Perrin Rich, a bartender at the Carousel Club:

> Counsel: Are you saying that Jack Ruby told you that when any member of the Police Department came in, that there was a standing order that you could serve them hard liquor?

Rich: That is correct.
Counsel: Did they pay?
Rich: Oh, no; of course not.
Counsel: Was that an order, too, from Mr Ruby?
Rich: That was.

This was not what the Warren Commission wanted to hear and it is no surprise that her testimony did not reach their Report. Rich also told them 'I don't think there's a cop in Dallas that doesn't know Jack Ruby' and this was easily borne out in other interviews. FBI agents were told by Mrs Edward Pullman, a hostess at the Carousel, that what Nancy Perrin Rich had said was true. Buried away in the Commission's hearings is evidence from a police lieutenant that 'Ruby was well known among members of the Dallas Police Department . . .' an example of this surfacing when Sergeant D.V. Harkness reported to his superiors that while he was on traffic duty he had recognised Jack Ruby standing near the assassination site on the day after the President was killed. Another instance is found when, at Police Headquarters, Ruby had tried to enter the room where Oswald was being interrogated. The police officer who stopped him called out, 'You can't go in there, Jack.' Examples could go on and on. The Jack Ruby the Warren Commission wanted the world to know was a different man, however. A man who had no particular connections with the Police Department. And they never mentioned anywhere the letter Hoover sent to the Commission in June 1964 telling them Ruby had been an FBI informant in 1959.

In fact, in return for his hospitality, Ruby was known to have received special treatment from his friends at headquarters. He himself boasted he 'got away with things'. The 'things' included twenty-five beatings-up, for which he was not troubled by the police, arrests for carrying a concealed weapon, allowing dancing after hours at his club and liquor offences which were not listed in police records. But in spite of this the Commission was able to record: 'There is no credible evidence that Ruby sought special favours from police officers or attempted to bribe them.'

The connections between Ruby and the underworld, also, were well known, though the Warren Commission recognised none of them. The Commissioners would only have had to inspect his telephone account to see whom he telephoned to find this out. Ruby placed calls to Irwin S. Weiner, Murray W. 'Dusty' Miller, Nofio Pecora and Hoffa's man, Barney Baker, among others. He made frequent calls to gambler Lewis McWillie, often called his mentor, and a little digging would have shown that he had been in contact with the likes of Joseph Campisi, Paul Roland Jones, Lenny Patrick and Russell D. Matthews. All those named were directly or indirectly associated with organised crime. It is interesting to note that an FBI report sent to the Warren Commission was incomplete when they quoted it. The first page was missing. The first page dealt with Ruby's gambling connections. In respect of their investigation into Jack Ruby's mob background, the Warren Commission stated: 'There is no evidence that he ever participated in organised criminal activity.'

Unbelievably, to establish whether Ruby had connections with organised crime, the Commission approached certain Chicago underworld figures directly to ask if Ruby was associated with them. Not surprisingly they denied he had contact with them. Were they likely to admit to such a thing? The Commission reported:

> Virtually all Ruby's Chicago friends stated he had no close connection with organised crime . . . unreliable as their reports may be, several known Chicago criminals have denied any such liaison.

What else?

Jack's house was clean, according to Earl Warren.

CHAPTER NINE

Lee Harvey Oswald

LEE HARVEY OSWALD WAS BORN on 18 October 1939 in New Orleans. He was born into a poor family whose father, Robert E. Lee Oswald, had died shortly before Lee was born. His mother, Marguerite Claverie Oswald, was left with three boys, John Pic Junior, seven, from a previous marriage, Robert, who was five years of age, and Lee, and the outlook for the family was not very bright. When Lee was born, Marguerite placed his brothers in an orphanage in Algiers, Louisiana, so that she might earn a living as she provided for her baby. John Pic and Robert were brought out of the orphanage when Lee was about a year old, when their mother managed to buy a small house, but all three boys were sent to another orphanage when the shop which Marguerite tried to run, failed.

Robert and John Pic Junior were later enrolled in a military academy in Mississippi, and Lee joined his mother in a new home in Dallas, from which they moved to Benbrook, Fort Worth, when Marguerite married again. Her new husband, Edwin Ekdahl, was an electrical engineer, but the marriage did not last, and she divorced him in 1948. Lee moved from school to school; before he was ten years of age he had attended six different schools. It is, therefore, hardly surprising that he became, for a while, a regular truant. This created problems when he and his mother moved briefly to New York, but Lee appeared not to suffer retardation for his truancy and was found to be a normal, bright boy with an IQ of 118, when a psychiatric report was made on him.

A few days after his seventeenth birthday, Lee joined the Marines. He did his basic training – ten weeks of boot camp – at San Diego, California, and when this was completed on 20 January 1957 he was posted to Camp Pendleton, about twenty miles north of San Diego. At Camp Pendleton he carried out combat training, and after two months became eligible for leave. He spent his leave with his mother at Fort Worth, and then went on to Keesler Air Force Base at Biloxi, where he began training in radar. Strangely, his weekend passes were spent in New Orleans, a hundred miles away, though not to see his relatives there. This became one of the many mysteries surrounding Lee Harvey Oswald in his time in the Marines. Lee passed his examinations and qualified in seventh place in his class as an Aviation Electronics Operator with the Military Occupation Speciality of 6741. He was then shipped overseas.

Lee Harvey Oswald was posted to Japan, to a base at Atsugi, whence the U-2 spy planes made their information-gathering trips at extraordinary heights over the USSR and China. The 'spy in the sky' plane was kept a mystery from the servicemen serving at the base, who recognised it only as the huge, curiously shaped plane which took off and landed, and which was not spoken of. Significantly, however, buildings allocated to the Joint Technical Advisory Group were also sited at the base, and these were later identified as a cover for the CIA's main operational base in Asia.

At first, Lee obtained the 'Confidential' clearance which was normal at the base. His friends were impressed, however, when this was raised to 'Secret' in respect of the work he was to do in the 'inner sanctum' of radar operations. Remarkably, Oswald was said to have later attained 'Crypto' level of clearance while at the base, the highest level possible, and became one of only five at Atsugi to do so. He was good at his job and got on well with those around him. His friends were surprised that he had begun to learn how to speak Russian. They were even more surprised to see this did not seem to bother those in command at the base.

When he returned to the United States in November 1958, his posting was to Santa Ana in California, and he took his thirty-day leave entitlement, which he spent with his family at Fort Worth. He resumed his study of the Russian language, spending nine months at Santa Ana. He read left-wing literature, which was delivered to him at the base, and earned the nickname 'Oswalskovich' in respect of his unconcealed interest in things Russian. He was ragged by his friends, which he took in good part, and once again his activities and leanings were ignored by those in command.

With only a few months left to serve in the Marines, Oswald told his friends he intended extending his education. He said he planned becoming a student at the Albert Schweitzer College in Switzerland and, indeed, made application to attend that institution. He became anxious to leave the service ahead of his scheduled time and made a special application for early discharge on the grounds that his sick mother needed him at home. This was granted without delay and Lee Harvey Oswald was very soon a civilian again.

When released from the Marines, Oswald little more than called at his home before embarking on a long journey which took him to England, then to Helsinki and then on to Moscow. An apparent defector, he told officials at the United States Embassy in Moscow he wished to renounce his American citizenship and stay in Russia. The Russians, for their part, were experiencing a season of young Americans attempting to enter Soviet bloc countries so that they could operate as US spies, and they told Oswald he must leave. Oswald, different from the rest in that he did not have the college education background common to most CIA recruits, was determined to stay, and it was claimed he attempted suicide by cutting his wrist. After being treated in hospital, he was eventually allowed to stay on sufference and was sent to Minsk to work at a factory there. He was well paid, and housed in relative comfort, but by February 1959 it appeared he was disillusioned with Communism and made his first approach to the US Embassy in Moscow for their help in returning home. This took time, and before his application for repatriation was completed he had married a young Russian girl, Marina Nikolaevna Prosakova, niece of a colonel in the MVD. This did not seem to slow down the process, however, neither did the addition of a child to their family, and on June 1st 1962, Lee Harvey Oswald, with Marina and baby June, began the return journey to the United States.

But then there was more to the Oswald story. Much, much more . . .

FIGURE 6

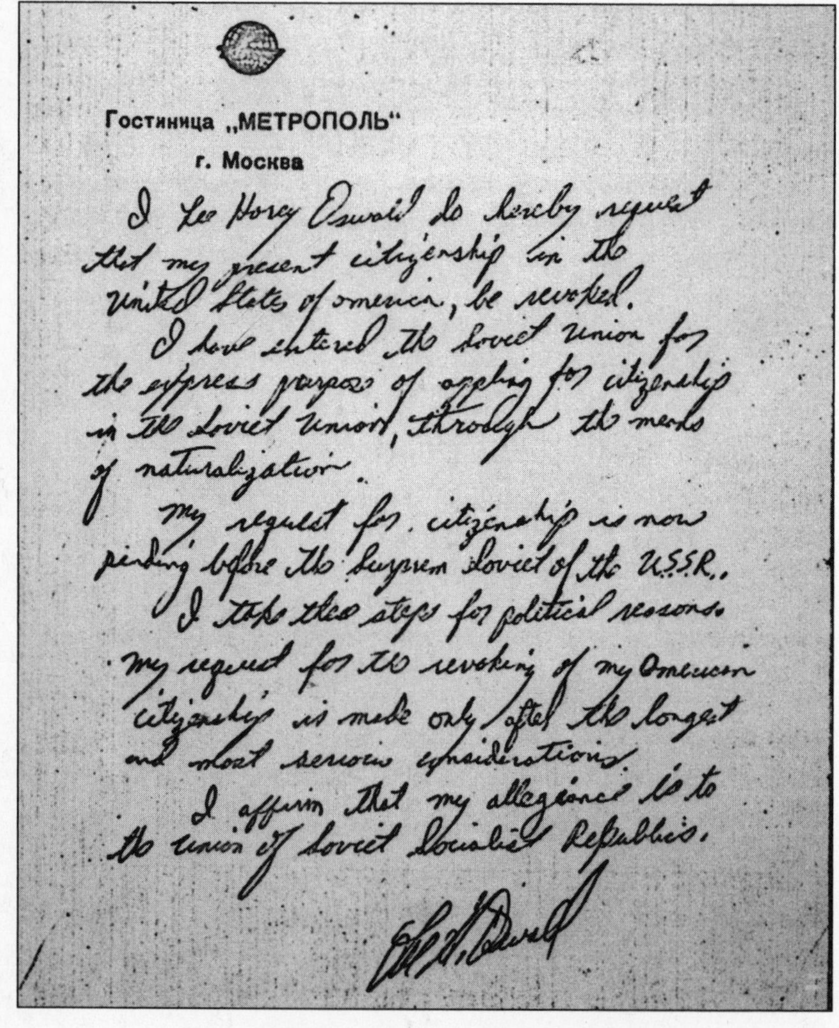

Гостиница „МЕТРОПОЛЬ"

г. Москва

I Lee Harvey Oswald do hereby request that my present citizenship in the United States of america, be revoked.

I have entered the Soviet Union for the express purpose of appling for citizenship in the Soviet Union, through the means of naturalization.

My request for citizenship is now pending before the Suprem Soviet of the U.S.S.R.

I take these steps for political reasons. My request for the revoking of my American citizenship is made only after the longest and most serious considerations.

I affirm that my allegiance is to the Union of Soviet Socialist Republics.

Lee H. Oswald

Oswald's letter 'renouncing' US citizenship. (Courtesy National Archives)

CHAPTER TEN

The Taming of the Medical Evidence

WHILE THE BODY OF President Kennedy lay in Trauma Room One of Parkland Hospital, members of the Secret Service were making plans to fly it back to Washington for autopsy. This by no means suited Earl Rose, the Dallas County Medical Examiner, who expected the body to remain at Parkland until he released it. It was, he said, to preserve the chain of evidence, which related to the assassin's rights. This did not impress the Secret Service, however, who, regardless, continued their arrangements to the point where they were literally about to remove the casket in which the body of the President had been placed.

Rose was adamant the body should stay and the Secret Service, in the person of Agent Roy Kellerman, was equally adamant it should not. A Justice of the Peace, Judge Theron Ward, was sent for to resolve matters, but he did nothing to help. Rose said if the body was removed it would be removed illegally. 'We are taking the President back to Washington,' was the reply, and it was at about this point that all hell let loose. For half an hour the battle raged and the scene looked very ugly. At length Kellerman snapped, 'Wheel it out,' and the casket was moved out towards the double doors leading to the hospital exit. Medical Examiner Rose puffed himself up and stood in the way of the trolley, arm outstretched and hand flattened. Matters had come to a head. At a signal, Secret Service personnel surrounded Earl Rose and a policeman who was standing beside him. 'Go screw yourself,' Kenneth O'Donnell, Kennedy's aide had retorted to Judge Ward. The police officer fingered his gun, but they were bypassed by the now mobile coffin. At this stage it had been well and truly taken without the permission of the Dallas County authorities, although at the last minute a release was rushed to the agents at the waiting hearse before it moved off.

This was a disgraceful spectacle, to say the least. For such a performance to have related to the mortal remains of any person is outrageous. For it to involve the remains of the President of the United States is unthinkable. It reflected both parties in the worst possible light. The question must be asked, why could an initial autopsy not be carried out in Dallas to satisfy the Dallas authorities? When we consider what followed at Bethesda Naval Hospital, we may find the answer.

The body of President Kennedy was taken to Air Force One, the President's aircraft, and flown to Washington DC, where it was taken to the Bethesda Naval Hospital for autopsy. There would be some satisfaction in being able to say that the offence to the mortal remains of the dead President had now ceased. Unhappily this was not so.

The autopsy was to be carried out by Commander James J. Humes, senior pathologist and director of laboratories at Bethesda Naval Hospital. Dr J. Thornton Boswell was in co-charge of the autopsy team, and Army Colonel Pierre A. Finck was brought in as a consultant. Navy hospital corpsmen James Curtiss Jenkins and Paul Kelly O'Connor assisted the principals. It appears that none of the doctors involved was a forensic pathologist and not one had conducted an autopsy before, and while later criticism of blunders and omissions tended – perhaps conveniently – to explain away incompetence, one has to wonder whether instructions from 'above' was not a greater factor. There was no shortage of 'top brass' in the autopsy room. It was apparently milling with people. In 1977 the Congress Assassinations Committee considered why Commander Humes had not dissected a wound and reached the conclusion it was because of the pressure on time. Dr Pierre Finck, more realistically, seemed to recall it had more to do with an order from an army general. It was, again, exerted pressure which prevented him from examining the President's clothes.

It was extraordinary that the autopsy team did not have access to the photographs taken of the President's body until three years after the time of the autopsy. In fact it was 1967 before they saw them, by which time one of the key photographs had disappeared. But this was an autopsy shrouded in extraordinary events. For instance, there are strong reasons for believing that the body of the President, despatched from Dallas in a polished bronze ceremonial casket, arrived at the back door of Bethesda Hospital in a grey metal shipping casket at about 6.45 p.m., after being flown into Andrews Air Force Base at Washington. It arrived in a black Cadillac hearse and was received by First Class Petty Officer Dennis David. The casket was opened and more than one witness recounted that the body of President Kennedy was there in a zipped-up pink-grey body bag. The polished bronze casket turned up at the front door in a navy ambulance accompanied by Jacqueline Kennedy and her brother-in-law, Robert. They arrived twenty minutes later, shortly after seven o'clock, observed from a second-floor window by First Class Petty Officer Dennis David. However, since nothing about the autopsy was straightforward and to add a dimension of confusion a casket team member, James Felder, said that when the bronze casket was opened in the morgue he saw the President's body there. Mr Felder's statement flew in the face of the evidence of those who said they witnessed the opening of the grey shipping casket. Who was right? Corroboration that the President's body had arrived in the grey shipping casket at the rear of the hospital came during the House Select Committee on Assassinations hearings which ended in 1979. A Lieutenant Richard A. Lipsey confirmed that a decoy ambulance was sent to the front entrance. He, personally, had attended the delivery of the body to the rear entrance.

Further confirmation of Lt. Lipsey's statement came in evidence given to researchers by Navy X-ray technician, Jerrol Custer. X-rays of the body of the President having being taken, Custer was carrying some of them down the corridor to have them developed when he saw Jacqueline Kennedy arriving with her brother-in law, Robert, at the main entrance, accompanying the bronze casket. Custer added he had already made previous trips with other film of the President before this arrival.

The body had left Parkland Hospital at Dallas wrapped up in a sheet, with the head wrapped in a towel. The principal wound was in the right rear of the President's head, where a gaping hole estimated at about three inches in diameter was present. It was thought that about two-thirds of the President's brain remained when the body left Dallas. When the body arrived for autopsy at Bethesda the hole in the right rear of the head now measured approximately five inches by seven, and there was little of the President's brain remaining. It was hardly surprising this raised questions and, indeed, caused deep suspicion.

The surgeons at Parkland Hospital confirmed they had carried out no surgery to the President's head, whereas as the body was received at Bethesda, FBI Agents James W. Sibert and Francis X. O'Neill, witnessing the cover being taken from the President's head, in a written FBI report, stated that surgery had been carried out, there being much blood in evidence. (See Figure 7.) This, and the change in caskets and body-wrappings, led to the belief by many that agents of the conspirators had contrived to examine the body, probably removing the incriminating evidence of bullets from the President's brain and leaving the body in a condition consistent with the fatal shots having come from behind the motorcade. Books written by David Lifton[1] and Noel Twyman[2] strongly support this theory.

It should not be thought that the only wound sustained by the President was

FIGURE 7

BA 89-30
FXO/JWS:dfl
3

transportation of the President's body back to the White House. AMC CHESTER H. BOYERS, U. S. Navy, visited the autopsy room during the final stages of such to type receipts given by FBI and Secret Service for items obtained.

At the termination of the autopsy, the following personnel from Gawler's Funeral Home entered the autopsy room to prepare the President's body for burial:

JOHN VAN HAESEN
EDWIN STROBLE
THOMAS ROBINSON
Mr. HAGEN

Brigidier General GODFREY McHUGH, Air Force Military Aide to the President, was also present, as was Dr. GEORGE BAKEMAN, U. S. Navy.

Arrangements were made .. for the performance of the autopsy by . the U. S. Navy and Secret Service.

The President's body was removed from the casket in which it had been transported and was placed on the autopsy table, at which time the complete body was wrapped in a sheet and the head area contained an additional wrapping which was saturated with blood. Following the removal of the wrapping, it was ascertained that the President's clothing had been removed and it was also apparent that a tracheotomy had been performed, as well as surgery of the head area, namely, in the top of the skull. All personnel with the exception of medical officers needed in the taking of photographs and X-Rays were requested to leave the autopsy room and remain in an adjacent room.

Upon completion of X-Rays and photographs, the first incision was made at 8:15 p.m. X-Rays of the brain area which were developed and returned to the autopsy room disclosed a path of a missile which appeared to enter the back of the skull and the path of the disintegrated fragments could be observed along the right side of the skull. The largest section of this missile as portrayed by X-Ray appeared to be behind the right frontal sinus. The next largest fragment appeared to be at the rear of the skull at the juncture of the skull bone.

The Chief Pathologist advised approximately 40 particles of disintegrated bullet and smudges indicated that the projectile had fragmentized while passing through the skull region.

FBI agents, Sibert and O'Neill, reported that surgery of the head had been carried out before the body arrived for autopsy. But by whom? The doctors at Dallas confirmed they did not conduct any surgery of the head.

the massive wound to the back of his head. A neatly drilled hole in the President's throat was identified by the Dallas doctors as a wound of entry, though later they were pressed to reconsider this. Wisely, the Parkland team had used the wound in the throat to perform a tracheotomy, when it was found to be required, instead of creating another entry. The wound, now enlarged, presented itself as an exit wound to the Bethesda doctors, and their opinion prevailed. The exact position of a bullet wound in the President's back caused much consternation, since it was marked on the autopsy sketch at a position about six inches below the collar line and slightly to the right of centre. (See Figure 8.) The Warren Commissioners argued the bullet entering there, exited at the throat. This suited the Commission's argument for the number of bullets fired but unfortunately it neccessitated two simultaneous changes of direction for the bullet, one from a downward to an upward direction and another from left to right. However, since details of a new investigation into the Warren claims are featured in the next chapter, I shall ask the reader to pick this point up later.

According to the Warren Commission, the wounds described above were the only wounds sustained by President Kennedy, and this sat very uncomfortably with the evidence of the Zapruder film, which arguably showed that the President had been hit three times. Interestingly, Lieutenant Richard Lipsey, whom we mention above, was also present throughout the autopsy. Elsewhere in his statement he says he saw three wounds (apart from the throat wound); the gaping head wound and two more, one in the top part of the neck and one further down in the neck. In making this statement, about which he was quite adamant, Lt. Lipsey appeared to be blissfully unaware that he had just sunk the entire Warren Commission case without trace, and with it the case against Lee Harvey Oswald. Perhaps, not surprisingly, the House Select Committee on Assassinations did not advertise what he had said. They buried Lt. Lipsey's statement, as though it had never been made, deep in the National Archives.

But as we said, there was nothing straightforward about the autopsy of President Kennedy. Commander Humes told the Warren Commission that the President's brain was examined separately by the three autopsy doctors two or three days after the autopsy, but in 1996 when he testified to the House Select Committee on Assassinations, Humes did not confirm that Dr Finck was present, and Dr Boswell said he was not there. Dr Finck, on the other hand, said he was there, but that he was not even called regarding a date for the examination of the brain until a week after the autopsy. There was further controversy when Dr Boswell was asked about photographs being taken of the brain. He said the only photographs taken were taken at the autopsy proper, whereas Pierre Finck said that both black-and-white and colour photographs were taken at the separate examination. All this led Douglas Horne, chief analyst for military records, to conclude that two examinations may have taken place. 'If true, Dr Finck's

FIGURE 8

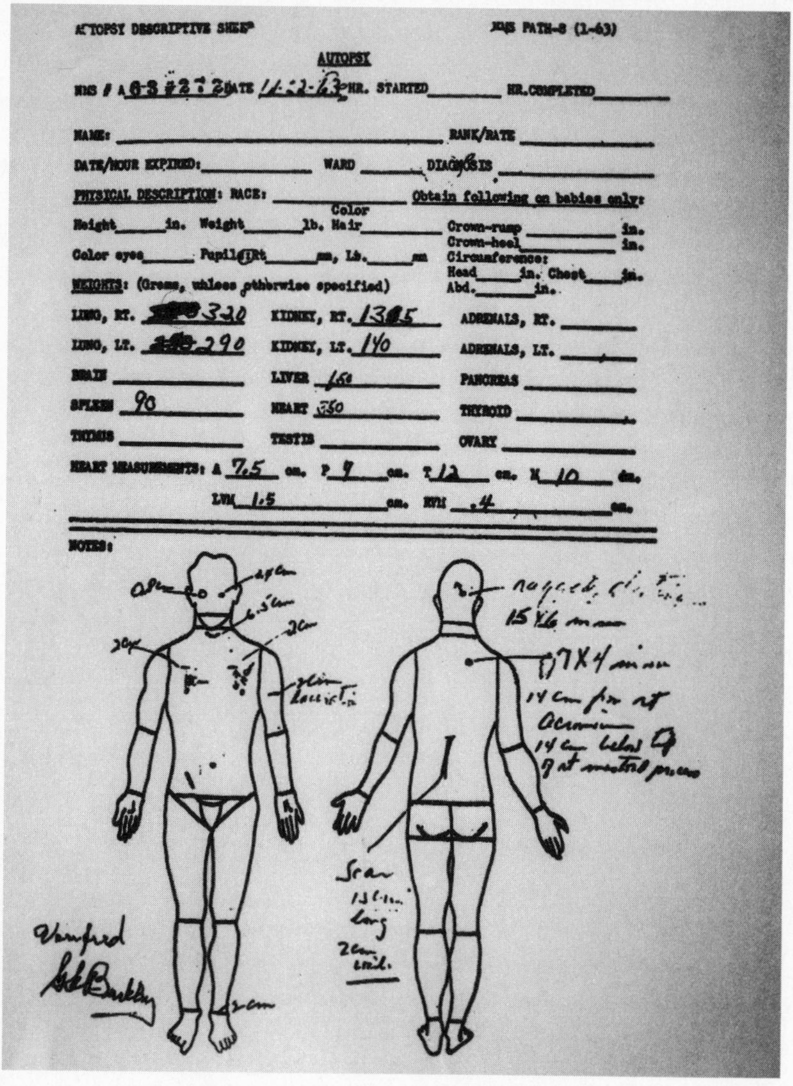

AUTOPSY DESCRIPTIVE SHEET NMS PATH-8 (1-63)

AUTOPSY

NMS # A 63 #272 DATE 11-22-63 HR. STARTED ______ HR. COMPLETED ______

NAME: ______ RANK/RATE ______

DATE/HOUR EXPIRED: ______ WARD ______ DIAGNOSIS ______

PHYSICAL DESCRIPTION: RACE: ______ Obtain following on babies only:

Height ______ in. Weight ______ lb. Hair Color ______ Crown-rump ______ in.

Crown-heel ______ in.

Color eyes ______ Pupil Rt ______ mm, Lt. ______ mm Circumference:

Head ______ in. Chest ______ in.

WEIGHTS: (Grams, unless otherwise specified) Abd. ______ in.

LUNG, RT. 320 KIDNEY, RT. 135 ADRENALS, RT. ______

LUNG, LT. 290 KIDNEY, LT. 140 ADRENALS, LT. ______

BRAIN ______ LIVER 1650 PANCREAS ______

SPLEEN 90 HEART 350 THYROID ______

THYMUS ______ TESTIS ______ OVARY ______

HEART MEASUREMENTS: A 7.5 cm. P 7 cm. T 12 cm. M 10 cm.

LVM 1.5 cm. RVM .4 cm.

NOTES:

15 X 6 mm

7 X 4 mm

14 cm from rt acromion

14 cm below tip of rt mastoid process

Scar 13 cm long 2 cm wide

Verified

GG Burkley

Autopsy Descriptive Sheet. (Courtesy National Archives.)

account of a brain exam separate and distinct from the first one would mean that Drs Humes and Boswell were present at two different brain exams,' he said.

US Navy photographer John Stringer added fuel to the controversy by testifying that he took pictures of the brain two or three days after the autopsy. Dramatically, he also claimed that the official photographs of the brain held in archives were not those which he took. He said the angles of the shots did not match those he recalls taking and the film was not the same. Former FBI Agent Francis X. O'Neill, whom we mention above, watched the President's brain being removed at the autopsy. He told the Assassination Records Review Board that when he saw the photographs of the brain they did not resemble what he saw. 'I did not recall it being that large,' he said.

We are, therefore, left with various possibilities. It would appear that two separate examinations of the President's brain were carried out and the doctors may have been looking at a brain which was not the President's on one of those occasions or, for that matter, both. Curiouser and curiouser.

Before we leave the realms of the curious, however, we should mention a receipt issued by FBI Agents Sibert and O'Neill, whom we have mentioned earlier. This receipt is in respect of a 'missile removed by Commander James J. Humes' during the autopsy. (See Figure 9A). It would be apparent to most people that this referred to a bullet, but the authorities argue that the agents

FIGURE 9A

22 November 1963

From: Francis X. O'NEILL, Jr., Agent FBI
James W. SIBERT, Agent FBI

To: Captain J. H. STOVER, Jr., Commanding Officer, U. S. Naval Medical School, National Naval Medical Center, Bethesda, Maryland

1. We hereby acknowledge receipt of a missle removed by Commander James J. HUMES, MC, USN on this date.

Francis X. O'NEILL, Jr.

James W. SIBERT

Another FBI report from Sibert and O'Neill. They recorded that a 'missile' was removed during the autopsy. It was later argued they meant a fragment of a missile, but in yet another report they refer to 'fragments' (see Figure 9B), which supports they meant a missile when they said a missile. But it disappeared.

FIGURE 9B

BA 89-30
FXO/JWS:dfl
4

During the autopsy inspection of the area of the brain, two fragments of metal were removed by Dr. HUMES, namely, one fragment measuring 7 x 2 millimeters, which was removed from the right side of the brain. An additional fragment of metal measuring 1 x 3 millimeters was also removed from this area, both of which were placed in a glass jar containing a black metal top which were thereafter marked for identification and following the signing of a proper receipt were transported by Bureau agents to the FBI Laboratory.

During the latter stages of this autopsy, Dr. HUMES located an opening which appeared to be a bullet hole which was below the shoulders and two inches to the right of the middle line of the spinal column.

This opening was probed by Dr. HUMES with the finger, at which time it was determined that the trajectory of the missile entering at this point had entered at a downward position of 45 to 60 degrees. Further probing determined that the distance travelled by this missile was a short distance inasmuch as the end of the opening could be felt with the finger.

Inasmuch as no complete bullet of any size could be located in the brain area and likewise no bullet could be located in the back or any other area of the body as determined by total body X-Rays and inspection revealing there was no point of exit, the individuals performing the autopsy were at a loss to explain why they could find no bullets.

A call was made by Bureau agents to the Firearms Section of the FBI Laboratory, at which time SA CHARLES L. KILLION advised that the Laboratory had received through Secret Service Agent RICHARD JOHNSON a bullet which had reportedly been found on a stretcher in the emergency room of Parkland Hospital, Dallas, Texas. This stretcher had also contained a stethescope and pair of rubber gloves. Agent JOHNSON had advised the Laboratory that it had not been ascertained whether or not this was the stretcher which had been used to transport the body of President KENNEDY. Agent KILLION further described this bullet as pertaining to a 6.5 millimeter rifle which would be approximately a 25 caliber rifle and that this bullet consisted of a copper alloy full jacket.

Immediately following receipt of this information, this was made available to Dr. HUMES who advised that in his opinion this accounted for no bullet being located which had entered

Sibert and O'Neill refer to 'fragments'.

meant a fragment of a bullet. In a report by the same agents on the examination of the brain, they refer specifically to 'fragments'. (See Figure 9B.) Why, therefore, should they use the word 'missile' in the receipt if they meant 'fragment'? One would have expected a receipt to be extremely accurate. It is my opinion they were referring to a bullet, a bullet which would, for instance, have likely proved without question the guilt or innocence of Lee Harvey Oswald. Where is the bullet? Vanished without trace . . .

The discovery by Dr David Mantik in 1993 of a metal object, 6.5 mm in diameter, showing in an X-ray, may, in fact, offer further evidence of the existence of this bullet. He came across this never-before-mentioned bullet while conducting an examination of the X-ray photographs in National Archives. Dr Mantik, a radiation oncologist and physicist, also identified what appeared to be clear evidence of forgery. He found that a radio-dense patch had been superimposed over an X-ray of the rear of the head where the gaping hole had been.

Whatever was left of the President's brain, assuming it was the President's brain, was preserved in a jar and sent to Robert Kennedy. To the dismay of all researchers, when it was sought it had disappeared and it has never been seen since. Whether it was stolen or whether it was respectfully disposed of by the President's brother, we do not know.

Commander James J. Humes, who was in charge of the autopsy and who wrote the autopsy report, may not have been altogether in charge of the proceedings, as we have intimated earlier. When he reported to the Warren Commission, he made a point of telling it that he burnt all of the original notes he made during the autopsy. One has to wonder whether or not this was his way, in some measure, of disclaiming what he had presented in the autopsy report. It was an unusual thing to do, to say the least, and has always appeared to researchers as an illegal act. Since there was no compulsion for Commander Humes to make this 'confession', it would seem he wanted the world to know that his spontaneous notes went up in flames. Did they contradict what went into the published autopsy report? Did they reveal he was under restraint at every step of the proceedings by senior officers present at the autopsy? We shall probably never know.

---

[1] David Lifton: *Best Evidence*, Macmillan Publishing Co. Inc, New York 1980.

[2] Noel Twyman: *Bloody Treason*, Laurel Publishing, Rancho Santa Fe, California 1997.

FIGURE 10

U. S. NAVAL MEDICAL SCHOOL
NATIONAL NAVAL MEDICAL CENTER
BETHESDA, MARYLAND 20014

In reply refer to

24 November 1963

C-E-R-T-I-F-I-C-A-T-E

I, James J. Humes, certify that I have destroyed by burning certain preliminary draft notes relating to Naval Medical School Autopsy Report A63-272 and have officially transmitted all other papers related to this report to higher authority.

J. J. HUMES
CDR, MC, USN

Commander J.J. Humes reported that he had burnt all his original notes on the autopsy. Was this on instructions? (Courtesy National Archives)

CHAPTER ELEVEN

New Light – Old Shadows

I RECEIVED A TELEPHONE call from an Essex company which marketed computer software among many other things. It was the director's secretary who was trying to track me down for a German designer and supplier of brilliant new software. 'I have been trying to find your telephone number. Herr Markus is very anxious to meet you,' she said. 'I eventually obtained your number by ringing a publisher. I hope you don't mind.' I said I didn't and promised to motor down to Essex the following week when Joachim Markus was visiting her company.

Joachim Markus had seen me on German television talking about the assassination of President Kennedy. 'I have this new method of handling photographs. I can turn a two-dimensional picture into a three dimensional image,' he said, and he demonstrated it then and there. It was staggering. From an ordinary photograph of a chapel featuring the front and side of the building, he projected – or created, if you like – the other side, the rear, the inside of the building and the roof. And we were viewing it in three dimensions. This was photogrammetry. Whereas photogrammetry normally required locations to be photographed by two cameras in order to calculate the third dimension, the system developed by Joachim Markus required only one picture. He could, therefore, take existing photographs and 'create' a third dimension from them.

'I want you to supply me with data so that we can create a three-dimensional model of the place where President John F. Kennedy was killed,' said Joachim. 'We can then rerun the assassination and make calculations which will tell us exactly what happened.' So began the most exciting piece of research I have ever had the good fortune to be involved in. I supplied photographs in many different forms.

Some were prints, some were transparencies, some were on videotape. Some were in black and white and others in colour. Joachim Markus was demanding. Some of the data I sent did not match his requirements and he came back for more. He came back many, many times for more. I found myself seeking material by phone from different parts of the United States and Canada. On and on it went over a period of four years. We talked on the telephone, we faxed messages to each other, and now and then we met each other. Sometimes Joachim visited England and we met, and other times I journeyed to the little town of Herdecke in Germany, where he lived, one of the most attractive towns I have ever visited.

There was one source of data I did not use. I drew nothing from the Warren Report. I bypassed it completely. It came to be thought of as 'tainted' data. Similarly, I would not have permitted data from any other questionable source to be used. I remembered well the saying, 'Garbage in – garbage out'. Everything put into the study was to be 'clean'. Though it had not been our direct intention, it became obvious to us that in seeking to know what had really happened in Elm Street, we could not avoid putting the Warren Report claims to the test. This became central to our work, though it was not our intention when we began.

Came the day when Joachim telephoned me and told me he had obtained the first results from our joint study. 'I followed the trajectory of the bullet from the President's back to the front and projected it to the rear,' he said. 'It was nonsense, so I wondered what would happen if I turned it round as though the bullet had come from the front.' My heart sank. We were not seeking to be controversial and, at the outset, this had not even been discussed as a possibility. 'How did you get on?' I asked. 'It was fascinating,' he said. 'The bullet could have come from the front, from the grassy knoll.' I pricked up my ears and we discussed the first findings in some detail. 'The Dallas doctors said the throat wound was a wound of entry,' I said. 'I think we just struck oil.'

We dutifully considered the Warren position on the first hit. The 'Single Bullet' theory was well and truly examined. This hit occurred – in Zapruder film terms – just as the President's limousine was obscured by the Stemmons sign. We took measurements of the angles involved in a bullet striking the President in the upper back, exiting his throat, striking Governor Connally in his back and exiting once again to find the Governor's wrist and finally, his left thigh. We knew long before we reached the end of the sequence that it was impossible, but we persevered. The whole notion was completely untenable. The bullet would have had to have changed direction after every point of contact veering upward or downward in combination with left or right, rendering the idea of the bullet behaving randomly totally unacceptable. (See Figures 11–17.) As we later detected, it was far more likely that Governor Connally was hit by two other bullets, one from behind and one from the grassy knoll.

FIGURE 11

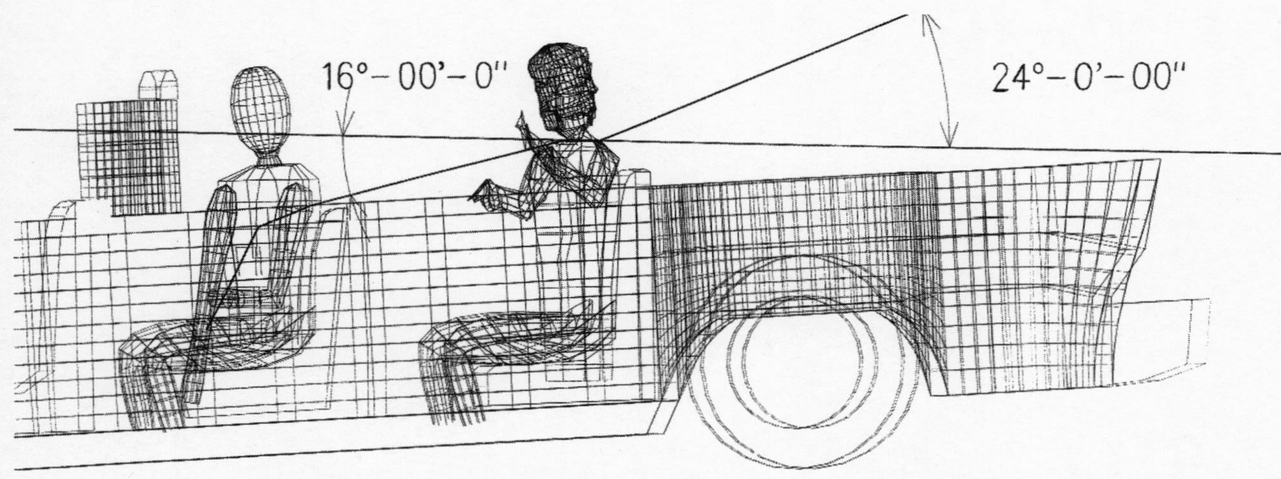

First hit (A). Close side view showing the flight path of the bullet the Warren Report claimed came from the sixth-floor window and the changes of direction which would have been necessary for it to have achieved all the wounds attributed to it. The trajectory of the bullet the computer attributes to a sniper on the knoll is also shown.

FIGURE 12

First hit (B). Overhead view of (A) with calculations.

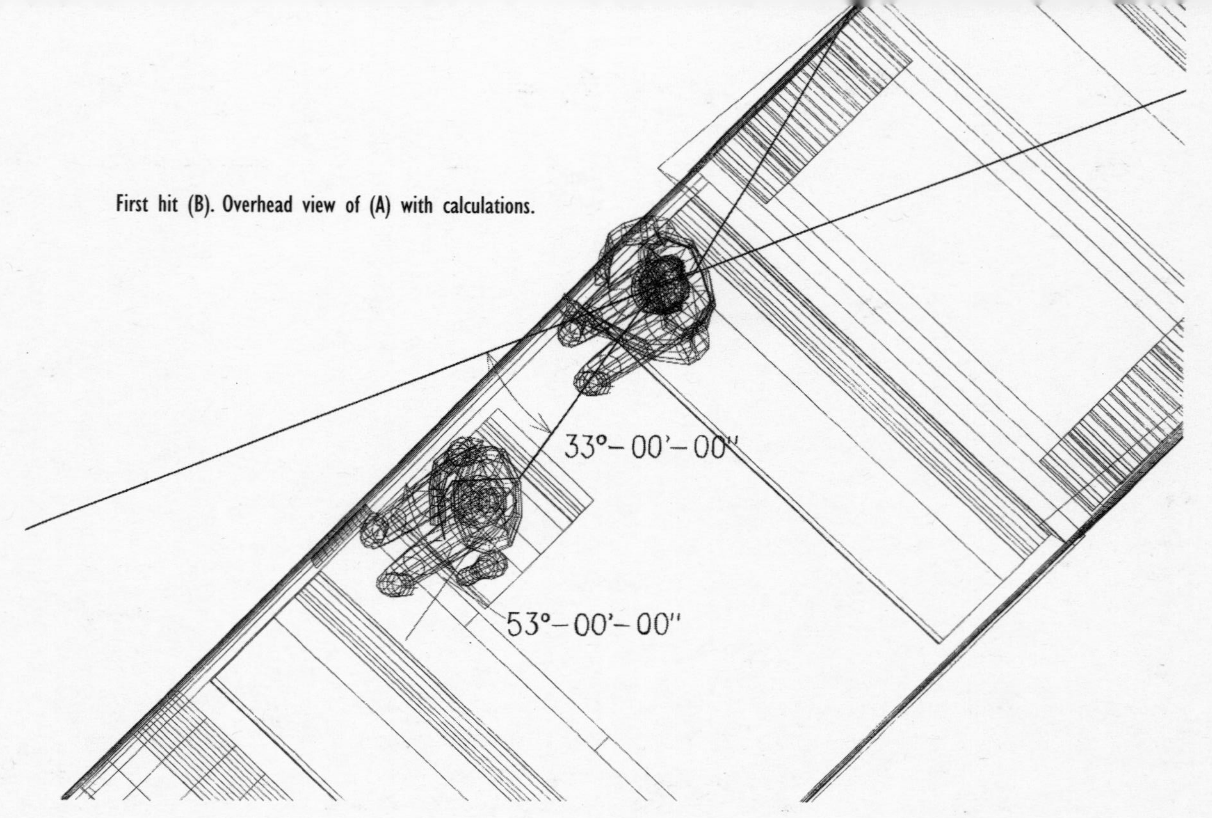

FIGURE 13

First hit (C). This long view shows the trajectory of the bullet from the knoll which struck the President in the thoat and exited his back. It also shows the hugely conflicting trajectory which would have represented a bullet from the sixth-floor window.

FIGURE 14

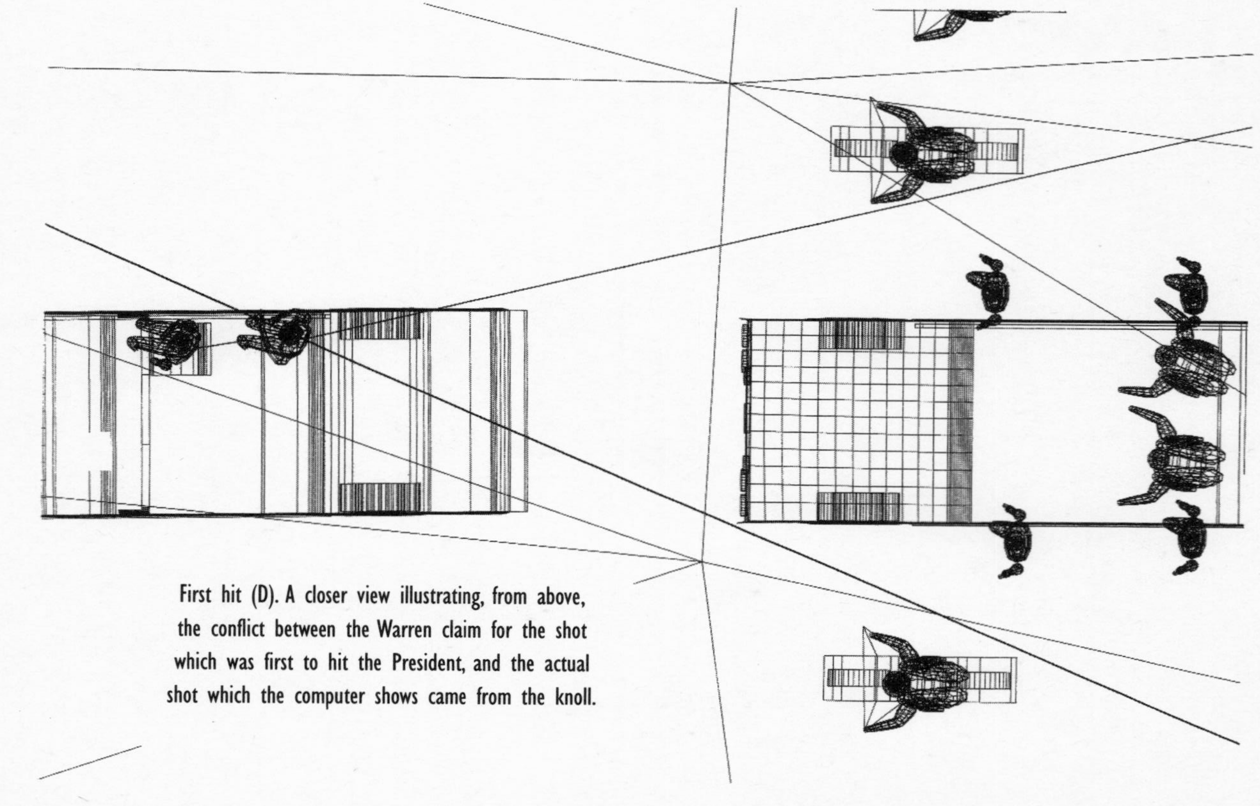

First hit (D). A closer view illustrating, from above, the conflict between the Warren claim for the shot which was first to hit the President, and the actual shot which the computer shows came from the knoll.

FIGURE 15

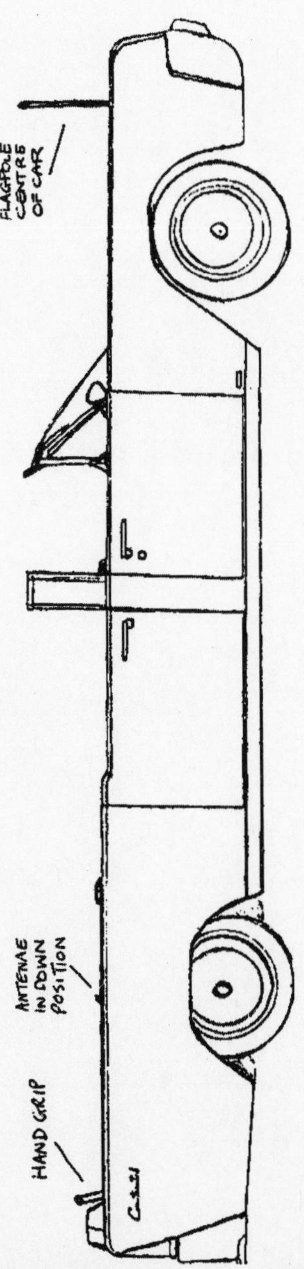

Scale: ½" = 1'.

SS 100 x 1961 Lincoln Continental
R.Side View. (Drawn by Colin McSween)

FIGURE 16

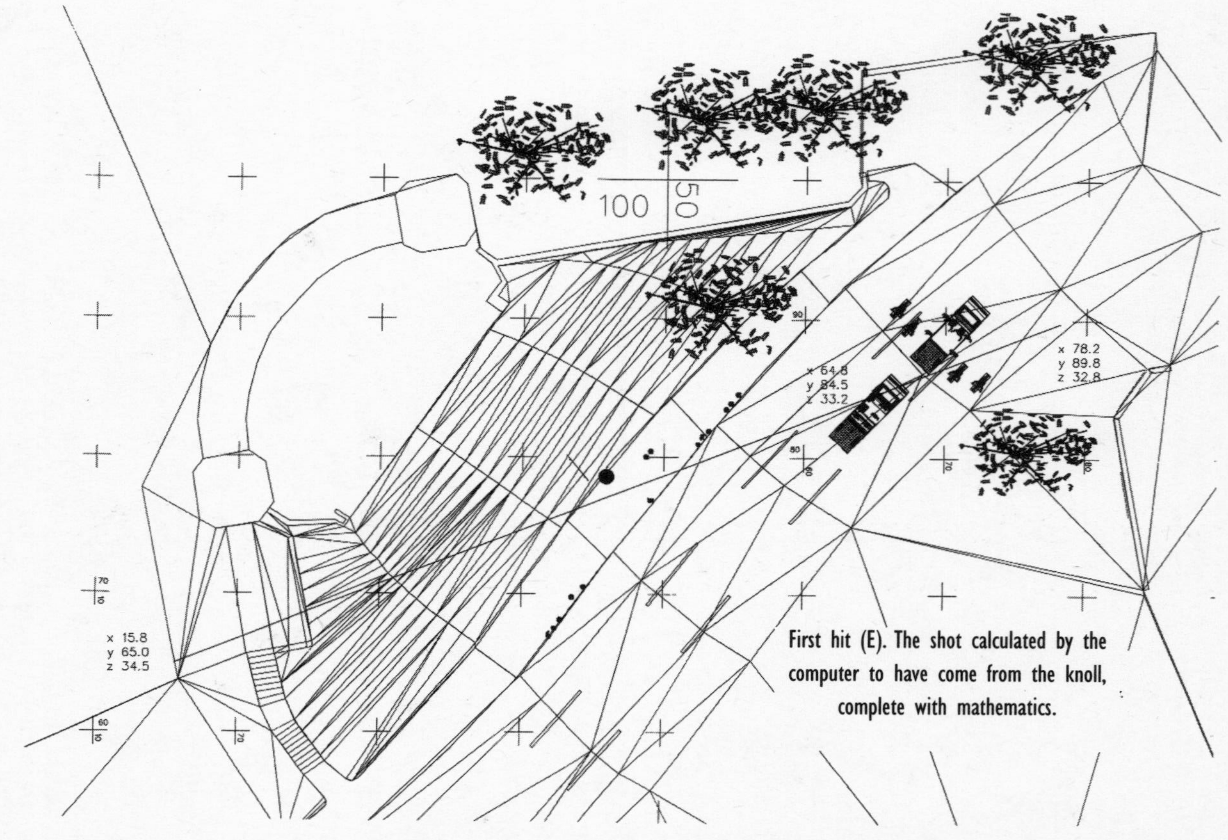

First hit (E). The shot calculated by the computer to have come from the knoll, complete with mathematics.

FIGURE 17

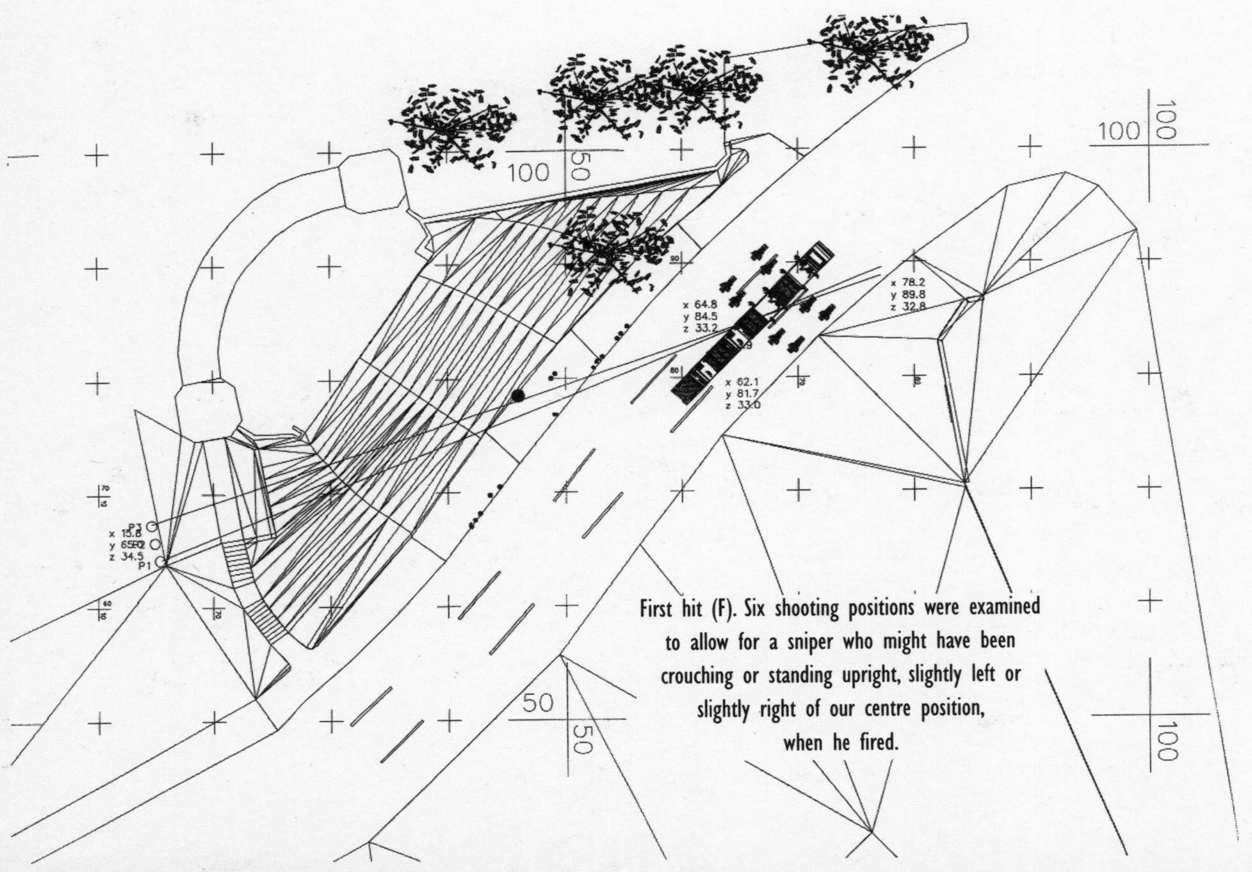

First hit (F). Six shooting positions were examined to allow for a sniper who might have been crouching or standing upright, slightly left or slightly right of our centre position, when he fired.

We examined our early finding carefully. To establish the trajectory of the bullet which passed between the President's back and his throat, Joachim had used two excellent-quality autopsy photographs, one showing the President's head from the front and the other from the back. He took measurements from the tip of the right ear to the back wound, and from the tip of the right ear to the throat wound. (See first picture section.) This gave us the exact direction the bullet took as it passed through the President's throat. Another vital task was to establish where the car was when this bullet struck and what the position of the President's body was. One of the Zapruder frames was extremely useful in this exercise and another was one of the Willis transparencies. Looking from Zapruder's viewpoint, the President was hit at the instant the car disappeared behind the Stemmons sign, when JFK was well turned to his right, waving to the crowds. His throat lined up with the fence on the knoll. (See first picture section.)

At first leaving this at one side, we looked carefully to see where the bullet would have come from if it had originated from behind. The sniper, we discovered, would have been lying in the middle of the road in great danger of being killed by the oncoming motorcade. This, of course, was quite absurd, as Joachim had said. I then ventured the opinion to Joachim that if this bullet had originated from the grassy knoll it must have come from well down the picket fence, towards the overpass. This gave Joachim the task of pinpointing the position occupied by the sniper. I was quite wrong. The sniper fired from the corner of the picket fence, at the side of the footpath leading to the car park, and just a couple of feet in the direction of the car park. In fact, this was the only 'window' of opportunity from which the shot could have been fired. Remarkably, this coincides with the point at which, for many years, others have argued the presence of a gunman, notably the 'Badge Man', derived from the Mary Moorman Polaroid photo, so named because there was the semblance of a uniform about the shadowy figure. (See first picture section.)

We next looked at the shot which hit the President in the back of the neck, which we termed the second hit. It most certainly came from behind, and therefore, from a different rifle. The Zapruder film shows it clearly at a point where the Lincoln has barely cleared the Stemmons sign. The President is pushed forward in his seat. In our three-dimensional computer model we had 'constructed' the sixth floor of the Texas School Book Depository building, from where Warren was adamant all the shots had come. The sixth-floor is not divided into rooms. It is one, long continuous storage area and, via the computer programme, we 'walked' down from one end to the other, starting at the window from where Warren said Oswald had fired the shots and moving down to the opposite end. As we went we 'looked' through the windows from where, with

FIGURE 18

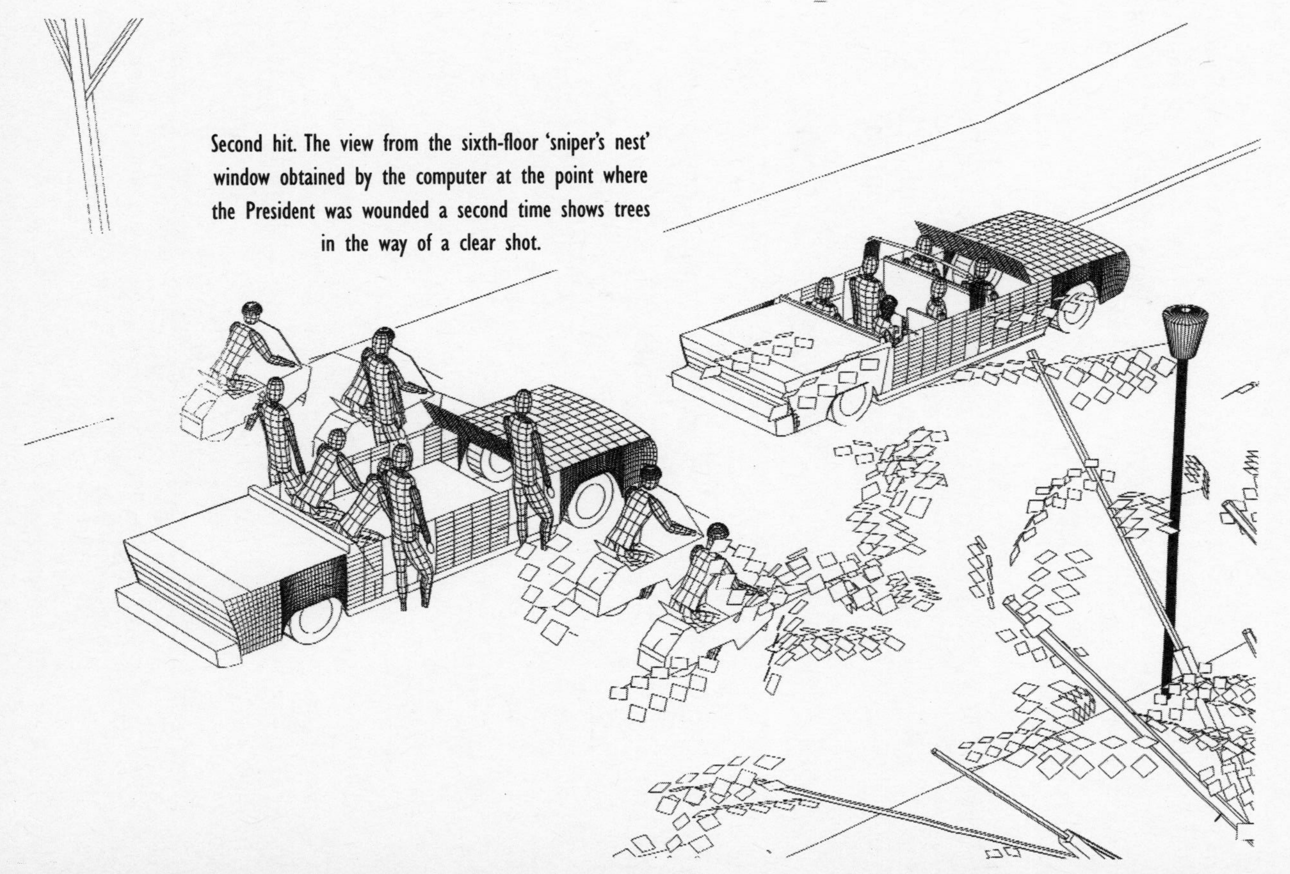

Second hit. The view from the sixth-floor 'sniper's nest' window obtained by the computer at the point where the President was wounded a second time shows trees in the way of a clear shot.

FIGURE 19

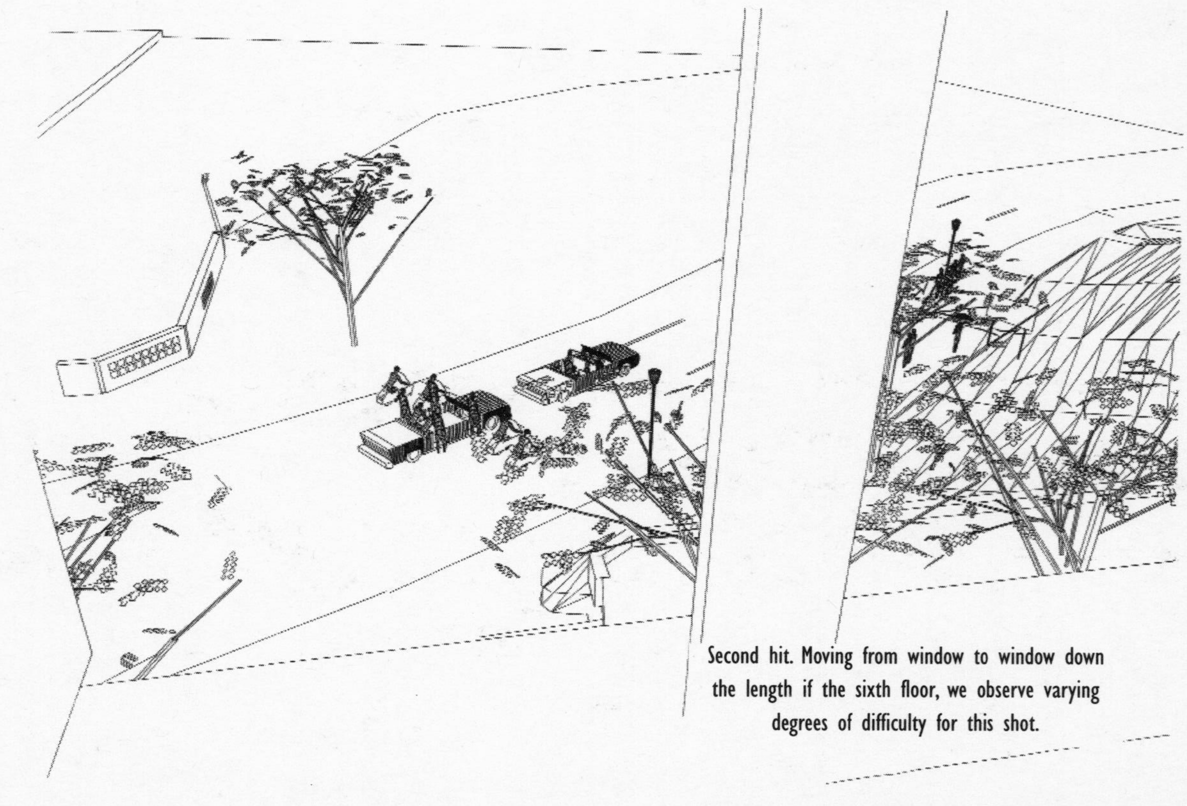

Second hit. Moving from window to window down the length if the sixth floor, we observe varying degrees of difficulty for this shot.

FIGURE 20

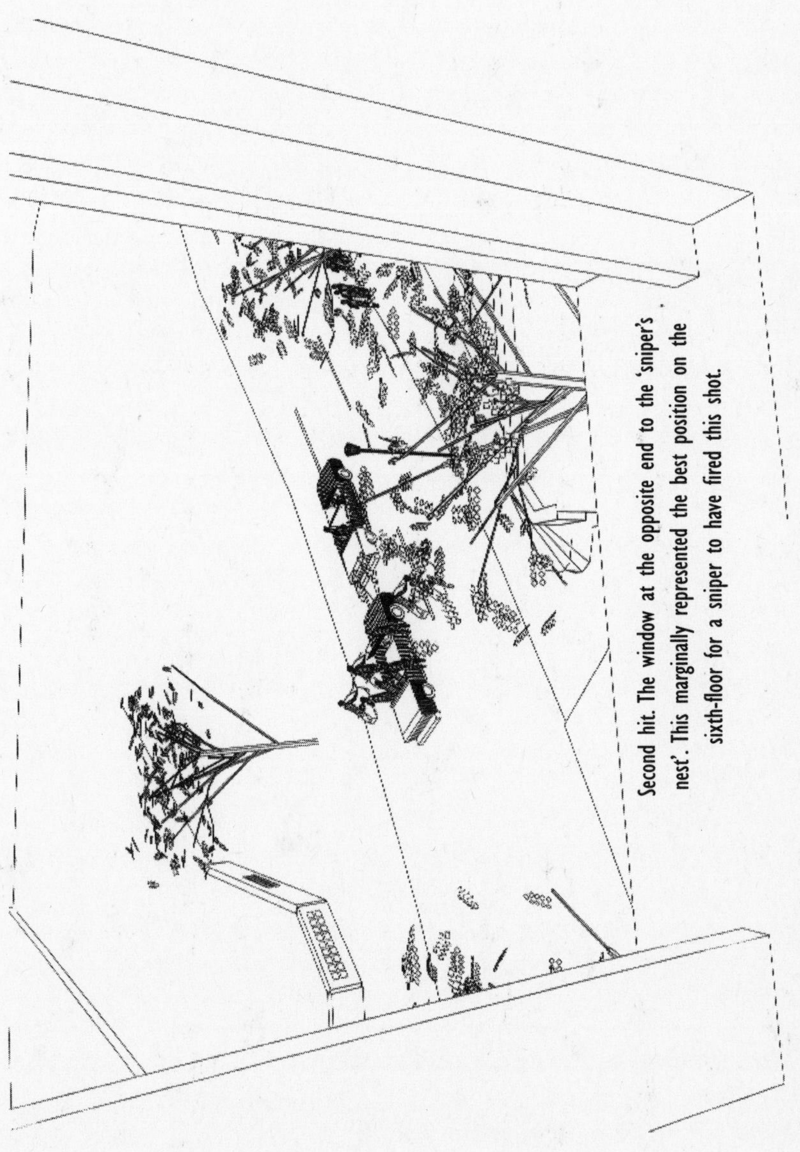

Second hit. The window at the opposite end to the 'sniper's nest'. This marginally represented the best position on the sixth-floor for a sniper to have fired this shot.

some difficulty, we could see the President's car, which we had 'stopped' at the point where this second hit took place. The difficulty arose because there were trees partly obscuring our vision in windows one, two, three and four. There was a relatively unhindered view from windows five and six and, perhaps, seven. Any sniper attempting a shot from the sixth-floor window Warren said was used (the 'sniper's nest') had his work cut out for him. One assumes the snipers involved in this high-precision ambush would have, at some time, walked the ground, so to speak. They must surely have viewed the position their target would occupy from their firing positions at some previous time, and it would seem odd if they chose a difficult firing position when there were far easier positions available. It would certainly be odd if Lee Harvey Oswald, for example, who had access to all parts of the sixth floor, chose one of the more difficult places to shoot from. Taking the overall view, it seemed more likely the shot in question came from another building, perhaps the Dal-Tex building. (See second picture section.)

After a shot from the front which exited the President's back, leaving one tear in the fabric of the jacket, a shot from behind entering the President's back was sure to have opened another hole, though no mention of this is made by Warren. I eventually found a report of a second opening in the fabric of the jacket in the report of the '1968 Panel Review of Photographs, X-Ray Films, Documents and Other Evidence Pertaining to the Fatal Wounding of President John F. Kennedy on 22 November 1963, in Dallas, Texas'. It first referred to the hole visible in the photographs of the jacket and went on to say, 'A smaller ragged hole which is located near the midline and about 4 cm. of the upper edge of the collar . . . appears to be unrelated to the wounds or their causation.' Is the writer arguing there was no cause for this second 'ragged hole'? Is he saying the President was wearing a holey jacket? We think not. We think we have found physical evidence to support our claims.

When we came to the final and fatal head wound, we again considered the Warren position on the wound first. Warren stated that the wound was made by a shot from the rear, from the sixth-floor 'sniper's nest'. We produced an animation showing the flight path a bullet fired from the sixth-floor window would have taken. The outstanding feature of such a shot would have been picking out JFK's head from the sea of heads which were in view. The other heads belonged to the Secret Service men who were standing on the running boards of the car immediately behind the President's Lincoln. As someone once said, it's hard enough to hit a rabbit, but to hit one particular rabbit in a gathering of rabbits is well-nigh impossible. It also must be remembered that the heads being viewed were not still. They were moving, changing position every second, and the distance for a shooter from the sixth-floor window would have been

FIGURE 21

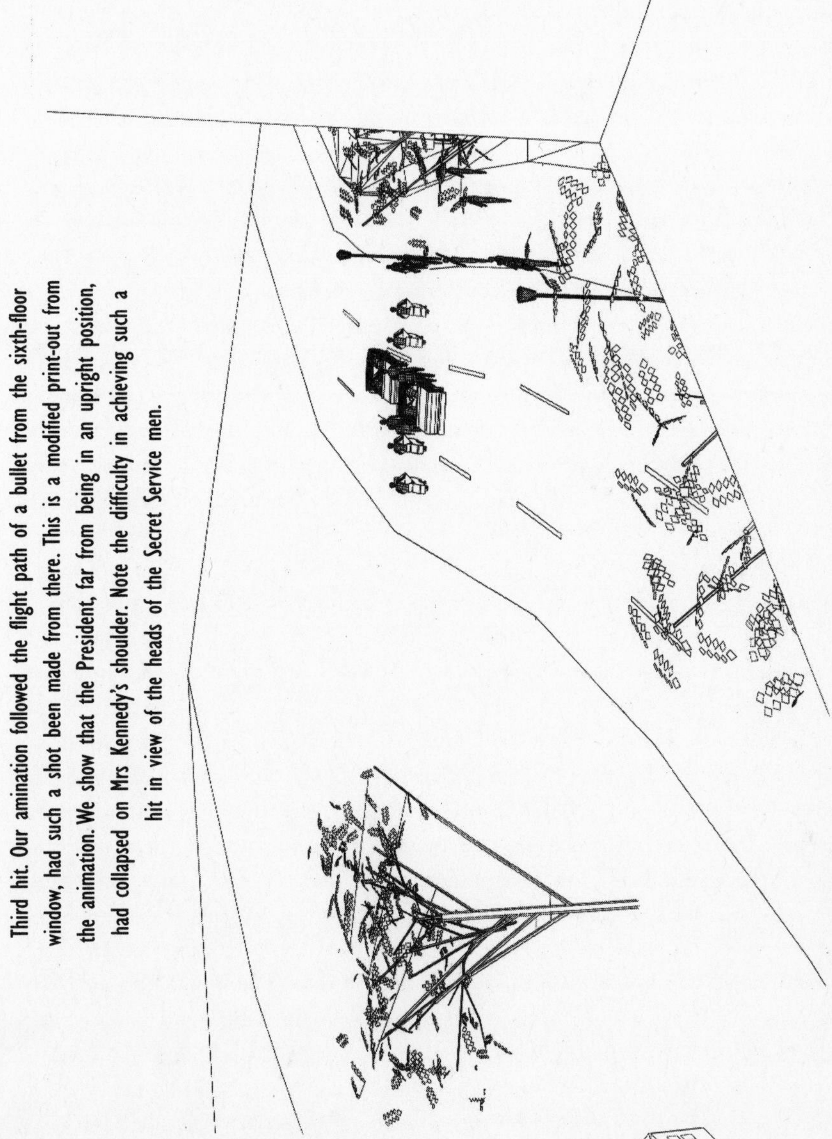

Third hit. Our amination followed the flight path of a bullet from the sixth-floor window, had such a shot been made from there. This is a modified print-out from the animation. We show that the President, far from being in an upright position, had collapsed on Mrs Kennedy's shoulder. Note the difficulty in achieving such a hit in view of the heads of the Secret Service men.

roughly 260 feet. An attempt at such a shot would have required time to set it up, and here Lee Harvey Oswald is ruled out. He certainly did not have time to set up anything. Warren's calculations barely gave him time to get three rounds off without painstakingly making calculations. This piece of our research found that the chances of the fatal shot having come from behind were so slim as to be easily dismissed. It also found that if anyone had, by any manner or means achieved such an incredible shot, it was clear it was not Lee Harvey Oswald.

A most compelling argument against the fatal shot having come from behind involved the position of Jackie Kennedy's head and face in relation to where the President's head was. This did not admit to a shot from the rear. Our calculations placed her virtually in front of him at the moment of this shot. She was almost face to face with him. (This can be seen in Zapruder frame 312, the frame before the fatal hit.) Had this shot come from behind, her face and hat would have been severely spattered with blood. This did not happen.

In asserting that the fatal head wound sustained by President Kennedy was not the result of a shot from the sixth-floor window, we have, of course, only confirmed what has been popularly believed for a long time. But we examined the possibility scientifically, and our results are supported by scientific calculation. We have taken the guesswork out of it. We now turned our attention to the question of where that fatal bullet had come from. We could not establish an accurate trajectory such as the one we constructed for the neck wound, for the gaping head wound involved made that impossible. We could, however, make calculations as to where along the picket fence such a shot might have been fired. This we did, and found two possible sites or 'windows' about halfway down the run of the fence. Our calculations might be upset should a sniper have thrust his rifle through a gap somewhere or other in the fence, but we regard this as unlikely. Remember that Governor Connally was hit in the wrist by a bullet which ended up in his left thigh, suggesting a broad trajectory which would indicate a bullet from the grassy knoll, we suggest that President Kennedy was hit from one site and Governor Connally from the other.

In another animation which we produced, the head of the wounded President was revolved in three dimensions. We entered first a trajectory representing a bullet from the sixth-floor window, if that had been possible. This showed that Jackie Kennedy would have been covered in a shower of blood in this case, and the wounds sustained by the President did not reflect this shot taking place. We then added another trajectory representing a bullet fired from the grassy knoll. This agreed with blood and tissue being blown behind and to the President's left (that is, into the middle road), and the wounds agreed with this bullet path. An outrider immediately behind and left of the President reported blood and tissue being blown on to him.

We did not deal with the claimed neat hole higher up on the back of the President's head, as we believe this may be an invention to support the fatal head shot having come from behind. If such a wound exists, it does not alter any of our findings. It would, however, add another to the wounds sustained by President Kennedy and drive the Warren claim of two bullets hitting the President further into fiction.

One of the outstanding results of this study relates to Lee Harvey Oswald. Clearly Oswald could not have fired the first hit, the neck-to-back wound, and neither could he have fired the shot which constituted the third, fatal hit. These were both fired from the grassy knoll. As for the one shot we know that came from the rear, it was unlikely the shot came from the sixth-floor window. **Taken at large, this means that the likelihood of Oswald's total innocence rates about 95 per cent which, in a court of law, would be beyond reasonable doubt**.

In Figures 22–27, details of how our calculations were obtained are shown. There is nothing up our sleeves.

FIGURE 22

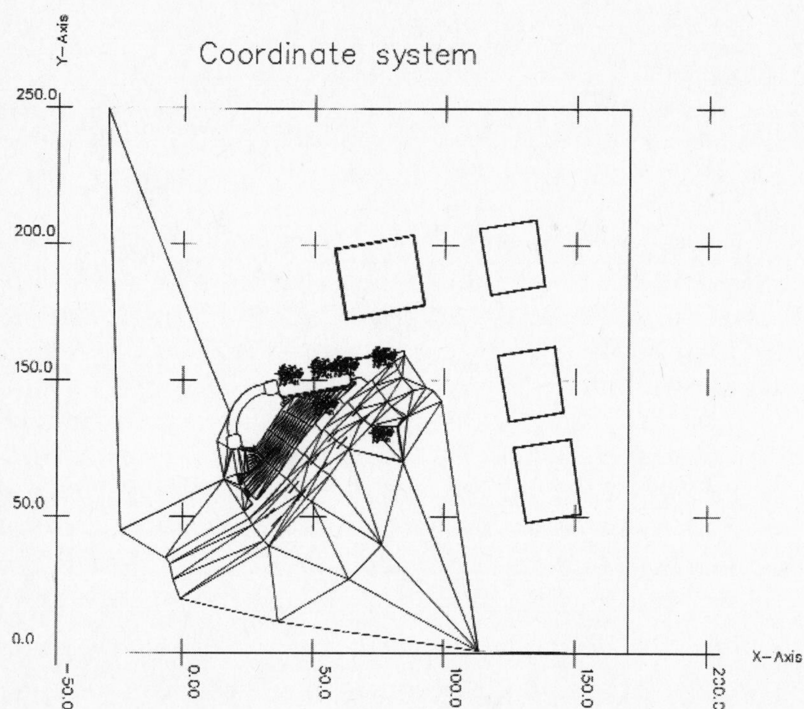

Coordinate system
Y-Axis
X-Axis
250.0
200.0
150.0
50.0
0.0
-50.0
0.00
50.0
100.0
150.0

FIGURE 23

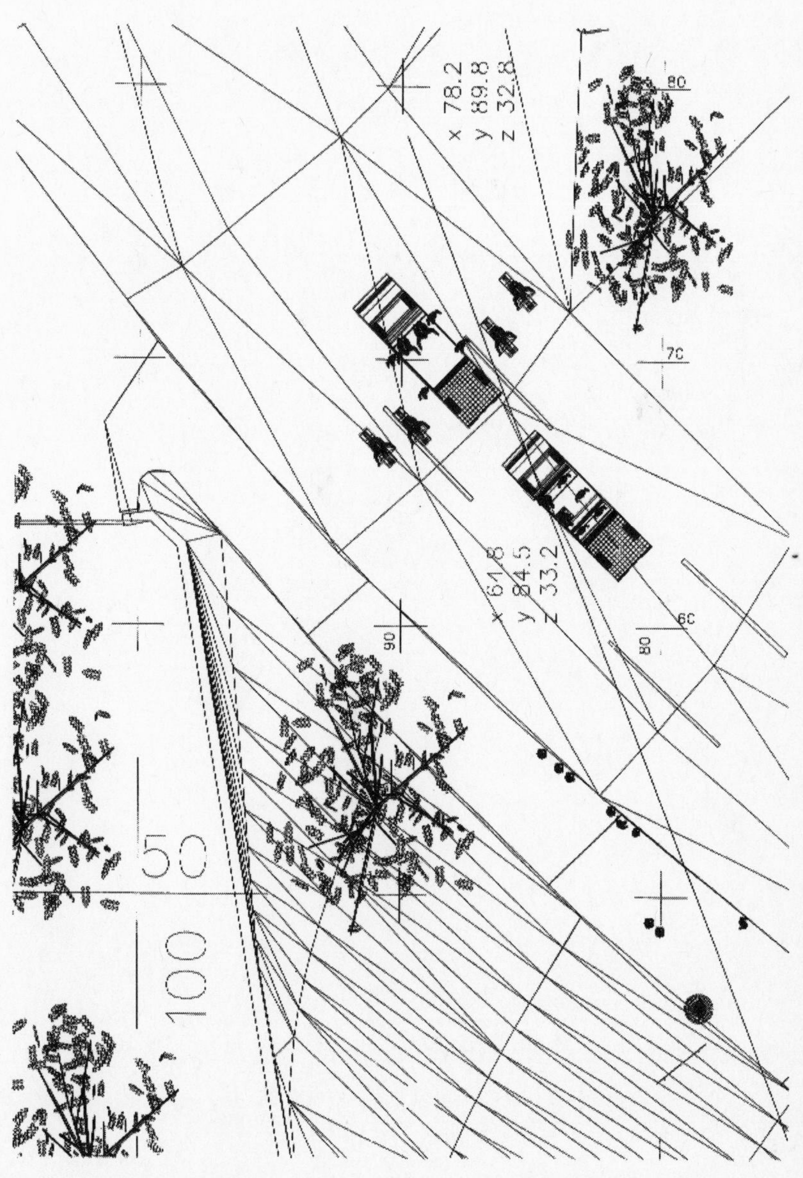

FIGURE 24

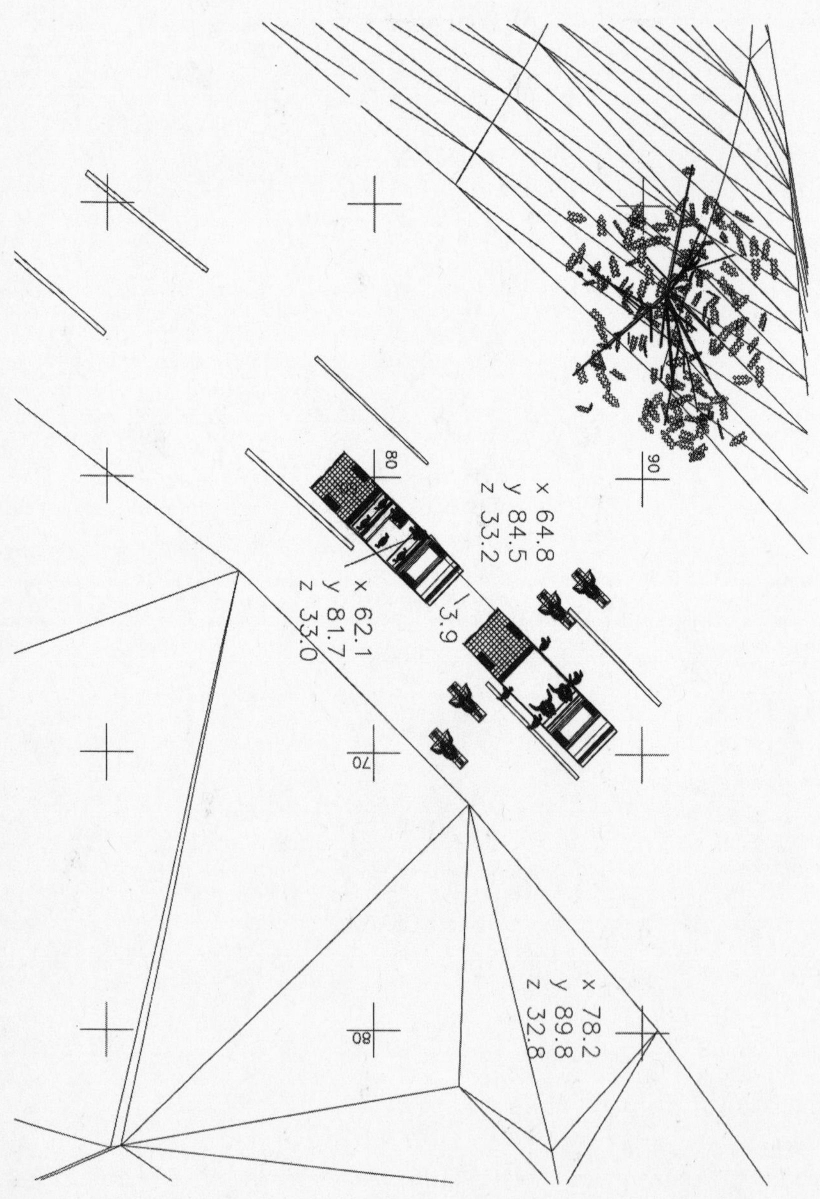

FIGURE 25

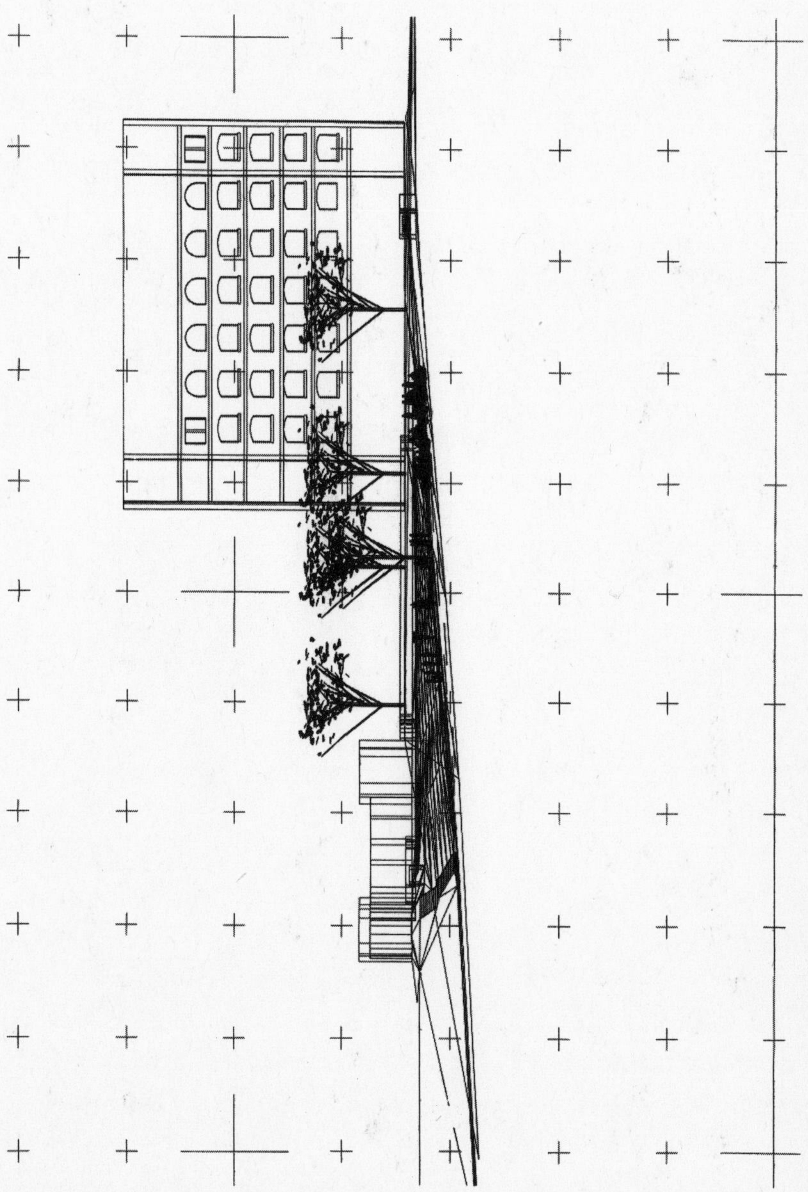

FIGURE 26

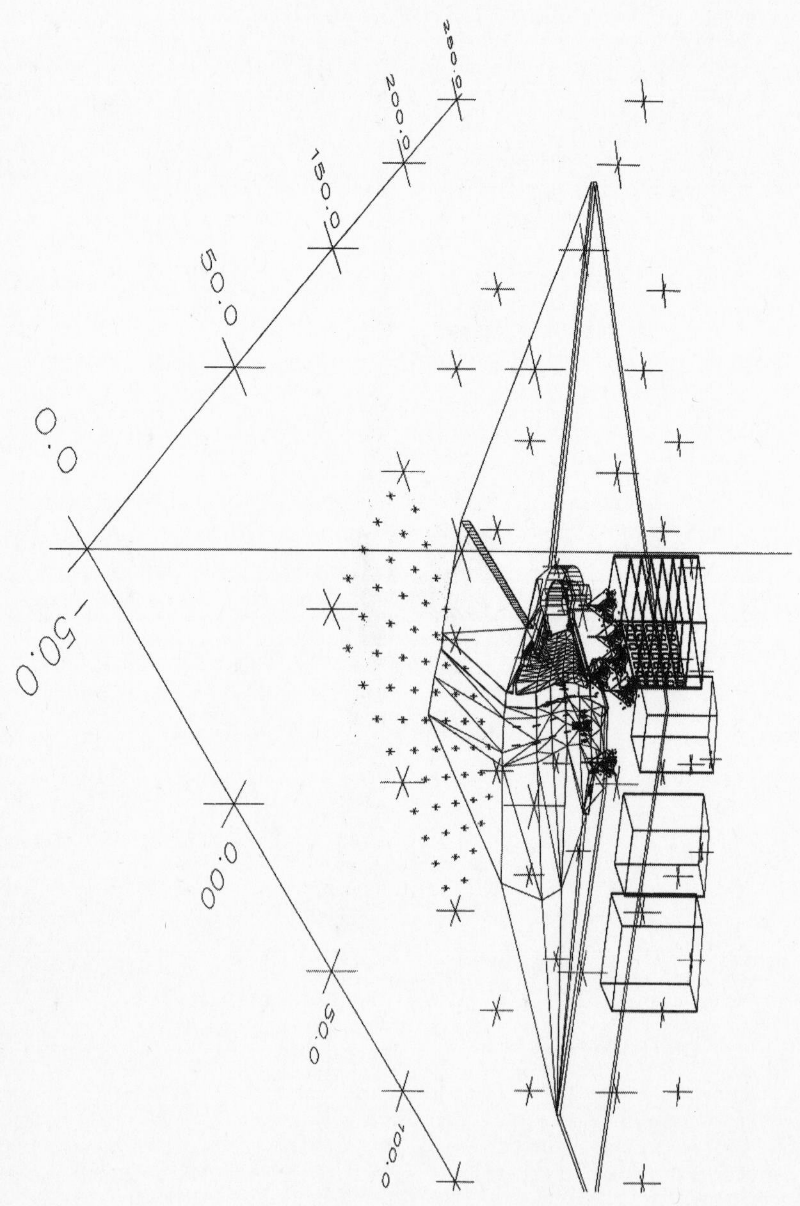

FIGURE 27

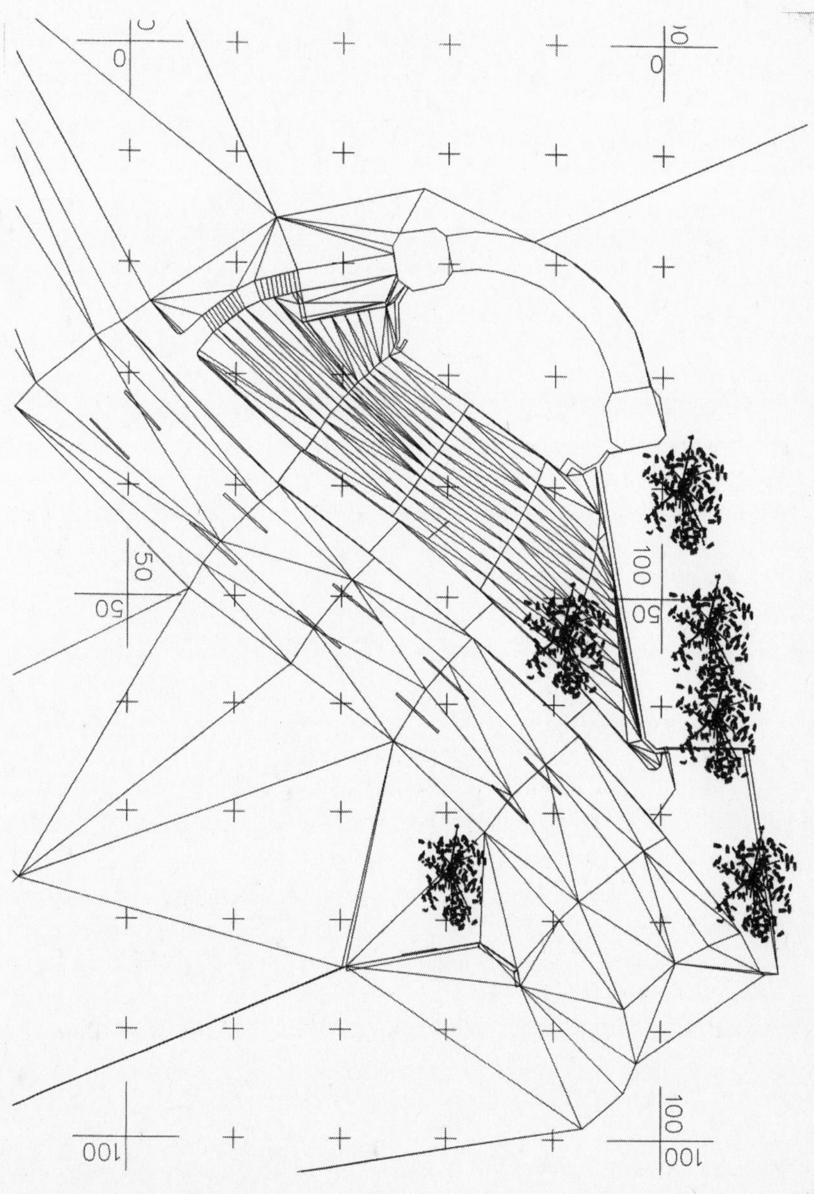

CHAPTER TWELVE

The Trouble with Warren

WHEN LYNDON BAINES JOHNSON became President of the United States, Order No. 11130, establishing a Presidential Commission on the assassination of President Kennedy, was one of the first the new President signed. On the face of it very commendable, but in fact this was a move to protect his own position. Johnson had wanted to leave the investigation to his friend J. Edgar Hoover and the FBI and, for the record, he had actually empowered Hoover to take this on four days before he signed Order 11130. What made him change his mind? He was worried he might lose control of the investigation. In the Senate and elsewhere, independent enquiries on an official level were being mooted and this made Johnson feel insecure. In a dramatic U-turn – and no doubt on the advice of those around him – he signed Order 11130, placing the inquiry in the hands of a Presidential Commission, and thereby superseding all other proposed enquiries. This move also cancelled his order to the FBI which, it might be said, did not please Director Hoover at all.

There are a number of questions which must be asked about this. Why did Johnson want to keep complete control of the investigation? Why did he not welcome as many independent inquiries as were offered? Why was he so apprehensive about the whole thing? It might be said he feared a war might result from the 'wrong' answers being found. This, of course, implies that the Presidential Commission found the 'right' answers. And it is only a small step away from saying they found the answers they were supposed to.

But there were other factors in this sticky equation. Lyndon Johnson was up to his neck in problems which related to corruption and sleaze when he gratefully sheltered under the protective umbrella of the presidency. In the *Dallas Times Herald* on the very day President Kennedy was killed, there were no fewer than three stories which would make Johnson squirm. They involved charges of influence-peddling and suspicion of irregular financial manipulation against Bobby Baker, a close associate of Lyndon Johnson. A storm had been gathering rapidly concerning this affair and it was only a question of time before it broke right over Johnson's head. His political survival was extremely doubtful, especially since there was another scandal looming in regard to his association with another shady friend, Billy Sol Estes. Billy Sol Estes had held government contracts for the storage of grain and federal cotton allotments, which had come under scrutiny for malpractices. Agricultural Agent Henry Marshall, sent to investigate, was found dead in a Texas ditch with five bullets in his body and was conveniently ruled a suicide without so much as a routine autopsy having taken place. The smell of this took a long time to penetrate Washington, but when it did, some years after the event, the body was exhumed and an autopsy was finally held. Marshall was found to have received a blow to the head and suffered carbon-monoxide poisoning before being shot. The verdict was now murder. Though not accused of murder, and federal charges being dropped after Johnson became President, the State of Texas brought charges and a 15-year sentence was handed down to Estes. Granted immunity from prosecution, Billy Sol Estes was eventually called before a Grand Jury investigating the death of Agent Marshall and, when questioned, implicated Lyndon Johnson in the murder. He said Johnson ordered the killing to protect his association with Estes from being exposed. By the time this happened, however, Johnson was dead. Estes was not the most reliable of witnesses, though with no risk of prosecution, this was a strange claim against an old friend if not true.

This was not the only death linked to Billy Sol Estes, however, who lived next door to Johnson. There were three others with question-marks hanging over them. Lyndon Johnson, a colourful character throughout his time in Texas politics, had brought his brand of colour to Washington where, slow to move but sure, the axe was on the point of falling when John F. Kennedy was killed. *Time-Life* had run a story, 'THE BOBBY BAKER BOMBSHELL', featuring a picture of Baker with Lyndon Johnson on 8 November, and on the very day the President was shot they ran another story, 'SCANDAL GROWS AND GROWS IN WASHINGTON'. *The Dallas Morning News* on that same day carried the headline, 'NIXON PREDICTS JFK MAY DROP JOHNSON'. This precariousness was probably the reason why Johnson insisted on being sworn in as President before leaving Dallas. Perhaps he felt events might even then overtake him. It was certainly the eleventh hour for Johnson. Baker was indicted on seven charges of income tax evasion, larceny and conspiracy in 1966 and came to trial in 1967. It is unlikely the Vice-President would have survived with his political skin intact had JFK not been murdered.

As was said earlier in this book, Madeleine Brown, Johnson's mistress, claimed in very positive terms that the Vice-President knew in advance the assassination was going to happen. This does not mean he was one of the conspirators. It would certainly mean, however, that Lyndon Johnson was party to the assassination. Sometime after the event, when Madeleine was discussing with Johnson the Warren documents sealed away until 2039, he said, 'Remember Box 13? There'll be no information there to hang LBJ, that's for sure.' The scandal of Box 13 involved votes cast in the election for the Senate. As the counting proceeded, Johnson's bid was in great jeopardy. He found himself in a corner and it all depended on the contents of Ballot Box 13. The first announced result, 765 for LBJ and 60 for his opponent, Coke Stevenson, magically became 965 for Johnson and 60 for Stevenson. 1,028 votes counted from a box for which only 600 ballot papers were provided. Johnson fought every way he knew to obstruct investigations of the Box 13 scandal. He fought in state court and federal court, and even resisted a re-examination of the votes cast in South Texas – including Box 13 – which had been ordered by a court. The remark made to Madeleine Brown was full of meaning.

The Chief Justice, Earl Warren, at first refused to head a Commission to investigate the assassination for President Johnson, before being leaned on very heavily by the new President. It is believed he was asked how his conscience would be if forty million Americans died in a war which might be the consequence of the assassination of JFK, should the right hand not guide the wheel. He is said to have left his interview with LBJ with tears in his eyes, having succumbed to the exerted pressure. Melvin Eisenberg, a Commission staff lawyer, reported that the President had convinced Warren that this was an occasion on which actual conditions had to override general principles. The interpretation of this could mean many things, not all good.

The other Warren Commissioners appointed were Senator John Sherman Cooper and Representative Gerald Ford, both Republicans; Senator Richard B. Russell and Representative T. Hale Boggs, both Democrats. Allen Dulles, a former Director of the CIA, and John McCloy, who had been US High Commissioner for Germany, made up the total of six. J. Lee Rankin was appointed Chief Counsel, and this team was supported by a substantial staff.

The Commission, according to Earl Warren, was to quash rumours and preclude further speculation, and it had to determine the truth, whatever that might be. It patently failed on all counts, and it is hard to understand why the

FIGURE 28

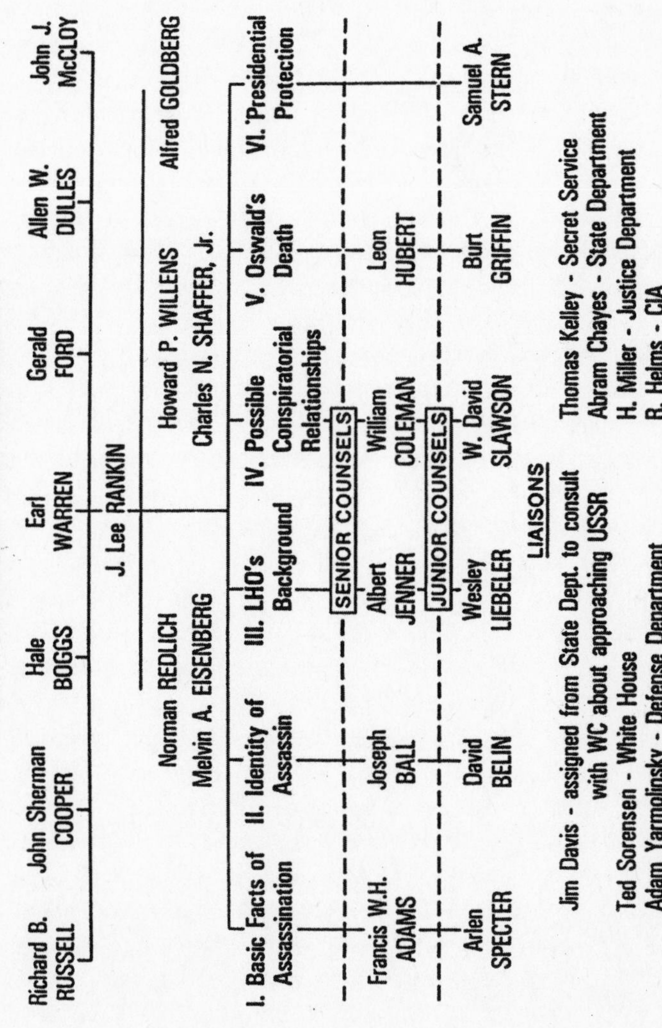

The Warren Commission. (Courtesy National Archives)

United States Government still honours it and goes on trying to prop it up. Indeed the Commission went out of its way to lay the blame for the assassination on Lee Harvey Oswald whom, they said, was alone and unaided. The Commissioners distorted the evidence, favoured anything, no matter how slight or flimsy, which supported their view and rigorously opposed evidence to the contrary. It was a Commission which did not reflect well on the government, and new evidence continues to erode any standing it once had.

Examples of the distortion of truth are numerous. One example relates to the survey commissioned by the FBI, who were doing the legwork for the Warren Commision in May 1964. It was to be carried out by Dallas City Surveyor, Robert H. West, with another prominent surveyor, Chester Breneman. They matched elevations and distances to the Zapruder film and submitted their findings to the FBI and the Secret Service. The results were published in the Warren Report but, to the horror and amazement of West and Breneman, their figures had been changed. Said Breneman, '. . . these figures were changed just enough that the Warren Commission could come up with the idea that another shot came from the same direction as the first.'

During the research necessary for the Smith-Vidit study, reported in Chapter 10, I came by a photograph of West's original survey for the FBI. In Figure 30 we show an enlargement of the vital box containing the figures. We can confirm their figures were falsified in the Warren Report, as Breneman said. Zapruder frame 168 became 161, 171 became 166 and frame 208 became 210. Not surprisingly, neither West nor Breneman were called to testify to the Warren Commission. The two surveyors were convinced from their work that the shots had come from two directions. Prior to the FBI survey, they had conducted an investigation for *Life* magazine on the Monday following the assassination. This also was a matching to the Zapruder frames which, amazingly, *Life* already had by that time. The results of the investigation showed to the *Life* investigator's satisfaction that the bullets could not have been fired by the same man.

The Warren Commissioners, who must have visited the scene of the assassination, never asked, it seems, what happened to the Stemmons Freeway sign which figured so prominently in all the Dealey Plaza photographs they looked at. The sign was dismantled and removed very soon after the assassination. Surveyor Chester Breneman who, with Robert West, as we have said, conducted a thorough investigation of distances and elevations in the Dealey Plaza three days after the assassination, noted the presence of a bullet mark on the sign. But the sign was never seen again. The evidence was lost. Another bullet to account for would certainly have been an acute embarrassment for the Warren Commission, to say the least.

FIGURE 29

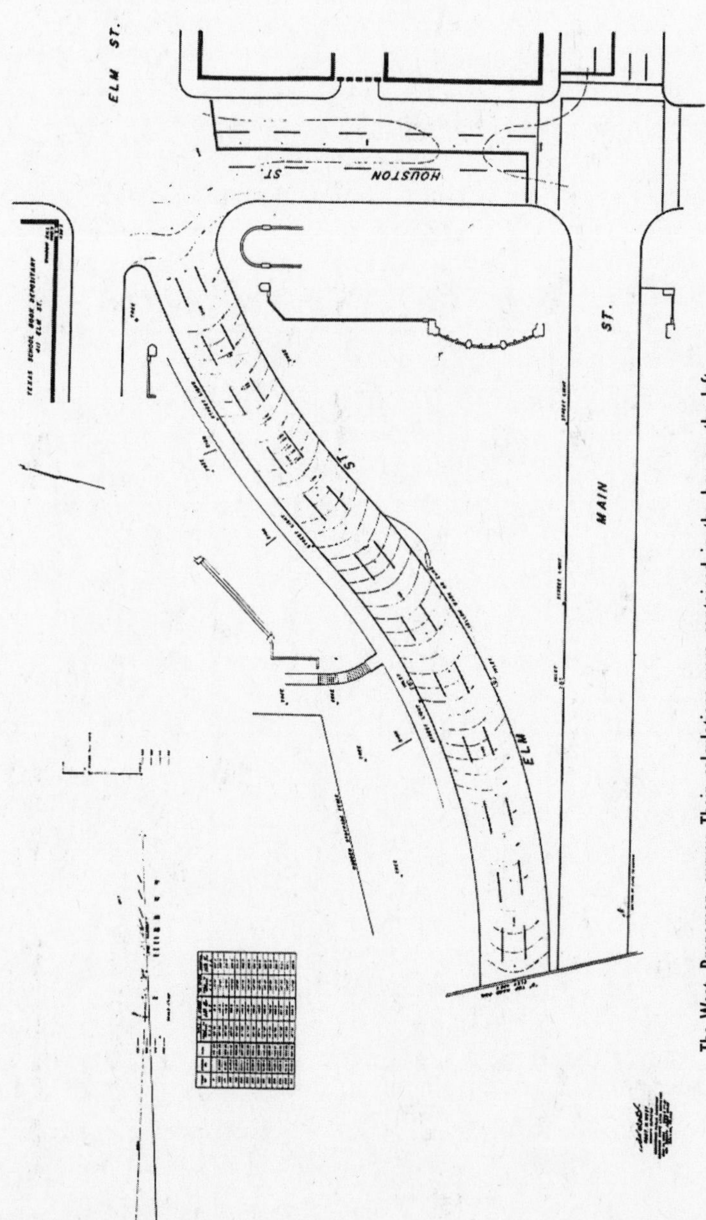

The West–Breneman survey. Their calculations were contained in the box on the left.
Both West and Breneman said the Warren Commission changed their figures.

FIGURE 30

	FRAME NO.	STATION NO.	ELEV.	RIFLE IN WINDOW: ANGLE TO HORIZON R-K-H	RIFLE IN WINDOW: LINE OF SIGHT DIST. K-R	TOP BRIDGE HANDRAIL: ANGLE TO HORIZON B-K-H	TOP BRIDGE HANDRAIL: LINE OF SIGHT DIST. K-B
	A		431.97	40° 10'	91.6	−0°27'	447.0
168	~~161~~	3+29.2	429.25	26° 58'	137.4	−0°07'	392.4
171	~~166~~	3+30.1	429.20	26° 52'	138.2	−0°07'	391.5
	185	3+49.3	428.13	24° 14'	154.9	+0°03'	372.5
	186	3+50.8	428.05	24° 03'	156.3	+0°03'	371.7
	207	3+71.1	427.02	21° 50'	174.3	+0°12'	350.9
208	~~210~~	3+73.4	426.80	21° 34'	176.9	+0° 22'	348.8
	222	3+85.9	426.11	20° 23'	188.6	+0° 24'	336.4
	225	3+88.3	425.98	20° 11'	190.8	+0° 26'	334.0
	231	3+93.5	425.69	19° 47'	196.0	+0° 28'	329.0
	235	3+96.8	425.52	19° 26'	199.0	+0° 30'	326.8
	240	4+02.3	425.21	19° 01'	204.3	+0° 34'	320.4
	249	4+10.0	424.79	18° 32'	211.9	+0° 40'	313.1
	255	4+16.4	424.46	18° 03'	218.0	+0° 44'	307.1
	313	4+65.3	421.75	15° 21'	265.3	+1° 28'	260.6

Hard evidence. The figures published in the Warren Report are shown here. The figures shown on the extreme left are the real figures submitted by West and Breneman which were changed by the Warren Commission.

Johnson: He was told at Murchison's party that J.F.K. was to be killed.

Nixon: In Dallas to meet Pepsi Cola boss Don Kendall. Nixon was another in the exclusive group at the party who learned what was to happen.

Hoover: Likely that he brought the news of the planned assassination.

Murchison: Wealthy oil man, publisher and banker, he threw the party the night before J.F.K. was murdered. He was friends with Hoover and had links with the underworld

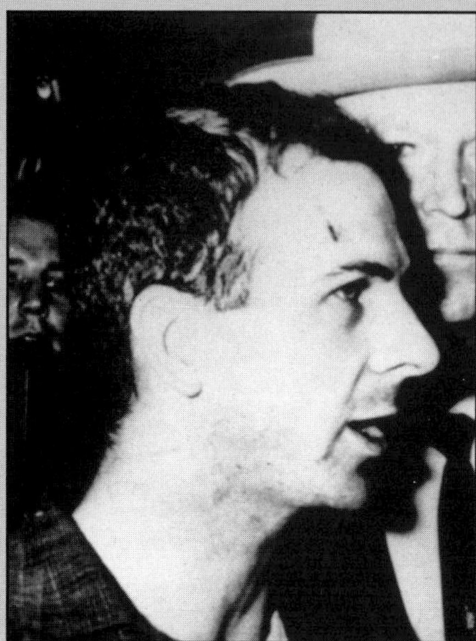

Lee Harvey Oswald: They said he shot President Kennedy alone and unaided. (Courtesy National Archives.)

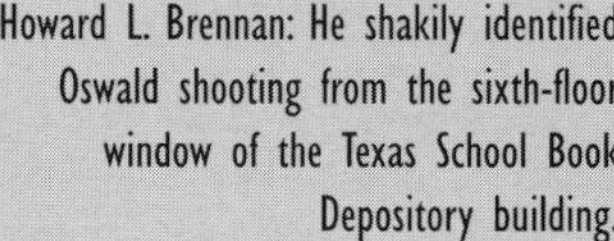

Howard L. Brennan: He shakily identified Oswald shooting from the sixth-floor window of the Texas School Book Depository building.

Howard L. Brennan: Sits where he sat when the shooting was going on. (Courtesy National Archives.)

DA Henry Wade: Holds a press conference the night of the assassination. He told the world the rifle discovered by the police on the sixth floor of the School Book Depository building was a German 7.5 Mauser. The rifle handed in to Police HQ, however, was an Italian 6.5 Mannlicher Carcano. This, they said, was the murder weapon, adding that it belonged to Lee Harvey Oswald. (Courtesy National Archives.)

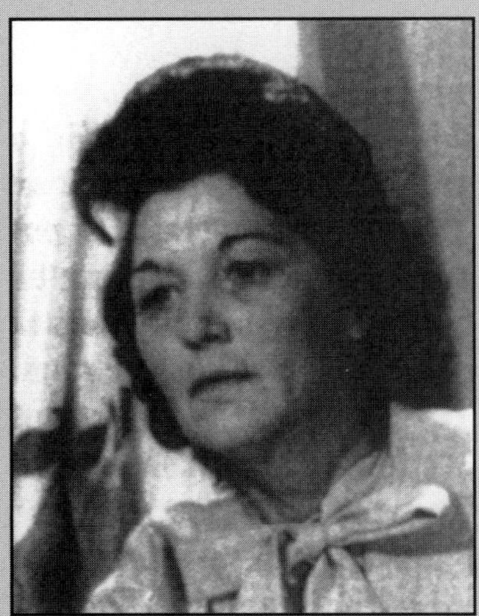

Mrs Helen Markham: Was not sure of what she saw at all. An 'utter screwball', said a member of the Warren Commission staff. But the Commission needed her 'testimony'.

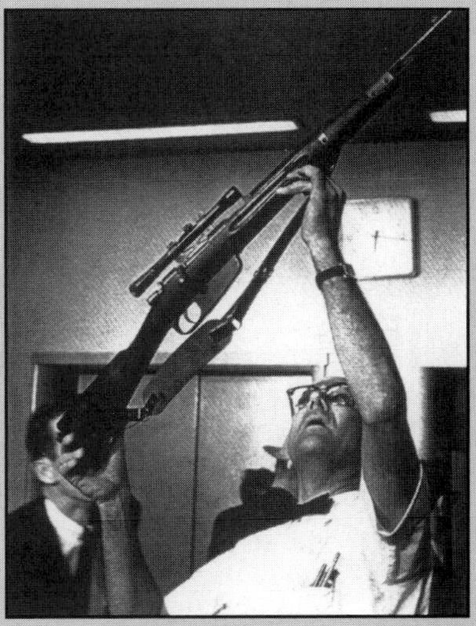

Lt J.C. Day: Shows the Mannlicher Carcano said to have been discovered at the School Book Depository. There were several rifles seen in the area that day, but this one, they said, belonged to Lee Harvey Oswald. (Courtesy National Archives.)

Jack Ruby: Shot Oswald in cold blood. 'I had to do it,' he told policemen. He wanted to tell all about how and why but only if he was moved from Dallas to safety in Washington. Earl Warren refused to do this and Ruby died – or was killed – without speaking.

Sam Holland: A railyard signal supervisor who saw puffs of smoke from shots behind the picket fence on the grassy knoll. This was proof of a conspiracy but the Warren Commission used Holland's evidence selectively, changed what was not to its liking and ignored what did not suit its case.

Lee Harvey Oswald: Was allowed a press conference. He had killed nobody, he said. He told them he

TOP: The Moorman Picture: Mary Moorman took her famous Polaroid photograph from the opposite side of the road to Zapruder. On analysis it showed a sniper behind the picket fence on the knoll. Appearing to wear a uniform of sorts, he was nicknamed 'The Badge Man'. (Courtesy Mary Moorman, now Mary Krahma.)

ABOVE: The President's jacket and shirt: This shows where bullets had struck. But there was another

L.B.J. and Bobby Baker: The Bobby Baker scandal and the Billy Sol Estes connection were about to engulf Johnson. Then Kennedy was killed.

George de Mohrenschildt: Had been Oswald's minder for the CIA while a new mission was being arranged for him, but CIA renegades side-tracked Oswald to take the blame for the Kennedy murder.

Marina Oswald: Beautiful then and still beautiful today. In fear of being deported to Russia, she told the Warren Commission 'what they wanted to hear'. She now believes implicitly in Oswald's innocence.

The Motorcade: J.F.K. was assuming a similar position when the first bullet struck. He had turned sharply round to face and wave to the people.

Johnson sworn in: L.B.J. was sworn in with unseemly haste in Air Force One while the plane sat at Love Airfield, before it returned to Washington carrying the body of Kennedy. He insisted Jackie Kennedy – bloodstained clothes and all – came to the cabin for the ceremony.
(Photograph by Cecil Stoughton, White House photographer.)

TOP LEFT: Walker's House at the rear: The photograph was said to be among Oswald's possessions. Note the car. A hole had been made through the print obliterating its number plate.

TOP RIGHT: Major General Edwin Anderson Walker: Someone took a shot at him and the Warren Commission tried to blame Oswald.

ABOVE LEFT: Oswald's Possessions: Had the photo of Walker's house been added? (Bottom left corner). It can be seen the hole through the print had not been made when this was taken. This print was published in a book written by Police Chief Jesse Curry – we would never have known that the hole had been made otherwise.

ABOVE RIGHT: Police Chief Jesse Curry: Was Oswald's death really due to sloppy policework?

RIGHT: Close up of the photograph of Walker's house from Oswald's possessions, but unfortunately not clear enough to read the car number. The hole had certainly been driven through whilst in the hands of the police. But whose car would they not allow to be identified?

Sam Holland was a railroad worker who stood with several other railroad employees atop the overpass to watch the motorcade. When the shooting started he saw a puff of smoke rising above the picket fence on the grassy knoll. He, with fellow railroad employees, ran to the point behind the picket fence to see what they could. Because it took them about two minutes to get there they did not expect to find a sniper waiting. What they found, however, was evidence that someone had stood there. Scattered cigarette butts and footprints showing in the mud supported this. There was also a car, the bumper of which was muddy, suggesting someone had stood on it to see over the fence. The group agreed on what they had seen, and this was offered to the Warren Commission as evidence. The Warren Commissioners ignored it. It clearly undermined their 'lone shooter' theory. Holland also gave evidence that he had seen a puff of smoke and told the Commission that he had heard four shots. They recorded that he had heard three shots, and dismissed his other evidence with, 'Holland . . . immediately after the shots, ran off the overpass to see if there was anyone behind the picket fence on the north side of Elm Street but he did not see anyone behind the parked cars.' Four shots were, of course, inconsistent with a single gunman having fired all the shots, and to have given credence to his evidence of another shooter behind the picket fence would also have destroyed their single gunman theory. If they had been interested, the Commissioners could have had the evidence of five other railroad workers who saw smoke on the knoll. Come to that, Ed Johnson, a reporter, wrote an article which his Fort Worth paper published the day after the assassination in which he said, 'Some of us saw little puffs of white smoke that seemed to hit the grassy area . . .'

When he saw a transcript of his Commission 'evidence', Holland protested it was inaccurate, and tried to make them understand that two minutes after the shooting he was not likely to see anyone behind the fence. With his lawyer, Holland went to correct his testimony. 'We red-pencilled that statement from beginning to end,' he said, 'but it made no difference. They simply ignored the corrections and published what they wanted.' This provoked Sam Holland to make one of the classic quotations in regard to this government investigation: 'When the time comes an American can't tell the truth because the Government doesn't, that's the time to give the country back to the Indians – if they'll have it.'

Carolyn Walther stood on Houston Street looking at two men in a window of the Texas School Book Depository shortly before the motorcade arrived and the shooting started. One, wearing a white shirt and with light-coloured hair, carried a rifle and she thought he was a guard. The other wore a brown suitcoat. They stood at a right corner window on the fourth or fifth floor, she said. Her evidence was recorded and broadcast to the world, but the Warren Commission ignored it. No doubt the Commissioners were unhappy that she identified the presence of two men. Two men constituted a conspiracy and the Commisioners were sticking rigorously to their single gunman theory. In any case, for Warren, she did not get the window right, either. Arnold Rowland witnessed seeing two men, one wearing a 'very light-coloured shirt' and holding a rifle at a sixth-floor window, but at the other end of the building from that identified by Carolyn Walther. (It should be remembered that the sixth floor of the School Book Depository was one continuous room: it was not subdivided.) Ronald Fischer said he saw a man wearing a white shirt holding a rifle at the same window. Lee Harvey Oswald wore a dark shirt on the day that the President was killed.

Jean Hill was standing across the road from the picket fence on the grass of Dealey Plaza and was only a few feet from the President as he passed in the motorcade. Looking across the Lincoln, she saw a man fire at the President from behind the picket fence on the grassy knoll, smoke rising from his rifle as he did so (corroborating Holland's story). The evidence of Jean Hill, one of the closest witnesses to the President when he was shot, was also ignored by the Warren Commission.

Jean Hill stood near to Mary Moorman, who took the now famous Polaroid picture showing what many believe to be a sniper on the knoll. (See first picture section). The shadowy figure is now identified as 'Badge Man', because he appeared to be wearing a police officer's uniform. The picture was never investigated by the Warren Commission, though researcher Gary Mack has derived more detail from enhancements.

Bill and Gayle Newman, with their two sons, occupied a position below the pagoda on the grassy knoll, from where they witnessed the assassination. '. . . I thought the shots were coming from directly behind us,' Newman said, and he and his wife gave a full account of what they saw and heard to staff at the Sheriff's office and, two days later, to FBI men who called upon them. But the authorities did not want to know. Assuming notes of their testimony was sent to them, the Warren Commissioners did not ask the Newmans to come to an interview.

Julia Ann Mercer was driving down Elm Street about half an hour before the motorcade was due and, in traffic, found her lane blocked by a pick-up truck. It was parked partly on and part off the sidewalk just by the grassy knoll, and she was obliged to wait to pass it. While she was waiting she observed a man take what she believed was a brown rifle case from the tool compartment of the truck. She calculated one end was about eight inches wide and it tapered to four or five inches, and he walked up the knoll with it. The man, she said, was white, wearing a grey jacket, brown trousers and a plaid shirt. On his head was a stocking hat with a tassel. When she was able to go, as she passed she took a good look at the driver, who sat in the cab. He also was white, she said, about 40 years of age, heavy set, wearing a green jacket and with fair brown hair.

She thought she had seen a Secret Service man moving into place, but when she heard about the assassination, she phoned the Sheriff's office and told what she had seen. She later went to the Sheriff's office to sign an affidavit, and the following day, Saturday, 23 November, she was visited by FBI men. They questioned her about what she had seen, and produced about two dozen photographs for her to examine. From these she identified the man she had seen in the cab of the truck. His name meant nothing to her until the following day when she witnessed on television the shooting of Lee Harvey Oswald. The man she had identified was Oswald's killer, Jack Ruby.

When Julia Ann Mercer saw her written-up statement, she complained about the fact that an addition had been made to what she had said. Added to her description of the pick-up truck was a sign on the side which read 'AIR CONDITIONING'. This had the effect of throwing private researchers completely off the scent. She also complained that another affidavit she signed had been altered. This time her search through the photographs was dated several days after it really happened. It was also stated that she could not make an identification from the photographs. These instances are hardly likely to be accidental, and it is interesting to observe that, as a consequence of them, it appeared to the world that Julia Ann Mercer did not identify Jack Ruby and, in any case, she did not look at photographs until well after the day Ruby shot Oswald. Make of this what you wish, but could it be that the authorities were anxious to keep Jack Ruby at large to carry out the shooting of Lee Harvey Oswald on the day after Julia Ann Mercer made her identification? Naturally, the Warren Commission did not call Ms Mercer to give evidence.

Ed Hoffman found himself in a superb place to see what happened behind the picket fence on the grassy knoll. Having first found a place on the Stemmons Freeway, he decided to move to a better spot and walked along to a point where Stemmons crossed Elm Street. Here he looked across and something moving behind the picket fence caught his eye. There he saw a man in a dark suit, tie and overcoat running behind the fence away from the School Book Depository (westward) and carrying a rifle. The man ran along to the end of the fence where a pipe railing was located and threw the rifle over the pipe to another man waiting near the rail tracks. This second man, who wore light-coloured overalls and a railroad worker's cap, caught it and ducked behind a rail-car, where, kneeling down, he quickly disassembled it and put the gun parts in what looked like a railman's brown toolbag. He then walked into the railyard in the direction of the tower, while the man in the suit and overcoat dashed back along behind the fence and then sedately walked towards the corner near the pagoda. He quickly linked this activity to seeing the President's car drive through the triple underpass, with the President slumped in his seat as they drove to Parkland Hospital. He then realised what had happened. Ed Hoffman was a particularly good witness. The senses he used were finely tuned, for he was profoundly deaf. But in this case the Warren Commission never heard of him: he could not get anyone to take any notice of him however much he tried, and at one point an FBI agent warned him to keep what he had seen quiet, or he might get killed. Pressed by his parents to say nothing, it is not surprising his complete story did not surface until more than twenty years later.

Further evidence that shots came from the grassy knoll came from a young serviceman, Gordon Arnold. This young man was behind the picket fence, after parking his car near the railroad tower, when he was ordered to leave the area by a man who showed a badge and said he was a Secret Service man. Since he wanted to film the motorcade, he wasn't going to go far, so he walked round to the other side of the picket fence at the end of the triple underpass end and occupied a spot there. When the shooting started he said he felt, rather than heard, a bullet fly past him. He said, '. . . it went right past my left ear . . .' and recounted how he had then fallen flat on the ground. He was accosted by two policemen, one of whom kicked him and told him to get up, while the other waved a gun around, weeping as he did so. The unnerved Arnold was asked whether he had shot film, and when he said he had, his camera was opened and the policeman ripped the film out of it. Arnold, a GI on leave from Alaska, was no doubt relieved to go back there. The policemen were not concerned with his evidence and, altogether, the young man had a rough time in Dallas. It is small wonder he did not approach the authorities, and he was not approached by the Warren Commission. If the Commission had invited him to testify, he had, it would seem, all the wrong evidence for them. He would have said that without doubt shots came from the grassy knoll.

Having just mentioned the tower in the railyard in Gordon Arnold's account of his experience, and in Ed Hoffman's evidence, it would be appropriate to recount the evidence of Lee Bowers Jnr. Bowers was a dispatcher for the Union Terminal Company and was located at the tower in question. He noticed a car, a blue and white 1959 Oldsmobile station-wagon, which drove into the parking area behind the picket fence on the grassy knoll. He timed its arrival as 12.10 p.m. He noticed also that it displayed a 'Goldwater' sticker on its bumper and it bore out-of-state number plates. The car drove round in a circle, its driver examining the terrain, perhaps, or maybe just trying to find a way out. It finally left the way it had come in. A few minutes afterwards, at 12.20 p.m., a black Ford of 1957 vintage drove in. The man driving this car appeared to be holding a microphone – or telephone – with one hand while he drove with the other. Three or four minutes later it left, driving out the way it came, in front of the Texas School Book Depository building. Shortly before the assassination took place, Bowers saw a third car circling the parking lot in front of the railyard tower. This was a 1961 or 1962 four-door Chevrolet Impala. White, but spattered with mud up to the windows, this was also an out-of-state car, bearing a similar licence plate to the first car he saw. The car paused at what would become the assassination site, but Bowers' attention was then distracted and he did not see what happened to it after that.

Bowers had more to tell, however. He saw two men between the tower and the triple underpass. One was middle-aged, heavy-set, wearing a white shirt and dark trousers. The other, a younger man in his mid-twenties, was dressed in either a plaid shirt or coat. They were looking across at the approaching motorcade. After the shooting he saw a motorcycle police officer run up the grassy knoll in the direction of the men he had seen. He said that the one in the white shirt, he could see, was still there, while the other in darker clothing was hard to make out. What Bowers wanted to tell the Warren Commission was that something had attracted his attention, '. . . a flash of light or smoke or something which caused me to feel that something out of the ordinary had occurred there'. He was cut short by the interviewer before he could say this, however. He had to wait until he was later interviewed by author Mark Lane before he could complete his eyewitness account. Commission interviewers seemed to make a habit of cutting off witnesses at a point where they were going to say something the Commissioners didn't want to hear. In the case of Lee Bowers, none of his testimony was welcome to the Warren Commission, it seems. They recorded it all, then completely ignored it.

It should be remembered that the Warren Commission investigated the murder of Officer J.D. Tippit, also. In general, the same set of rules appeared to apply. If a witness could support their case against Oswald, the testimony was used. If the testimony supported Oswald's innocence, it was ignored. We have already quoted the thoroughly unreliable testimony of Mrs Helen Markham, who at first picked a policeman out of an identity parade, and who dithered until she was outrageously prompted by her interviewer to identify Lee Harvey Oswald as Tippit's killer. Mrs Markham emroidered her eyewitness story claiming she spent twenty minutes alone with Tippit as he lay dying, trying to speak to her, whereas in fact a crowd gathered very quickly and it would appear he died instantly. The evidence she gave, shaky though it may have been, was nevertheless seized upon by Warren in his case against Oswald. Similarly that of William Scoggins, who didn't actually see the shooting of Officer Tippit, but was prepared to identify Oswald as the killer. Evidence pointing in another direction, including clear descriptions of an assailant who could not have been Oswald, were noted and ignored.

There are numerous other examples of the bias the Warren Commission showed in its investigation of the death of President Kennedy. It could be believed that it was decided before the Commissioners began their work that the young man who had been shot and killed in Dallas Police Department custody was guilty. Of course it was always the case when an American President was assassinated that the blame was attached by the government to a lone-nut killer, regardless of what really happened. So it was with Lee Harvey Oswald.

CHAPTER THIRTEEN

Curiouser and Curiouser

AS WE SAID EARLIER, there is much to tell about Lee Harvey Oswald, and it is time to begin to add flesh to the bare bones we presented in Chapter Nine. It might be said that to understand Lee Harvey Oswald is to understand what happened when President Kennedy was assassinated.

When he went into the Marines on 24 October 1957, Oswald did his ten weeks of boot camp at San Diego, California. He coped well with the rigours of his new life, though, ironically, his skill on the firing range left much to be desired. With a struggle he qualified on the range, and finished his basic training four months after his enlistment. Posted to Camp Pendleton, north of San Diego, he next did his combat training, and went on to Keesler Air Force Base at Biloxi, Mississippi, to train in his chosen speciality, radar.

It is from about this time that we can detect an influence on Oswald's behaviour which suggests that, even at this early stage, he may have been of interest to the intelligence services. His weekend passes, for instance, provided a mystery which has still not been resolved. It seems he spent his free time in New Orleans, a hundred miles distance from his camp, but what was he doing there and with whom? He only once visited the relatives he had in New Orleans and there is nothing known of his movements or involvements during the rest of his off-duty time there. Was his aptitude for intelligence work being tested and measured in New Orleans?

He qualified as an Aviation Electronics Operator, having achieved seventh place in his class in his examinations, and was ready for a posting overseas. He was sent to Japan, to the First Marine Air Wing base at Atsugi, where his work was good and he made friends among his fellows, as well as with the officers under whom he served. When it came to his leisure time at Atsugi, at first he was content to find his pleasures alone, not shunning his friends, but not getting into the swim of whatever they were doing. Though he later changed, he did not drink, neither did he gamble with the boys nor take an interest in the girls when he first arrived at Atsugi. He was considered a likeable man, well read and good natured. He played chess and watched football games on television. And Oswald the Marine was not short of friends.

Oswald bought himself a .22 calibre pistol by post from the United States, for reasons which are unclear. Not known for being a troublemaker, he found himself on a charge only twice during the time he spent in Japan and the gun was the cause of one of those occasions. It seems he injured himself with the weapon and tried to disguise the wound as one made by a bullet from a service revolver. The bullet was recovered and recognised as being of .22 calibre, however, and he was disciplined for possessing a personal firearm. His friends were puzzled by the fact that he was detained in hospital for some three weeks for what was little more than a graze. It would seem the three weeks spent in hospital were for another reason. Some thought he had deliberately discharged the weapon to injure himself in an attempt to evade being sent on a mission with the others to the Philippines. If that had been the case he was unlucky. Assigned mess duties, Oswald joined his unit, known as 'Coffee Mill', and spent four months in the Philippines.

Atsugi base was home to more than the Marine unit. The Joint Advisory Technical Group, which was a cover for the CIA's main operational base in the Far East, was also located there. The Marine personnel could not fail to observe the secretive operations at the airfield attached to the base. A long, sleek and very mysterious aircraft was produced from its hangar – a hangar surrounded by armed guards – and took off at an amazing speed. Coincidentally, those in radar – including Oswald – heard conversations between the pilots and base, and became aware that the aircraft was extraordinary for another reason. It required data relating to flying at heights unknown to pilots of any kind of aircraft, ninety thousand feet, for instance, and maybe higher. This 'utility' plane, as it was called by those connected with it, was the U-2, which gathered intelligence, photographing military bases and other sites in the USSR and China, and flying so high that neither aircraft nor missiles could intercept it. Oswald took a special interest in the U-2's comings and goings, but then, so did many others on the base. Oswald, however, also took photographs around the base.

Several months after the Philippines, Coffee Mill carried out another mission, this time to Formosa (Taiwan), on which they took their radar equipment. They were to assist the Chinese Nationalists who were fighting the Communist forces and coming off worst. It was here Oswald was involved in a strange incident, about which we do not know enough. On guard duty one night the sound of shots was heard, causing the duty officer to make a dash to where Oswald was, to find out what had happened. He found him in a distressed state, literally shaking. Oswald explained he had seen men in the woods who had not responded to his challenge and he had opened fire on them. What happened next was even stranger. He was airlifted back to Japan for 'medical treatment' and then sent on to another unit at Iwakuni, four hundred miles southwest of Tokyo.

It was at Iwakuni that he began to learn Russian and had Communist literature sent in the post to him. This amused those around him, who called him 'Oswaldski' or 'Oswaldskovich' which he took in good part. Some, however, had doubts about what 'Oswaldski' was up to and expected their superiors to take him to task, for he made no secret of his preoccupations. The officers did not seem to mind, however. They made no fuss. The only man at Iwakuni who knew Oswald from training days, an Owen Dejanovich, said that Oswald shunned him. It suggests that Oswald was sent there because it was believed he was not known to anyone. Judging by his activities, it would appear that the reason for this was so that he could engage in preparation for intelligence work. He was displaying a number of classic signs of having been recruited by the CIA.

It was about this time that Oswald made his first application for early discharge on the grounds of his mother's hardship. Although an unrealistic request, since it was out of the question for a Marine to be shipped back to the United States for anything less than a major crisis, when seen in the context of what was eventually to happen, this may be taken as Oswald being given more of the necessary background for forthcoming work with the CIA. The .22 gunshot wound may also be seen in this context, since, to the 'watchers' outside the base, notably a group of Communists in Tokyo with whom Oswald had become involved, it advertised young Oswald was no wimp: he was capable of breaking rules when it suited him, and he was the kind of man who had reasons for possessing his own gun.

Again, the other incident which blotted an otherwise spotless record may also be seen in the light of creating a 'background' for Oswald. This was when he poured a drink over a sergeant's head while carousing in a bar, the Bluebird Cafe at Yamato. Conducting his own defence at court-martial for this offence, he argued that it had been an accident, and was successful in having the charge reduced to uttering 'provoking words'. This resulted in him being sent to the brig for eighteen days. He also collected the sentence for the gun incident, which had been suspended, and was locked up for a total of forty-six days. Curiously however, another inmate at that time saw Oswald only once during the period he was supposed to be there. He said he was wearing civilian clothes. And no other inmate could remember seeing him at all. When he was released from the brig, Oswald seemed a changed man, his friends said. The fun-loving Marine had now become withdrawn and serious.

Oswald's 'love life' in the Marines seemed to be linked to the specific demands of his service involvements. During this period Oswald was seeing a Eurasian girl – half Russian – who was helping him with the Russian language. Earlier, he had been having a 'fling' with a beautiful Japanese hostess from the Queen Bee nightclub in Tokyo. The hostesses there were believed to be collecting information for Russian intelligence, questioning personnel from the base about their work. The question arises here – was the hostess pumping Oswald or was it, as would seem more likely, the other way around? Oswald was obviously supplied with money for his visits to the Queen Bee, since one evening there cost more than a rating received in a month, and his forays involved two-day trips to Tokyo. Of course, his two-day visits to Tokyo may have also involved other duties, such as taking part in further intelligence-training sessions. His 'duties' with the hostess brought unpleasant consequences for Oswald, however. He was found to have contracted a mild form of gonorrhoea known as urethritis. Personnel found to have gonorrhoea were often disciplined, but not Oswald, whose record was marked, 'Origin: In line of duty, not due to own misconduct.'

On 2 November 1958, Oswald returned to the United States by sea. He was now due leave and made his way to Fort Worth, where he shared his thirty-day break between his mother and Robert, his brother. His next posting was to El Toro, in California, where he was attached to Marine Air Control Squadron No. 9. He became part of a radar crew. As before, his interest in things Russian continued and developed, particularly in learning the Russian language, an extremely difficult tongue to master. Again, because this was so incongruous an interest for a US Marine, it was expected command would be down on him in a big way with drastic consequences following. Not so. The officers were sublimely indifferent to Oswald's activities. It appeared they knew and approved.

On 17 August 1959, Lee Harvey Oswald made a move which was ultimately to decide the direction the rest of his life would take. He made another application for early release from the service on the grounds of his mother's hardship. This now makes sense of his earlier application in Japan, for a *second* application made it easier for the Corps to give priority to his request and process his departure with speed, and without attracting too much attention. It would seem he did not finish his intelligence preparation until August, and that he was now rushing to meet some kind of imposed deadline. The Marine Corps obliged by processing and granting his discharge in two weeks. Oswald's rushed discharge was patently a mechanical procedure for, although he provided the necessary paperwork – statements from his mother, her doctor, an attorney and two friends – no enquiries were made about his mother's well-being, for instance. Had they investigated they would have found she was in fairly good health. She had had a minor fall some time earlier but had recovered and was certainly not in urgent need of her son's assistance.

The speed with which Oswald's passport was granted was also something of a record. A mere six-day wait coincided with Oswald's discharge from the Marines. He had openly stated his interest in travelling to Russia, among various other countries, but this raised no questions. On 11 September he was discharged from the service, armed with a brand-new passport to travel to Russia.

The pattern of Lee Harvey Oswald's activities appear to leave little doubt that he became an intelligence agent. The CIA and other intelligence agencies have never confirmed that he was working for them, but in view of what was to come, this was hardly surprising. What might be called oblique confirmation has, however, been obtained from differing sources. One was the former CIA paymaster, James Wilcott. He told the House Committee on Assassinations Oswald had been '. . . recruited from the military for the express purpose of becoming a double agent assignment to the USSR'. He claimed he had unwittingly handled funds for Oswald's mission, and quoted colleagues who had told him that Oswald worked for an intelligence agency in Japan. The HCA considered this evidence and discarded it. Apparently one CIA colleague quoted was not in Tokyo at the time Wilcott said he was, and because all the others quoted by Wilcott denied any knowledge, the evidence was deemed unreliable. In view of the fact that CIA agents are master purveyors of deceit and untruth, it is surprising more was not made of what Wilcott claimed, and less of what his detractors had to say. Perhaps he confused one agent serving in Tokyo with another. Such an error would hardly be a sound reason for 'throwing the baby out with the bathwater'. After all, he was giving evidence some eight or nine years after the event.

Another example of 'oblique' substantiation for Oswald's status as an agent was given at a secret meeting of the Warren Commission. General Counsel, J. Lee Rankin, was engaged in filling in the background of Lee Harvey Oswald, and it was a period during his posting at El Toro, in California, before his rushed discharge, which was under review, it appears. 'We are trying to run that down,' he said, 'to find out what he studied at the Monterey School of the Army in the way of languages.' The Monterey School of the Army became the Defense Language Institute, which gave top-class crash-courses in languages for service personnel. Lee Harvey Oswald became extremely proficient in the Russian language, so much so that his wife, Marina, said that when she first heard him speak she mistook the imperfections in his speech merely as a Russian dialect in one who hailed from another region of the USSR. Where did Oswald learn the language so well? It appears the answer was being given by Lee Rankin to the secret session of the Warren Commission. Russian was obviously the language being studied by Oswald at Monterey. The bigger question to which they might have sought an answer was – why? In view of all we have learned about Oswald in the Marines, there would seem to be no doubt why.

It is greatly to the Warren Commission's discredit that an account of the Rankin/Monterey enquiry was not made available to the public until a Freedom of Information suit was brought, through which details were obtained.

Researchers have discussed Oswald with many of those who served as his fellow Marines at his various postings. Here were ample indications that Oswald was recruited for intelligence work. Sergeant G.P. Hemming, who was with Oswald in Japan, was recruited into the CIA and believed Oswald was too. Another was a Marine named Bucknell who told researcher and writer Mark Lane of interviews at El Toro where he and several of his friends, including Lee Harvey Oswald, were interviewed by the military Criminal Investigation Department with a view to recruitment to covert operations in Cuba. Oswald was apparently called back for reinterview several times. Bucknell said that Oswald told him he knew the man who interviewed him. He had been his contact at Atsugi. Bucknell told also that on another occasion Oswald confided he was being discharged to go to Russia for American intelligence.

CHAPTER FOURTEEN

They Do It with Mirrors

LEE HARVEY OSWALD PAID a brief visit to his home when he was discharged from the Marines and then he left, telling his mother he was taking up a job in New Orleans with an import-export company. Contrary to popular belief, his mother Marguerite appeared to know that Lee would not be staying. She had borrowed a bed for him from a neighbour, saying she would only require it for a couple of days. On 20 September 1959 Oswald sailed for Europe on the *Marion Lykes*, arriving first at Le Havre in France and going on to Southampton, arriving there on 9 October. His passport was stamped 10 October as he departed from England to Finland, but his arrival in Helsinki and registration at his hotel the same day causes some problems. There was no direct flight which would have taken Oswald to Helsinki on 10 October and we are now unlikely to find out how he did it. The most likely means would seem to have been by a military aircraft laid on specially for him.

At Helsinki he applied for a visa to visit Russia but, probably because the waiting time was too long for his purposes, he flew to Stockholm and obtained his visa promptly. He then flew back to Helsinki, whence he travelled to Russia, on 15 October, by train. Before Oswald left Fort Worth he had withdrawn all his savings, $203, from the bank, of which he left $100 for his mother. The cost of his travel plus the expensive hotels he used in Helsinki – he stayed at first at the Torni Hotel and then moved to the less expensive but still costly Klaus Kurki Hotel – and the extra journey to Stockholm in Sweden clearly could not be funded by the sum he brought from his savings. He told Customs in Southampton he carried $700 and, since he had paid $220.75 for his passage to

Le Havre, and allowing for sundry expenses, it seems he had at least $1,000 with him. This gives us a strong indication that Oswald was working for American intelligence.

When he arrived in Moscow, Rimma Shirokova, Oswald's Intourist guide, was almost certain to be the first to hear the news that he had come to Moscow to defect. He was interviewed in his hotel room by Leo Setyaev, a reporter for Radio Moscow and probably a KGB agent, and later by two American newspaper reporters, Aline Mosby, who worked for UPI, and Priscilla Johnson of the North American News Agency. Mosby received the full 'defector' treatment from Oswald. She said, 'I felt we were not carrying out a conversation.' Oswald was preoccupied in advertising his feelings about Russia and the ideologies he claimed to have embraced. 'As he spoke he held his mouth stiffly and nearly closed. His jaw was rigid. Behind his brown eyes I felt a certain coldness.' Mosby tried to bring Oswald to discussing his mother and family but he wasn't having it. 'She doesn't know [about my defection],' he said. 'She's rather old. I couldn't expect her to understand. I guess it wasn't quite fair of me not to say anything, but it's better that way. I don't want to involve my family in this. I think it would be better if they would forget about me. My brother might lose his job because of this.' For a two-hour interview Mosby had not done particularly well, and she tried to set up a dinner date with Oswald, no doubt hoping he would melt a little. 'Thank you,' he politely said, but he didn't turn up.

Oswald had a hard time with the Soviets. Plainly, they were simply not interested in him. This was a period during which the United States was running a programme to infiltrate its agents into Soviet bloc countries. The college boy types which had been the norm for CIA recruitment were now becoming more easily identified by the KGB, and the Agency was beginning to send different types of young men on this kind of mission. But after thirty years in which a US defector to Russia was a rare event, the sudden interest young American men developed in living in Russia after the Iron Curtain was dropped was distinctly observable. When the week permitted by his visa had elapsed, Oswald was told his plane left in two hours and to be on it. He clearly had to act fast if he was to stay on in Russia.

Oswald responded by slashing his wrist, feigning a suicide attempt, which was probably exactly what he had been schooled to do should the need arise. Rushed to the Bodkin Hospital, he was admitted to a ward for the insane, about which he was quite miffed, though he was later transferred to another ward. A week later he was discharged, and since his dramatic action was still not having the desired effect, he decided to use another ploy. On the following Saturday morning he went to the US Embassy and asked to see the Consul. When he faced Richard E. Snyder across his desk, he threw down his passport and noisily denounced the United States and all it stood for, telling the Head Consul he was renouncing his citizenship and taking up residency in Soviet Russia with a view to taking up Soviet citizenship. This was, no doubt, a charade anticipating the embassy was well bugged by the Russians, as indeed it was. Snyder, who had been recruited by the CIA, played his part well, trying to get this young man to see sense and not to act too hastily. John McVickar, a senior consul also present at this interview and, apparently, not briefed about what was going on, was aghast to hear Oswald say he would pass to the Soviets the classified information he had regarding his radar work in the Marines, not to mention something which would be of 'special interest' to them. Oswald produced a letter (see Figure 6) he had already written, which ran:

> I Lee Harvey Oswald do hereby request that my present citizenship in the United States of America be revoked.
>
> I have entered the Soviet Union for the express purpose of applying for citizenship in the Soviet Union, through the means of naturalization.
>
> My request for citizenship is now pending before the Supreme Soviet of the USSR.
>
> I take these steps for political reasons. My request for the revoking of my American citizenship is made only after the longest and most serious consideration.
>
> I affirm that my allegiance is to the Union of Soviet Socialist Republics.
>
> Lee H Oswald

Oswald ranted on about how 'his eyes had been opened to the way America oppresses and colonises foreign people, from observing . . . actions in Okinawa'. In response, Snyder, who had, only a few days before Oswald appeared, sent a confidential letter to the Officer in Charge of USSR Affairs in Washington asking advice on how to deal with an attempted renunciation of citizenship, cleverly told Oswald his application could not be processed on a Saturday morning and he should come back on Monday. His citizenship was never revoked.

Well-schooled in the business he was about, Oswald wrote a protest note at being put off the revoking of citizenship:

> My application, requesting that I be considered for citizenship in the Soviet Union is now pending before the Supreme Soviet of the USSR. In the event of acceptance I will request my government to lodge a formal protest regarding this incident.

Those who monitored the signals in and out of the embassy would carefully report on the official notifications of the defection of ex-Marine Oswald and the threats of treachery he had made. The embassy telegraphed details to the State Department, the CIA, FBI and the Office of Naval Intelligence. The naval attaché to the embassy cabled Naval Operations: 'Oswald, a radar operator in the Marine Corps states he is to give information he possesses on radar to Soviet Intelligence.' Curiously, the same naval attaché had, a week before this time, already despatched a cable to Washington about Lee Harvey Oswald. He referred to him as 'a former Marine and . . . .' The next forty-three spaces were covered up with strips of paper before it was copied. What was under the strips? Was the naval attaché about to blow Oswald's cover?

The reply from the Office of Naval Intelligence was extremely interesting. It did not instruct the embassy staff to prevent Oswald from defecting at all costs, neither did it even advise persuasion. It requested to be informed of 'significant developments in view of continuing interest of HQ, Marine Corps and US intelligence agencies', with copies to FBI, CIA, INS, Air Force and Army. Significantly, it was marked 'INTELLIGENCE MATTER'.

The Soviets, however, no doubt impressed by what they saw in the cables and heard from the embassy bug, finally allowed Oswald to stay. They did not grant him citizenship, but he was issued with residency papers which, in turn, allowed him to obtain an identity card for a stateless person. Oswald then dropped completely out of sight until 29 December when he was sent to Minsk to work in a radio factory. The last person to see him before he left Moscow – on 16 November – was the reporter, Priscilla Johnson (later Priscilla Johnson-McMillan). Priscilla Johnson had been collecting her mail from the embassy when she encountered John McVickar. McVickar told her about Oswald defecting and that he was staying at the Hotel Metropole. Priscilla went to find him and a hotel employee directed her to his room, No. 319.

It was early evening when Oswald opened his room door to Priscilla Johnson. He was quite happy about her interviewing him and he said he would come to her room at 9 p.m. that night. The interview lasted some four to five hours, during which the reporter got her story and more besides. She wrote a sympathetic article for her paper, nowhere mentioning his threat to pass on radar secrets or the 'something of special interest'. It was thought that this might have been because he didn't tell her about it, but she certainly had the full story when she replied to questions from the Warren Commission:

> I had the impression, in fact he said, he hoped his experience as a radar operator would make him more desirable to them (the Soviets). That was the only thing that showed any lack of integrity in a way about him, a negative thing. That is, he felt he had something he could give them, something that would hurt his country in a way, or could, and that was the one thing that was quite negative, that he was holding out some kind of bait.

In a more recent interview with researcher and author John Newman[1], she was asked why she did not put this headline-making material in her original story. 'I know, that it is terrible,' she said, 'that it is so unprofessional.' There may have been a strong reason for her keeping quiet about it, of course. Priscilla Johnson had links to the CIA, and it may have been that she – or they – did not want to scandalise their latest man in Moscow in the US papers.

When Lee Harvey Oswald was despatched to Minsk, he was given 5,000 roubles by the Red Cross, which generally indicates involvement on the part of the MVD, the Soviet internal security organisation. On his arrival, he was greeted by no less than the mayor of the city, supplied with a luxurious apartment, and was given an allowance which, in addition to the wage he earned, gave him a higher income than the manager of the factory at which he worked. For the next year very little was heard about him or from him. It was during this period a U-2 spy-in-the-sky plane was brought down by the Soviets while it was on an espionage mission over Russia.

The pilot of the U-2, Gary Powers, baled out and landed safely. He was taken prisoner and it was while he was in Soviet hands that he was apparently observed by Lee Harvey Oswald. Oswald wrote to his brother, Robert, 'He seemed to be a nice bright American-type fellow when I saw him in Moscow.' The question then was whether radar data relating to U-2 flights was the something of 'special interest' which Oswald dangled as bait before the Soviets, and it would be easy to reach this conclusion. But there are many aspects relating to the downed U-2 which bear careful consideration before making any kind of judgment. What was known to very few at this time was that there was a suspected 'mole' at CIA Headquarters and, from a reliable source in Russia, the CIA learned that U-2 secrets had been compromised. How much the Soviets knew about the spy-in-the-sky programme, however, was unknown. (This was before the time Oswald was sent to Russia.) The CIA chief of counter-intelligence, James Jesus Angleton, was extremely worried about this situation, which remained a close secret, and it has to be wondered whether there was a direct link between the 'mole', the leaking of U-2 secrets and Lee Harvey Oswald's mission. Had the CIA given Oswald peripheral data to hand to the KGB in the hope he would find out exactly what they knew and unearth something which would help them to identify the enemy agent at the heart of the CIA? It is not beyond the realms of possibility that the CIA had decided to abort the U-2 programme and sacrifice one of their top pilots in order to 'place' Oswald. Then again, among many possibilities, there must also be the question of whether Oswald was sent to Russia merely to take the blame for the U-2 leak, which no one as yet knew about. This has support is some quarters.

Gary Powers was returned to the United States in exchange for the spy Rudolph Abel, and wrote a book about his experiences, *Operation Overflight*. The fact that he had not flown out of Atsugi, the base at which Oswald had been located, but from another secret base, tended to undermine the idea of Oswald's involvement, though Powers, in his book, said the Soviets seemed to know quite a lot about Atsugi Base. He said the data Oswald could have provided may have given them the means of shooting down a U-2 plane.

New insight was gained in 1977, however, when Powers, in a radio interview, said he believed his plane had been sabotaged. He told his listeners he believed a bomb had been placed on board his aircraft. If this were true, it may mean that the Soviets, unable to bring the plane down by other means, had succeeded by secreting a bomb in it. It is not by any means impossible, however, that the cause was a CIA-organised controlled explosion arranged to ensure the downing of the plane while giving Powers every opportunity for survival.

The idea of the loss of the plane being linked to the abortion of the U-2 programme suddenly becomes more realistic. This could have been the CIA's way of dealing with the leaked knowledge the Soviets then had. It would suggest to the Soviets the United States was now bereft of any means of large-scale information gathering. This was untrue, of course. Another breakthrough had occurred via progress made in the space programme. The time for spying by satellite had arrived. To a large extent this made the U-2 programme obsolete.

Strangely, Gary Powers was killed in a helicopter crash soon after the radio interview we have just mentioned.

Lee Harvey Oswald's year in Minsk – if that is where he spent his time, and we really don't know – was apparently a period when he was under close observation and unable to carry out his mission, whatever that was. He began to give the impression he had lost his zeal for living in the USSR and, in a letter dated 5 February 1961, made overtures to the US embassy in Moscow to return home to America. It was during this period he met Marina Nikolaevna Prusakova at a dance at the Palace of Culture, and six weeks later married her.

But the waters certainly began to muddy at about this time. In an account of his time in Russia, probably written at a much later date, he said that in Minsk 'I was in the Foreign Language Institute', which he amended to 'I was visiting friends in the Foreign Language Institute'. The Foreign Language Institute was located very near to a KGB spy school in Minsk. This set off alarm bells that he might have been recruited by the KGB and had become a double agent. To those who knew, however, this is likely to have been precisely what he was there to achieve. The decision to return to the USA followed by a speedy marriage to a Russian girl did not make the best of sense, and the ease with which both he and his wife obtained permission to leave Russia was also somewhat unnerving.

What was most impressive, however, was the response from the US State Department. This supposed vile traitor, scoundrel of the first water, villain who may have been recruited by the KGB, found his return to the United States was made as easy as could be. Of course all the motions were gone through for the benefit of the Soviets. Oswald wrote to the embassy saying he would like to return to the US '. . . that is, if we could come to some agreement concerning the dropping of any legal proceedings against me'. Oswald was to repeat this request over and over again, though no undertaking was ever given. Since the Soviets were monitoring all mail to the US embassy, however, Oswald had to play the defensive 'defector' all the time, and such concern about legal proceedings would have been uppermost in the mind of a genuine defector. When Oswald visited the embassy, he questioned Snyder about this again, this time receiving a verbal assurance from him, but with the rider that he could not speak for the State Department. Via the Soviet bug, that would satisfy the listeners he had made as much progress as was possible, his satisfaction with Snyder's response consistent with that of a returning defector.

'Coincidences' at this time were quite intriguing. At the embassy Snyder had received from the State Department a 'Welfare Whereabouts' enquiry on Oswald which was despatched on 1 February 1961. This came within a few days of a request for information from Marguerite, Oswald's mother, who had travelled by train the enormous distance from Texas to Washington to raise enquiries about her son. Oswald's letter of 5 February, asking to return home, was received at the embassy on 13 February. It stretches the imagination to believe this was a coincidence. Rather more, it suggests that the CIA had been in touch with Oswald all the time and his return to the US was ordered by them. If this was the case, any liaison he had with the Foreign Language Institute was likely to have been at the behest of the CIA, and any idea for him to play the double agent for the KGB, if such a thing ever occurred, was likely a CIA ploy. The 'odd move out', so to speak, was Oswald's marriage to Marina. If the Agency suggested this marriage, so soon before his departure, the reasons remain obscure. One thing is sure, however. His marriage did not impede his return to the USA; neither did the birth of a daughter, June, shortly before he left Russia.

As far as the Soviets were concerned, they had no further use for Oswald in Russia. It was costing them money to support him and he was a drain on their manpower resources, since they were watching him day and night. But again, it was Marina who provided the puzzle. The Soviets were not usually so obliging when it came to allowing Russian nationals out of the country, but they made no fuss about the departure of Marina and baby June. It did, however, conform to something of a pattern seen in the context of returning defectors. Over twenty other defectors had taken Russian wives home by this time.

Oswald barely knew Marina when he was sent to hospital for an adenoids operation, but Marina was a regular visitor to the man she knew as 'Alik', and it was in the Fourth Clinical Hospital that they got to know each other. Oswald proposed to Marina before he left his hospital bed, and a few weeks later they married. When Marina first met Lee Harvey Oswald she mistook his imperfect accent for that of someone from one of the further-flung parts of the Soviet Union. She said it came as a surprise to learn that he was an American. Marina had qualified as a pharmacist in 1959 and lived with her uncle and aunt. Her uncle, Ilya Vasilyevich Prusakov, was a colonel in the MVD and no doubt had serious misgivings about his niece marrying an American, but he did not interfere. They married on May Day, 1961. Oswald wrote to the US embassy in Moscow:

> Since my last letter I have gotten married . . . My wife is Russian, born in Leningrad, she has no parents living and is quite willing to leave the Soviet Union with me and live in the United States. I would not leave here without my wife so arrangements would have to be made for her to leave at the same time I do.

Was it was another indication of his status that the embassy accepted the situation without blinking? Or was it that they were expecting it to happen? What did concern the embassy people was that Marina found it necessary to obtain a replacement birth certificate with which to support her application to accompany her husband. If she had no birth certificate how had she satisfied the paperwork requirements for getting married? Was Marina concealing secrets with the help of the Soviet authorities? The investigation the CIA ran on her only made matters worse. They found the name Lev Prizentsev in her address book which produced a blank when fed into the computer. But they next fed his address in, Kondratyevskiy, Prospkt 63, Apartment 7, Leningrad, and obtained the response of it being matched to the address of Robert Edward Webster. Webster was another 'defector' at just about the same time as Lee Harvey Oswald and there were parallels and confusions between the two. Webster returned to the United States within weeks of Oswald. Marina told a friend some years later how Lee had gone to Russia with an exhibition and had decided to stay there. This was entirely untrue of Oswald, but exactly the case with Webster. Had Marina been part of a KGB programme for 'placing' suitable girls with Americans, with the intention of sending them to the US? Was she first attached to Webster before Oswald? Webster would have had no interest in her for he had quickly established himself with a commom-law wife, and already had a wife in the United States. None of this made any difference. A technicality raised by the Immigration and Naturalization Service was quickly buried. The fact Marina said she had not been a member of a Communist organisation when this was untrue, was ignored. The State Department said it was 'in the interest of the United States to get Lee Harvey Oswald and his family out of the Soviet Union and into the United States as soon as possible'.

When he was planning his return home, Oswald asked the embassy to return his passport to him. He thought it could assist in obtaining an exit visa. The embassy was concerned, however, lest the Soviets intercepted the document and used it to introduce a KGB agent into the US. They decided to hang on to it as long as possible, but as the Oswald family's departure time grew close, the passport was reaching its expiry date. Oswald made the 450-mile trip to Moscow to fill in his passport renewal application, where he received the assistance of Consul Snyder. Filling in the form, Oswald was asked to respond to a question relating to any act or acts which might expatriate him or make him ineligible for renewal of his passport. He had to 'delete that which does not apply' and honestly deleted the 'have not' entry in favour of 'have'. Passport renewal in a returning defector's case was normally an extremely uncertain procedure, and such an entry should have disqualified him automatically. An application for renewal connecting with the 'lookout' card attached to a defector's file would, in any case, have sent correspondence flying from department to department causing endless delays, while a decision was reached relating to the desirability of readmitting the applicant back home. But no 'lookout' card had been posted to Oswald's file and, regardless of the deleted 'have not' entry, the speed and ease with which the renewal of passport was achieved constituted a nasty slip on the part of his CIA masters. The KGB were well aware of the difficulties returning defectors had in obtaining passport renewal and Oswald was extremely lucky this did not – at the eleventh hour – leave him exposed.

While Oswald was in Moscow dealing with his passport, he met two American tourists, Rita Naman and Monica Kramer, and they conversed, to the annoyance of the ladies' Intourist guide. This by itself was not remarkable, but they bumped into one another again, ten days afterwards, a Mrs Marie Hyde being with the women this time. A coincidence? A coincidence when Oswald had returned home in that ten days and the second 'chance' meeting took place 450 miles away in Minsk? The ladies were severely reprimanded by the authorities before leaving that city. Mrs Marie Hyde travelled home via Poland and was given another hard time by Polish officials. A snapshot they took which included Oswald in the group found its way into CIA files. Surprise, surprise!

Marina gave birth to their first child, June Lee, on 15 February 1962, amid much excitement. Oswald was a happy father and June a most welcome baby. The need arose for another letter to the US embassy in Moscow requesting travel arrangements to the US for three now, instead of two. This was dealt with without any problem being raised.

Before leaving Russia, Lee Harvey Oswald wrote some letters. One was to Texas Governor John B. Connally on the subject of his Marine discharge, which had been changed from 'honourable' to 'undesirable' while he had been away. It is noted that it had not been downgraded all the way to 'dishonourable', but 'undesirable' would still give him a hard time getting work when he returned home. He asked Connally to have it reversed since his time spent in Russia had 'always had the full sanction of the US Embassy . . . and hence the US Government'. It was an angry letter, probably for the benefit of the KGB letter-openers, and its contents are very interesting, since they more than hinted that he had come to Russia in the service of his country. Another letter on the same topic, posted after Oswald left Russia, was sent to Senator John Tower. This was by no means hostile. Similarly another letter was posted to the US Naval Review Board after his departure. In this, in addition to arguing his corner, Lee Harvey Oswald asked the Review Board to restore him to the Marine Corps Reserves, offering them 'the special knowledge I have accumulated through my experiences since my release from active duty in the Naval Service'. Oswald's discharge status remained the same until his death, probably due to the need for continued cover in the service of the CIA.

Oswald did not have the money to fund his journey home, so he asked the US Government for a loan. The rule was that an applicant must have already applied to a charitable fund, and been turned down, before being eligible to seek a government loan. Oswald routinely filled in and sent off an application to the International Rescue Committee Incorporated but, without waiting for a reply, he then filled in his application for a government loan. Without problems he was granted $435.71. On 1 June 1962 the Oswald family boarded a train for the first leg of their journey from Moscow to the United States.

Although not the most reliable of sources, KGB files which have become available since the demise of the Soviet Union suggest Oswald betrayed no secrets. The Russians never took his 'defector' story seriously and assumed he was an American spy.

---

[1]John Newman, *Oswald and the CIA,* Carroll & Graf, New York, 1995.

CHAPTER FIFTEEN

Homecoming

WHEN IT CAME TO HINTS that Oswald was an intelligence agent, the US embassy in Moscow seemed to spread them liberally. The International Rescue Committee wrote a letter to the Warren Commission which included:

> A few days later we received a letter from Mrs Harwell of the Wilberger County Chapter, Vernon, Texas (Red Cross), dated January 14 1962, to which, to the best of my recollection, were attached copies of a letter written by Consul Norbury, American Embassy, Moscow, to Lee Harvey Oswald, dated December 14 1961, and of a letter addressed to the International Rescue Committee, dated January 13 1961 (sic), and ostensibly written by Oswald . . . To the layman's eye it would appear that both copies were typed on the same typewriter . . . What is most puzzling, though it did not then attract my attention, **is that the letter from Oswald, dated January 13, could have reached the United States by January 14 and that it reached us via Texas . . . [Author's emphasis]**

This raises very good questions to which there are intriguing answers. It appears that Oswald carried such status that someone at the embassy, anxious to ensure that the repatriation of 'our man' went without a hitch, and knowing the rule about a money loan depending on a previous application to a charitable organisation, wrote to International Rescue on his behalf and sent it via the diplomatic pouch. Oswald's own letter to International Rescue did not turn up until February.

The overland rail journey to Amsterdam involved a border check at Helmstedt. Marina's passport showed the required stamp but, strangely, Oswald's did not. The significance of this is not known, but an illegal crossing obviously meant that Oswald did not want to meet the border authorities. Perhaps he felt there was a risk of being identified as a CIA agent. In Amsterdam the Oswalds did not stay in a hotel. They were provided with accommodation at a private residence. Marina recalled a three-day stay at Amsterdam, which suggests Oswald was intensively debriefed there.

They travelled to the United States on the SS *Maasdam*, and docked at New Jersey. On the way, Oswald had prepared some notes, no doubt in readiness for questions from officials who knew nothing of his mission. In fact he prepared a second lot of notes from the first before reaching home, and it appeared he had someone helping him as he wrote. But on landing, there was not one single official to question him, to greet him or scold him. Not one. Had it not been that a representative of Traveler's Aid of New York, Spas T. Raiken, was waiting to be of assistance to him, Lee Harvey Oswald would have slipped into the United States completely unnoticed. When it is considered that, on the face of it, Oswald was a returned defector and traitor, that was extremely remarkable.

Raiken tried to question Oswald, but he didn't cooperate. He merely said he had been 'a Marine . . . attached to the Embassy [in Moscow]'. He was annoyed to be met by the Traveler's Aid representative. Raiken spoke of how he normally had the willing assistance of the senior Immigration and Naturalization Service officer, Louis Johnson, in identifying those whom his organisation had sent him to find. In Oswald's case, he said, he was surly and reluctant to help. Did Johnson's surliness stem from a belief that Oswald was a returning defector? Or had he been instructed to see that the tired Oswalds were left in peace?

Traveler's Aid provided a hotel for Oswald and his family for the one night they were to stay in New York. They stayed at the Times Square Hotel, and it was probably there that travel arrangements to Dallas were hammered out. Oswald did not have the fare for the journey and demanded the State Department was asked to pay it. Instead, Traveler's Aid contacted Robert, Oswald's brother, for the money which necessitated him mortgaging his car. Oswald was extremely annoyed at their interference and, at first, refused the money. His demands for them to get in touch with the State Department being ignored, he had no option but to take the $200 Robert had promptly sent – a lot of money, to a working man in 1962 – and promised himself he would sort it out when he got home. He would, naturally, have expected the State Department to provide his expenses, but was unable to explain why.

When the Oswalds arrived at New York, they had with them seven bags. Two they sent on by train because of the cost of excess baggage by air, but when they arrived in Dallas they had only two. The riddle of the missing bags stems indirectly from the exposure of the American spy, Oleg Penkovskiy. Penkovskiy was a top-level agent for the United States and had made a huge contribution to the intelligence input of the West. He was caught at about the time Oswald was making his final arrangements for leaving Russia, and the ripples were about to flow. Lee Harvey Oswald and Marina had to have medicals at this time before their journey home, and the examinations were carried out at the Moscow embassy by an Air Force flight surgeon, Doctor Alexis Davison. A pleasant man, he chatted to the Oswalds, telling them about his Russian-speaking mother who lived in Atlanta, Georgia, and inviting the couple to meet her when they returned home. Doctor Davison had been a contact man for Penkovskiy, however, and he was quickly despatched from Russia before the spy's trial began on 6 May 1963. Penkovskiy was found guilty and shot. It would seem that in anticipation of a hasty departure, Davison had asked Lee Harvey Oswald to take his luggage home for him. This explains the roundabout route Oswald took from New York to Dallas, travelling via Atlanta City. He didn't visit Davison's mother, but he no doubt dropped off three bags belonging to the doctor to be delivered to her home.

Robert, Lee's brother, and his wife, Vada, met the Oswalds at Love Field airport and took them home to stay with them until they found a place of their own. His mother, Marguerite, who was at that time living at Cromwell, then moved to Fort Worth and the Oswalds moved in with her. His family were to learn nothing about Oswald's work in intelligence, but on odd occasions hints were dropped. One such hint came after the time Oswald had routinely been called in by the FBI for interview. Lee had demonstrated some impatience with this and Robert was curious about what had happened. 'They asked me . . . was I a secret agent,' said Oswald, and Robert asked what he had replied. Oswald retorted, 'Well, don't you know?' Another occasion was when, for some reason, Lee was discussing his return home with his mother. 'Not even Marina knows why I have returned to the United States,' he said. And he was saying no more, though his mother had detected he was working in intelligence long before this time, when he was in Russia, if not even before he went.

Oswald set himself the task of writing about his experiences in Russia. He paid a girl he knew to type up his work, and when his funds would not permit him to pay any more, she offered to do it for nothing, a kind gesture Oswald declined. It seems he wrote about Kiev, a city he had not mentioned living in. His time there probably coincided with the 'lost year' when he had dropped completely out of sight. There are indications he may have travelled widely in Russia during that period.

It was clear from the events of this period of time after his return that Lee Harvey Oswald was still working for US intelligence. It seems he worked not only for the CIA but for the FBI also, and possibly another agency as well. This doubling or tripling was not unusual. During this period he spent a lot of time with the mysterious George S. de Mohrenschildt, who 'babysat' him for the CIA during his wait for a new mission. This was confirmed by author Edward J. Epstein, who interviewed de Mohrenschildt on the day of his death, though he did not write about the interview until 1983. He said the Baron told him that the CIA asked him to 'keep tabs on Oswald' for them. The man asking was probably the CIA's 'local' man, J. Walton Moore, whom de Mohrenschildt knew well. In Dallas, de Mohrenschildt was well connected to the Dallas Russian-speaking community. This group was strongly anti-Communist and, whilst showing affection for Marina and June, they were suspicious of Lee because of his supposed defection.

De Mohrenschildt, believed to be of aristocratic stock, was born in Russia and brought up in Poland, where he was taken to escape the rule of the Bolsheviks. Well educated in Poland and Belgium, he came to the United States before the commencement of World War II. He had links with intelligence and was probably in the employ of French intelligence when he arrived in the United States. Much later, he admitted he had worked also for the Germans. He travelled to Cuba, Mexico, Guatemala, Africa and Yugoslavia, where he was shot at by President Tito's guards when boating near the President's residence.

George de Mohrenschildt, who, it seems, had a genuine entitlement to be called Baron, took a master's degree in petroleum geology at the University of Texas. It would appear, however, that he used his qualifications mainly in the cause of intelligence-gathering, his brush with the Yugoslavs being an example. From that mission, he brought back 'intelligence data' for the CIA which occupied ten separate reports. His connections with the CIA had begun in OSS days and, it appears, they were to continue for the rest of his life.

De Mohrenschildt and Oswald got on well together. Oswald was employed as a metalworker but soon gave this up in favour of a job George found for him. Jaggars-Chiles-Stovall produced high-class print, specialising in those techniques so much in demand by glossy magazines and other publications, including those of the United States Army Map Service. The maps they printed for the government included data from U-2 flights. The government demanded strict security arrangements at Jaggars in return for the contract, and it has puzzled many that Oswald, overtly a returned defector and Communist sympathiser, could be employed there. At first it appears the firm did not keep up the strict security required, but at a closer look it is more likely that de Mohrenschildt's word was all that was required. Oswald was to profit greatly from his proximity to such sophisticated photographic techniques. He learned a lot, and supplemented his new knowledge by learning to type in the evenings. Oswald got on well with those he worked with as, indeed, he did wherever he worked. One of his friends, Dennis Ofstein, told how Oswald did a little private work for him. He remembered how once he enlarged a photograph of a military headquarters he had taken in Russia. The same man recalled Oswald explaining to him what a microdot was, a highly sophisticated intelligence technique at that time.

Lee's relationship with Marina was not happy, according to de Mohrenschildt. They were breaking up, he said. More than once he tried to separate the two, placing Marina and June with an emigré family, but the family stayed together. What de Mohrenschildt's motives were in trying to separate the Oswalds is uncertain. It looked as though he knew something they didn't, and was planning ahead. Perhaps he had advance news of the new mission for Oswald, and realised that Marina would be on her own for an extended period. It is hard to say. Indications from another source showed there was nothing amiss in the relationship between Oswald and his wife. His New Orleans cousin, Marilyn Murret, said, 'They were a real cute couple . . . perfectly happy. He was devoted to Marina [and] seemed to love his child very much . . .'

There were indications that a new mission was pending. The money owed by Oswald to the State Department for his return passage home was still largely unpaid, and at the rate Oswald could afford to repay it, it would be some time before he was out of debt. It may have been something of a charade that Oswald owed anything to the government at all, but outward appearances were to be kept up. The approaching mission caused something of a problem, however, for when money is owed to a government body, the file of the debtor is flagged so that a new passport cannot be issued until the debt is paid. The obvious thing to do was to pay Oswald more so that he could pay off the debt, and this is what they did. If he had to rely on what he could have afforded from his wages, Oswald would have had to have worked excessively to produce the extra cash. As it was, the debt reduced very quickly over a short period of time. Similarly, the money borrowed from Robert for the air fares from New York to Dallas was quickly paid off. Oswald applied for his new passport and, incredibly, it was provided within twenty-four hours.

In March 1963 Oswald purportedly ordered two weapons by post; a handgun and a rifle. They were ordered under the name of A.J. Hidell, and delivered to Oswald's post office box. With hindsight, this was the first concrete sign that there was something odd about Oswald's new assignment, and that he was being railroaded into a conspiracy to kill the President. No doubt the instructions to buy a handgun and a rifle came from his Agency masters, and he would not hesitate to act upon them at once. He probably thought it was curious, however, to be ordered to buy items by mail order when he could have gone into any one of many gunsmiths' shops and bought what he wanted over the counter. This would have had the added benefit of being able to see what he was getting.

As would later happen, a case was manufactured against him as the killer of John F. Kennedy, largely based on his possession of these weapons and the fact that he had bought them could be proven without dispute because he had done so by mail-order. Had he walked into a gun shop on any street and given the name of Hidell – or any other name, for that matter – the chances of linking him to those weapons would have been virtually nil. Oswald had fallen into the hands of a group of CIA agents who were operating outside of the Agency; 'renegades' who had joined with others determined to get rid of the young President they blamed for the CIA-organised Bay of Pigs débâcle.

CHAPTER SIXTEEN

Towards the Root of the Problem

WHEN KENNEDY TOOK OFFICE, he found that his predecessor, Dwight Eisenhower, had agreed to a plan hatched by the CIA to recruit and train Cuban exiles. They were to be sent back into Cuba as a band of guerillas to oust pro-Communist Fidel Castro, who had usurped the Batista government. The new President was told that delay would allow the militarily weak revolutionary army in Cuba to be bolstered and equipped by the Russians. The Head of the CIA, Allen Dulles, publicly supported the plan by speaking of:

> a group of fine young men who asked nothing other than the opportunity to try to restore a free government to their country ... [They were] ready to risk their lives ... Were they to receive ... no sympathy, no support, no aid from the United States?

Kennedy agreed to let the plan proceed, and in doing so he allowed his inexperience to be glimpsed at this one point. Kennedy made it quite clear, however, that he was permitting Cubans to undertake this invasion of their own country; the United States would not be involved more than they already had been, in assisting and training them. In a press conference before the operation began he said:

> ... there will not be, under any conditions, any intervention in Cuba by United States armed forces, and this government will do everything it possible can ... to make sure that there are no Americans involved in any

> actions inside Cuba . . . the basic issue is not one between the United States and Cuba; it is between the Cubans themselves. And I intend to see that we adhere to that principle . . . this administration's attitude is so understood and shared by the anti-Castro exiles from Cuba in this country.

What President Kennedy did not know was that the CIA had expanded the plan agreed by Eisenhower and had enlisted a greater number of men, training and equipping them as a conventional invading army. He also did not know that, unbelievably, planning continued on the basis of the availability of US military support, or at least on the basis Kennedy could be pressured to provide it if need be.

The invasion was an unmitigated disaster, CIA planning being founded on, of all things, inaccurate intelligence. It was expected that the Cuban people would rally to the army of exiles and that Castro would be cast aside. Not so. The people rallied to Castro, and the invasion became a massacre on the beaches of the Bay of Pigs. Believed to have little by way of air defences, the Castro air force displayed its supremacy in the skies. Those on the blood-stained beaches, which included many CIA personnel, radioed for air assistance in their hour of need. It appears Kennedy never received their signal, although had it reached the President's office, it would next have raised the issue of whether the United States could have involved itself in hostilities against Cuba without risking an all-out war which could have brought in the Soviets. As predicted, Kennedy was pressured by the CIA and Joint Chiefs to send in military support for the exiles. He refused to engage in an all-out war on an ad-hoc basis and that was that. The President did, however, in spite of all, agree to unmarked Navy jets going in to protect the exiles' own planes – elderly B-26s – as they made a bid to provide air cover to those on the beaches. Probably due to a time-zone error, the Navy planes took off an hour too late to provide the needed cover. By the time they got there the B-26s had either been shot down or had returned to base.

The President, who gallantly took full responsibility for the CIA's disastrous enterprise, was hated and despised by the CIA agents who survived the tragedy. They blamed him for abandoning them to their fate and because the President had received the aid and support of his brother, Attorney General Robert Kennedy, during this tense period, they hated and despised him just as much. The CIA had, during this period, become its own master, answerable to no one for its policy. It was observable that whilst the government might say one thing, the Agency would do another. This irked President Kennedy, who determined to put this particular part of his house in order. It was only a question of time before the CIA would be brought to heel.

CHAPTER SEVENTEEN

Frame Up

PRESIDENT KENNEDY HAD HAD Major General Edwin Anderson Walker, a well-known citizen of Dallas, 'retired' from army service. An avid right-winger in his political affiliations, the general had been fired for circulating right-wing propaganda among the troops under his command in the 24th Division of the US Army in West Germany. An unacceptable thing to do in any case, it was blatantly sailing against the wind when the literature was hostile to President Kennedy.

Another occasion when Walker ran up against Kennedy was over the President's anti-segregation policy at the University of Mississipi in 1962, when there was a violent confrontation in which two were killed and many injured. When it came to right-wing politics the general was usually found sticking out his chin: he was politically abrasive, so much so that for his personal protection he found it necessary to employ 'aides'.

One such aide, Robert Alan Surrey, noticed two men acting suspiciously one night in April 1963. They were peering through the general's windows. He kept them under surveillance until they got into a Ford sedan and drove off. He then followed them in his own car, but lost them in the city traffic. On another occasion a 1957 Chevrolet was seen by another aide circling the general's house. The general was warned: someone was stalking him.

On 10 April, a bullet was fired at Walker through a window and narrowly missed him. The general, unhurt, was covered in plaster dust; it had been a close thing. The gunman was not identified and, as time passed, no arrest was made for the attempt on Walker's life. After an unproductive investigation, the case remained unsolved. When the Warren Commission were putting together a case

President John F. Kennedy: Because of the scandals breaking over his head, Johnson needed the Presidency.

Clay Shaw: Implicated by New Orleans DA, Jim Garrison, for complicity in the murder of J.F.K. The powers that be were determined he would be acquitted, however. And he was.

Jim Garrison: Took on the CIA agents in New Orleans in his famous case. Little did he know he was taking on the government also.

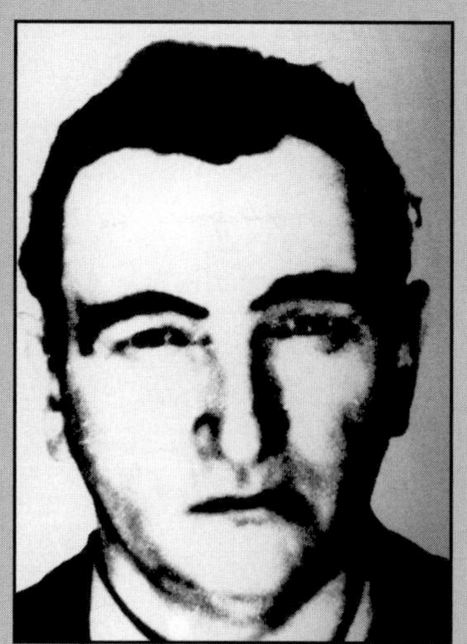

David Ferrie: Worked with Banister and also knew Shaw. Linked to Oswald when he was in New Orleans being 'sheep-dipped' by the CIA.

Guy Banister: Worked for the CIA and FBI. Led Oswald to believe he was carrying out CIA instructions, but he, Shaw and Ferrie had an agenda of their own.

LEFT: The 'Backyard Photo': Famously entered as evidence of Oswald's guilt. When Oswald saw the print he said at once what had happened. Someone had pasted his head on a body which was not his.
(Courtesy National Archives.)

BELOW: Putting the lie to it: Enlargements from one of the above series of prints. Oswald's cleft chin (pictured left) is compared to the pasted-up chin (centre left). A much later generation print (centre right) shows this quite clearly. (Right picture for indicator.)

Lee Harvey Oswald: Is led away in handcuffs. As far as Johnson was concerned they had their man. But the new President knew better.

Roger Craig: Identified the rifle as a Mauser, along with others. They were persuaded to change their minds, but not Craig. In a later challenge to the young deputy, Fritz denied an account Craig gave relating to seeing Oswald in his office, adding that Craig was never there. The above photo shows Fritz's office at the time Oswald was being interrogated. Craig is clearly shown extreme right

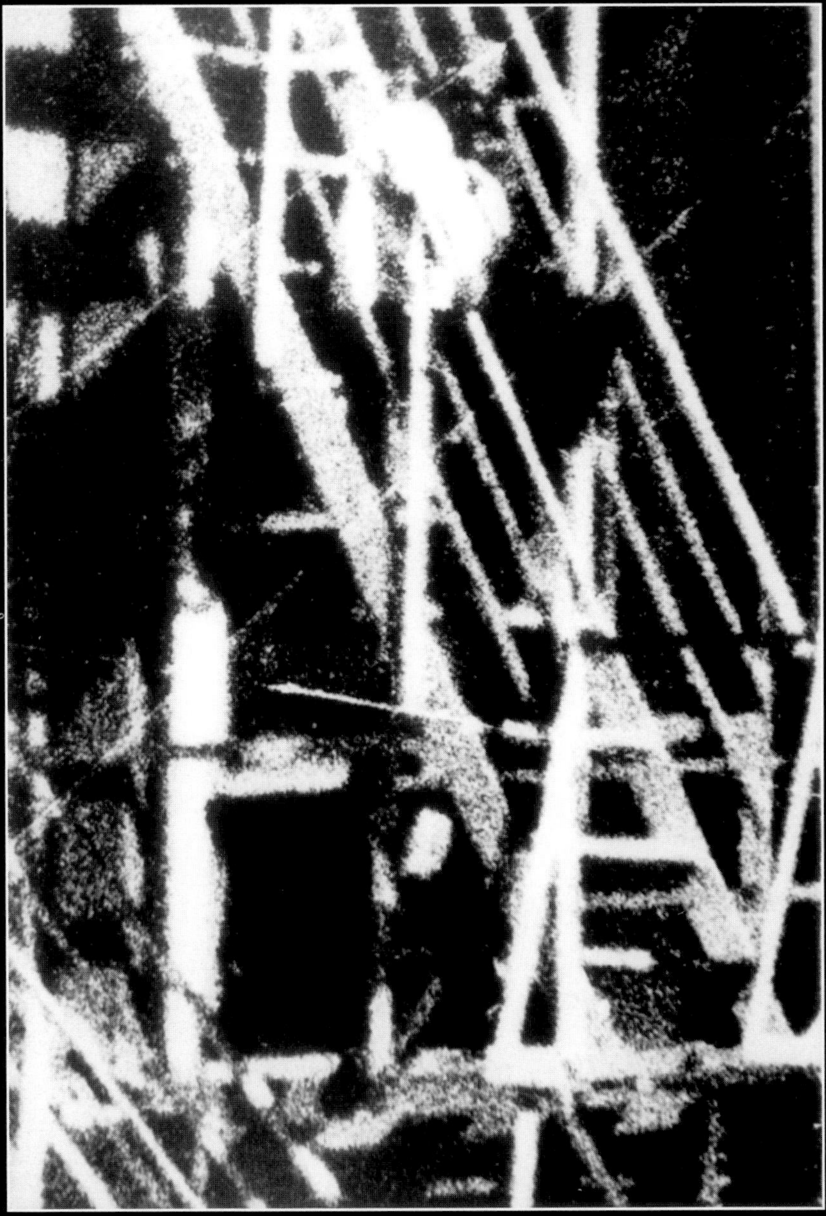

Dal Tex Building: Who was on the fire escape at the moment the shots were being fired? Was he a member of the assassination team? Then there's another figure below looking out of a window. (See Smith–Vidit Study, Chapter Eleven).

Oswald is Arrested: Lee Harvey Oswald is unceremoniously bundled away from the Texas Theatre, where he was arrested by a small army of police officers. It appears they swarmed to the theatre because someone was reported entering without paying. (Courtesy National Archives.)

Jack Ruby: Pictured with some of his girls outside the Carousel Club. It appears that when he killed Oswald he signed his own death warrant. (Courtesy National Archives.)

TOP LEFT: Madeleine Brown: Johnson's mistress who saw him at Murchison's party. Early next day, in a phone call, he said, 'After today those xxxx Kennedys won't be poking fun at me any more.'

TOP RIGHT: E. Howard Hunt: Was it to him that Oswald addressed a note seeking information? There were other Hunts but this one was the front-runner. A CIA man later involved in the Watergate scandal, he was in Mexico at about the time the note was written.

ABOVE LEFT: CIA Director Richard Helms: Admitted eventually that Clay Shaw had been a contract agent for the CIA. Garrison's case against Shaw collapsed due to lack of this evidence.

ABOVE RIGHT: FBI Agent James Hosty: Destroyed what might have been vital evidence on instructions said to have emanated from the top. He still tells a tale inconsistent with the waves caused by a note from Oswald.

TOP LEFT: Chief Justice Earl Warren: Chaired the Warren Commission but McClone, Dulles and Rankin controlled it.

TOP RIGHT: Rose Cheramie: One of the many who lost their lives for what they knew about the assassination of John F. Kennedy.

ABOVE: President John F. Kennedy: Stoops to kiss his aged and ailing father

against Lee Harvey Oswald as the President's assassin, however, Oswald was named as the culprit in an attempt, it seems, to give him a background of violence. The evidence to link Oswald to the shooting was extremely tenuous at best and somewhat ludicrous at worst. It was Marina who testified that her husband had been out on the night of 10 April and had returned in a lather, saying he had taken a shot at General Walker. He had buried his rifle and would retrieve it later, she said.

Marina was a frightened woman after the assassination of President Kennedy. She had become somewhat notorious as the wife of the man who, they said, had killed the popular young John F. Kennedy. She dreaded that she would be deported back to Russia where she would be even less popular at a time when the Soviets were asserting their innocence of any involvement in the crime. She told the Warren Commissioners what she thought they wanted to hear: she lied, contradicted herself, was evasive, and changed statements she had already made. She was anxious to please the Warren Commissioners, the FBI agents and any of the other officials who questioned her. In other words, her evidence was worth nothing. The only witness to the Walker shooting attempt, a fourteen-year-old boy named Walter Kirk Coleman, who lived nearby, said he saw two men running from Walker's house, and a Ford car speeding away down the alley. One man got into a black Chevrolet; there was a pause while he put something on the back floor of the car, after which he drove off quickly. Walter Coleman was told by the 'authorities' not to discuss what he had seen with anyone. He was not called by the Warren Commission when the crime was attributed to Lee Harvey Oswald.

But the two-car getaway, by itself, ruled Oswald out. He had no car, and couldn't drive anyway. There was no mention of a third man who fled on foot. Marina had testified Oswald had a file in which there were pictures of the general's house which he had taken. He also had the timetables for buses serving the area and other data, she said. As might be expected, however, the file and its contents had been destroyed. The 'buried rifle' evidence fell apart when the de Mohrenschildts told how they had seen the rifle at the Oswalds' home during the time it was supposedly buried. The only other substantial 'evidence' against Oswald was a police claim that the bullet fired had been of 6.5 calibre, the calibre of Oswald's rifle. It was later discovered, however, that it was widely reported at the time of the shooting that the remains of a 30.06 missile had been found at the scene of the crime.

When it came to the photographs of Walker's house, Marina said she was shown a copy by an FBI agent who had searched her house, which inspires no confidence at all in her testimony. Interestingly, shown the print, when giving evidence to the Warren Commission, she pointed out that a hole in the print that had not been there when she had seen it before. The hole obliterated the licence plate number of the car, a Chevrolet. The hole was never explained. The only other time the picture was seen was in a photograph, published in a book by the Chief of Police, Jesse Curry, years later, of what was claimed to be Oswald's possessions. The picture was among them, minus the hole. It now becomes clear in whose hands the picture was when the hole was driven through. Unfortunately, the photograph of the photograph was not good enough for the number to be read. (See first picture section.)

All in all, trying to link the Walker shooting to Lee Harvey Oswald was a shabby manoeuvre on the part of the Warren Commission, aided and abetted by the Dallas Police Department who, with their knowledge of the calibre of the bullet, had concrete evidence that Oswald was not the shooter in the Walker case. Even General Walker took a dim view of the description of the 30.06 bullet being changed to 6.5 in order to try to pin the shooting on Oswald.

There have been suggestions that the general himself arranged the rifle-shot and 'near miss' for reasons that were best known to himself.

CHAPTER EIGHTEEN

To Fall Among Thieves

LEE HARVEY OSWALD was required to move from Dallas to New Orleans, where a 'sheepdipping' operation was started. 'Sheepdipping' was the term given to the procedure of giving an agent a specific background which would equip him for a new mission. In this case, the background involved the Cuban exiles and the politics which pertained to the post-Bay of Pigs situation. Marina and June went to Irving to stay with Ruth Paine, who wanted to learn to speak Russian. The Oswalds had met Ruth, whose husband was later found to have CIA connections, through a friend of de Mohrenschildt.

Before leaving Dallas, Oswald had handed out leaflets in Main Street in support of the Fair Play for Cuba Committee, and had sent to their headquarters in New York for a fresh supply. George de Mohrenschildt and his wife, Jeanne, left Dallas for Haiti where George was purported to be involved in the oil and sisal business. In fact they called at Washington en route, no doubt so that George could receive instructions about intelligence work they were to carry out in Haiti. He had wielded enormous influence on Lee Harvey Oswald, and Marina, for that matter. And now, suddenly, he was gone. The timing of his trip to Haiti appears in retrospect to be quite significant for he was far, far, away when the bullets cut down President Kennedy in Elm Street.

Lee Harvey Oswald stayed with his aunt and uncle, the Murrets, for a short time when he arrived in New Orleans. It appears likely that his cousin, Marilyn, had been involved in his being recruited into the CIA. Marilyn, a teacher of languages, travelled extensively. When she was in Japan, she met Lee's half brother, John Pic, who was stationed there in 1959, and it was Marilyn who told him that Lee was in Russia. The question was, however, how did she know? That remains a mystery, for the news had not been released at that time, in newspapers, radio, or television. Even the family did not know his whereabouts. But someone who moved around the world as extensively as Marilyn was a likely candidate for involvement with the CIA. When the Agency was seeking young men for a new programme of infiltration behind the Iron Curtain it would not be unlikely she told them of her cousin who had joined the Marines. How else would she be so well informed? And since not all CIA personnel would know of recruitment for a new undercover programme, Marilyn's special knowledge could be explained by her recommendation of Lee, and her continued interest in what was happening to him.

Oswald refused financial help from his aunt and uncle and soon got a job. He went to work for the Reily Coffee Company as a maintenance man, and sent for Marina and June to join him. William B. Reily was highly committed to Cuban interests, but his politics were not pro-Castro. He gave financial help to the Cuban Revolutionary Council and supported the Crusade to Free Cuba. His business address was Magazine Street, the street on which the Oswald family had their house. Ruth Paine motored down with Marina and June and spent a few days with them before driving home. Oswald wrote to the New York Headquarters of the Fair Play for Cuba Committee telling them he was starting up a chapter of their organisation in New Orleans. He also said he was renting an office at his own expense. They replied telling him he should not rent an office and should proceed with caution. He wrote back to them several weeks later saying he had rented an office anyhow, but it had been closed down by the people in charge of renting.

Oswald's motives for promoting the FPCC had nothing to do with benefiting that organisation. He recruited only one member, A.J. Hidell – himself – and operated out of the last place in New Orleans which would have been suspected of links with the Fair Play for Cuba Committee – 544 Camp Street. This was the address of an office block known as the Newman Building, which seethed with *anti*-Castro activities. The particular office from which he ran FPCC was that of private detective Guy Banister. Since few of Oswald's leaflets bore the Camp Street address, it would seem that Banister was unaware that Oswald had used the address for his literature. As soon as Banister found out, he quickly enlightened him that he should find an alternative address to display. Oswald then used the address of his new home, 4907 Magazine Street, and a PO box number. Interestingly, Magazine Street was just round the corner from Camp Street, and Camp Street was close to the premises of the Office of Naval Intelligence and the FBI.

FIGURE 31

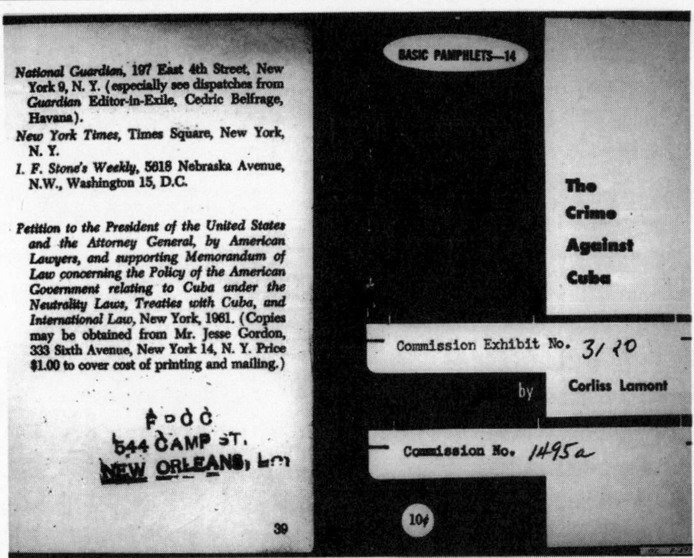

National Guardian, 197 East 4th Street, New York 9, N. Y. (especially see dispatches from *Guardian* Editor-in-Exile, Cedric Belfrage, Havana).

New York Times, Times Square, New York, N. Y.

I. F. Stone's Weekly, 5618 Nebraska Avenue, N.W., Washington 15, D.C.

Petition to the President of the United States and the Attorney General, by American Lawyers, and supporting Memorandum of Law concerning the Policy of the American Government relating to Cuba under the Neutrality Laws, Treaties with Cuba, and International Law, New York, 1961. (Copies may be obtained from Mr. Jesse Gordon, 333 Sixth Avenue, New York 14, N. Y. Price $1.00 to cover cost of printing and mailing.)

FPCC
544 CAMP ST.
NEW ORLEANS, LA

39

BASIC PAMPHLETS—14

The Crime Against Cuba

Commission Exhibit No. 3120

by Corliss Lamont

Commission No. 1495a

10¢

Literature handed out by Lee Harvey Oswald showing Banister's Camp Street address.

FIGURE 32

HANDS OFF CUBA!	**HANDS OFF CUBA!**
Join the Fair Play for Cuba Committee	**Join the Fair Play for Cuba Committee**
NEW ORLEANS CHARTER MEMBER BRANCH	NEW ORLEANS CHARTER MEMBER BRANCH
Free Literature, Lectures	*Free Literature, Lectures*
LOCATION:	**LOCATION:**
L. H. OSWALD 4907 MAGAZINE ST NEW ORLEANS, LA.	A J HIDELL P.O. BOX 30016 NEW ORLEANS, LA.
EVERYONE WELCOME!	**EVERYONE WELCOME!**

The Camp Street address (see Fig 31) was soon replaced by Oswald's own address – with a PO box number for his alias, A.J. Hidell.

Guy Banister had a background of intelligence connections running back to World War Two and long before. He had worked for the FBI, and had played a part in the capture of the notorious John Dillinger. His work earned the approval of Director J. Edgar Hoover who, in the 1940s, rewarded him with the post of Chief of the FBI's Chicago branch. During the war he became a Naval Intelligence Agent and eventually went on to become second-in-command of the New Orleans Police Department. When he left that job he opened his detective agency, which provided cover for his links with the intelligence agencies, notably the FBI and CIA, for whom he worked. Banister was anti-Communist in the extreme, a right-winger belonging to the John Birch Society, the Louisiana Committee on Un-American Activities and the Minutemen.

Banister's secretary, Delphine Roberts, told how Oswald applied to become one of Banister's 'agents'. As part of his activities on behalf of the Fair Play for Cuba Committee, he passed out leaflets on the streets of New Orleans, visited a college campus, and picketed the docks where the aircraft carrier, USS *Wasp* was berthed. Some of Banister's agents saw him doing this and reported it to Banister, who reassured them. 'Don't worry about him,' he laughed. 'He's with us.' Oswald was heavily involved in Cuban affairs as part of his 'sheepdipping' operation, and firmly under the control of the CIA's Guy Banister and his associates. These included David Ferrie, Clay Shaw and Jack Martin, and there is some evidence that George de Mohrenschildt had links with this group.

Lee Harvey Oswald made contact with an anti-Castro group, making a point of meeting one of their leaders, Carlos Bringuier. Bringuier owned a shop, and visiting it one day, Oswald got into conversation with a group of people there, and made an offer to help train their recruits. He told them of his Marines experience and how he was knowledgeable about sabotage techniques. He returned to the shop the following day and left his copy of the Marines training manual. Whatever impression these gestures made on Bringuier were quickly reversed when, a few days later, the latter was told that Oswald was on the streets handing out 'Hands Off Cuba' literature. Bringuier was incensed and, finding where Oswald was, ranted at him for being two-faced. Bringuier's anger did not seem to trouble Oswald, and the rebel-leader's blood pressure rose faced with Oswald's attitude. Tempers erupted when a smiling Oswald said, 'Okay, Carlos, if you want to hit me, hit me . . .' The police soon appeared and Oswald and Bringuier were arrested for a breach of the peace. Curiously, Oswald had, a week before this time, contacted the Fair Play for Cuba Committee, telling them he had been involved in a street fracas and had been cautioned by the police. He told FPCC, 'This incident robbed me of what support I had leaving me alone. Nevertheless thousands of circulars were ditrubed [sic] and many, many pamplets [sic] which your office supplied . . .'

The street brawl was obviously exactly what Oswald wanted. He had engineered it, apparently, to explain to FPCC why he had no new members in his branch. While he was in jail, Oswald asked for a message to be sent to the local FBI agent, John Quigley. Others might have asked for word to be sent to a lawyer, but not Oswald. He wanted to see Agent Quigley. The chances he had of obtaining a response on a Saturday morning were arguably slim to non-existent but, remarkably, Quigley turned up. Not only that, but he spent an hour and a half with Oswald.

There was a court hearing at which, in the segregationist courtroom, Oswald sat with the blacks while Bringuier sat with the whites. The charges against Bringuier were dropped, but Oswald was fined ten dollars. His fine was paid by one of the Murret family and he was released, having skilfully had his record endorsed with details of his FPCC activities, all part of the 'sheepdipping'. The notes taken by Agent Quigley at the extended meeting in the jail were all later destroyed. Oswald now became the centre of attention from radio and television interviewers, and he milked the situation dry. He paid for help to hand out more of the Fair Play for Cuba leaflets outside the International Trade Mart, and the local television station had a film crew there within minutes. Oswald was bent on obtaining every ounce of publicity he could make from his new notoriety. He took part in a radio debate with Carlos Bringuier. The programme was entitled 'Conversation Carte Blanche', in which Oswald's 'defection' to Russia was brought out. Oswald held his own admirably until he was asked how he had supported himself in Russia. 'Well, as I, uh, well,' he stammered, 'I will answer that question directly, then, since you will not rest until you get an answer. I worked in Russia, I was under, uh, the protection of the, uh . . . of the, uh, that is to say, I was not under the protection of the American Government. But that is I was at all times an American citizen.' Taken off his guard, it sounded as though Oswald had very nearly exposed his intelligence role in Russia, but he quickly covered up his slip. Both sides had to be pleased with the outcome. Oswald had succeeded in putting forward a case for the FPCC, whilst, in fact, the Cuban rebels came out rather better in the long run.

Another slip made by Oswald took place in the garage next to Reily's, where he worked. This particular garage provided transport for both CIA and FBI agents working in the locale, and Oswald often spent time there talking to the manager, Adrian Alba. Alba distinctly saw a white envelope slipped to Oswald by an FBI agent whom he knew. Though the envelope was quickly concealed, it was not quick enough to prevent Alba from becoming aware of Oswald's FBI connections. Probably because of spending too much of his working time at the garage – or possibly because of his FPCC connections being publicised, remembering that Reily was a strong supporter of the other side – Oswald was sacked from his job with the coffee-maker. Saying goodbye to Adrian Alba, Oswald was far from downcast. 'I have found my pot of gold at the end of the rainbow,' he said, and, retrospectively, his remark may clearly be understood. He was, it seems, delighted with the new mission he believed he was going on. But as time would tell, however, his comment might well have been tempered with 'All that glistens . . .'

He now became active in his operations from 544 Camp Street. Run by Guy Banister, Oswald was involved in a strange occurrence at the township of Clinton, less that a hundred miles north of New Orleans. Oswald, with two others, arrived in a long sleek black Cadillac which crept into the little town and glided down the main street. It was the day for registering for a vote, and the blacks in the community had been rallied to stand in line to obtain this right. The line was very long and registration was made as difficult as could be by the white organisers. The blacks did not react: they stood in line peacefully and introduced a holiday atmosphere to the occasion. The black Cadillac stopped by the registration station and Oswald got out. He stood in line with the blacks while those left in the car stewed in the heat. David Ferrie was identified as one of the car occupants and the driver, not identified with certainty, was believed to be Clay Shaw.

When at last, hours later, Oswald reached the registration point he told registrar Henry Palmer he wanted to register because he wanted a job in the township and thought he would stand a better chance if he was registered. Palmer examined his Navy ID card but told him what he undoubtedly knew already: he could not register because he was not a resident of Clinton. Oswald joined the others and the Cadillac drew away and left the area. If the reason for the incident is not obvious at once, this is understandable. It would seem, however, there was no more complex an explanation than Oswald standing out like a sore thumb again supporting another unpopular cause, the cause of the blacks in the segregationist New Orleans area.

Come September, Oswald sent Marina and June back to Irving to stay with Ruth Paine, telling them they 'might not meet again until they met in Russia'. It appears his new mission was about to begin. After they left, his first job was to secure an entry visa to Mexico, which he obtained without any difficulty. Standing in the same line, in front of Oswald, was CIA agent William Gaudet. Oswald's 'shadow' was in position.

Putting all the available clues together, it seems Oswald was being sent back to the Soviet Union. He had not left there under any cloud, in fact the ease with which the Soviets facilitated the return of the Oswald family to the United

States suggests that they might have held out some hopes that he could prove more useful to them there than in Minsk. This time Oswald would return to Russia via Cuba, where, as a man with all the right credentials – an established background in pro-Castro activities – he could ingratiate himself by handing over intelligence items which would pave the way for his re-entry into Russia. His first task was to persuade the Cuban embassy in Mexico City to grant him a visa to travel to Havana. This, it appears, is what the CIA had planned for him. What actually happened from this point reflected the intentions of the group of CIA renegades who were involved in the conspiracy to murder President John F. Kennedy. Oswald was an ideal selection from the point of view of the agents to whom he had been sent for 'sheepdipping'. They had chosen him to be the 'patsy'.

CHAPTER NINETEEN

Now You See Him . . .

LEE HARVEY OSWALD'S SOJOURN in Mexico City introduced one of the biggest mysteries ever to be associated with the assassination of President Kennedy. On the face of it, he travelled by bus from New Orleans, setting out on 26 September. He stayed at the Hotel Comercio and visited the Cuban embassy to try to obtain an entry visa which would allow him to travel on to Russia. Since the Cuban Embassy insisted he had to have acceptance for entry to the USSR before they would consider helping him, he visited the Soviet embassy to plead his cause. All of this was to no avail, and eventually, after a hectic week, he returned to New Orleans.

The Warren Report tells us little more than this. The Commissioners really didn't want to know what went on in Mexico City it seems, for what really happened there would have persuaded many people at the time that the Kennedy slaying was the work of Castro's Cubans. It was not, but then the plot to ensnare Lee Harvey Oswald had suddenly thickened when he arrived in Mexico City.

On Tuesday, 27 September, the attention of the consulate assistant, Senora Silvia Tiradodu Duran, was drawn to an American who wanted to go to Russia via Cuba, spending a couple of weeks in that country before the long haul to Russia. He produced a file containing documents which showed that he was Lee Harvey Oswald, and that he had been to Russia before. He also presented cards which showed that he was the President of the New Orleans chapter of the Fair Play for Cuba Committee, and newspaper cuttings which evidenced his FPCC leafleting, and his involvement in the street brawl and subsequent arrest. One picture which caught Silvia Duran's eye was one of Oswald flanked by police officers. The effect was overwhelming. It was a dramatic oversell and had the opposite effect to that required. She was suspicious, and sent the over-zealous applicant off to obtain photographs, four of them, to append to copies of an application form.

Oswald returned with the forms filled out and photographs in place. Where the photographs were taken was a mystery, for none of the local photographers could remember taking them when later asked. How he came back with the forms already completed might have been another mystery, as forms were normally filled out at the desk, but Silvia Duran admitted she sometimes made exceptions. She told Oswald he should return in about a week's time since she could do nothing immediately, and this caused an outburst. 'Impossible,' he said, 'I can only stay in Mexico three days.' Senora Duran offered no alternative and Oswald left, only to return just as the consulate was closing. He said he had been to the Russian embassy and it had been agreed he could enter the Soviet Union, and since this was settled, could he now have his visa to enter Cuba?

But Silvia Duran dutifully checked with the Soviet embassy, only to learn Oswald had not told the truth. The visa to enter the USSR would take some months to come through. When Duran faced Oswald with this, he exploded. He flew into a rage, causing such a disturbance that Eusebio Azcue, the Consul, was drawn to the scene to find out what was happening. Azcue persevered with Oswald, doing his best to calm him down and getting him to listen to reason. He was wasting his time, however; the aggrieved Oswald continued to erupt and the Consul finally lost patience with him. He told him his type of person did nothing to help Cuba, and eventually Oswald left.

Oswald returned another day to the Cuban embassy, doing nothing to help his case by getting into another argument with Azcue. The production of a membership card for the American Communist Party only served to add to the suspicion of him, since it was in pristine condition, and, finally, another row with the Consul in which he made insulting remarks resulted in him being thrown out. He paid several more visits to the Soviet embassy but, all in all, he had blown it. He was not likely to stampede the Soviets into rushing through an entry visa to Russia for him, and even if he had achieved that, there was no way the Cubans were going to grant him entry into their country. But in a matter of weeks, when Oswald was accused of killing President Kennedy, this whole episode was put under a microscope, with astounding results.

The man who had visited the Cuban embassy clearly was not Lee Harvey Oswald. When Consul Azcue was given his photograph he was adamant it was not the man who had made himself so unforgettable because of his unpleasantness, and Silvia Duran, after first agreeing with an identification of the photograph, described the man she saw, and it was clearly not Oswald she was describing. The man who visited the Soviet embassy was also an imposter. The man spoke in poor, broken Russian to those he met, whilst the real Oswald was extremely fluent in the language. This was all confirmed by no less than the CIA personnel serving at the Mexico City station. Asked by the Warren Commission to supply photographs from the surveillance cameras in use at the embassies, they sent pictures of a stranger. It was certainly not Lee Harvey Oswald. Asked to supply tapes made of surveillance sound recordings at the bugged embassies, they sent tapes, the voice on which was not Oswald's. The Agency tried to explain the wrong pictures away by saying the cameras were not operating at the times in question, but this convinced no one. The sound recording tapes containing the voice of the bogus Oswald were, unfortunately, routinely wiped, said the CIA.

However, documents lately released, some as recently as the late '90s, show that a package was flown in by a Navy plane the day after the assassination occurred, arriving at 4.00 a.m. EST. Six hours later J. Edgar Hoover[1] told President Johnson, 'We have up here the tape and the photograph of the man who was at the Soviet embassy using Oswald's name. That picture and the tape do not correspond to this man's voice, neither to his appearance. In other words, it appears that there is a second person who was at the Soviet embassy down there.' It would seem that the story of the tapes having been erased was a lie. The man taking Oswald's place also explains the Warren Commission's reluctance to go further into what was happening in Mexico City. Not only did it smell of conspiracy, the fake Oswald met and talked to the notorious Valeriy Kostikov when he visited the Soviet embassy. Kostikov was described by the CIA as a 'case officer in an operation which is evidently sponsored by the KGB's 13th Department responsible for sabotage and assassination'. When Kostikov and his KGB colleague, Oleg M. Nechiporenko, saw Oswald's photograph they both said he was the man who visited the Russian embassy. However, they then went on to describe him, speaking of his dreadful Russian. 'His pronunciation was bad. He really mangled the grammar,' said Nechiporenko.[2] Whoever they thought they had been looking at, it was quite clear they had not been listening to the accomplished Russian of Lee Harvey Oswald.

The events at Mexico City produced some interesting issues. The 'Oswald' who visited the Russian embassy, still speaking in broken Russian, said he feared the FBI were going to kill him. Breaking down and sobbing, he produced a gun and told Kostikov and Nechiporenko he had to carry it for protection. 'I'm afraid they're going to kill me. Let me in,' he begged. This took place on a Saturday morning when the staff were there only for recreational purposes. Later that same morning, the Russians got a phone call from Silvia Duran who told them

Oswald wanted to speak to them. She passed over the phone and he again spoke in poor Russian, we are told. But the whole telephone episode is problematic. The Cuban embassy does not open on Saturday mornings, so the call did not emanate from there. More than this, Silvia Duran denied it ever took place.

The House Select Committee on Assassinations investigator, Edwin Lopez, in his now well-known report, referred to a claim that Silvia Duran had been Lee Harvey Oswald's mistress while he was in Mexico, a claim first confirmed by Ms Duran but later denied. This links with a report that Oswald and two other Americans attended a 'twist' party given by Silvia Duran's cousin, Ruben Duran, but, even if true, raises the question of which 'Oswald' was invited. Knowledge of the affair, which appears to derive from post-assassination CIA documents, is hard to substantiate from elsewhere. More likely the story originated from a source anxious to strengthen the conspiratorial element to the Mexico episode, whilst at the same time attacking Oswald's moral character. The moral character of Ms Duran had, apparently, been compromised before meeting Oswald.

The day after President Kennedy was assassinated, the CIA requested Silvia Duran's secret arrest by the Mexican authorities:

> With full regard for Mexican interests, request you ensure that her arrest is kept absolutely secret, that no information from her is published or leaked, that all such info is cabled to us, and that fact of her arrest and her statements are not spread to leftist or disloyal circles in the Mexican government.

Duran was in custody for several days and only released after she identified Lee Harvey Oswald as the man with whom she had had dealings with in the Cuban embassy. She talked freely after her release, which inspired a new CIA cable requesting she be arrested again, and asking the Mexican authorities to take responsibility for this. At all costs Silvia Duran was not to know the CIA were behind her rearrest.

Silvia Duran was careful about what she said when she was released next time, resolutely asserting her identification of Oswald. Many years later, however, she confessed she really was not sure. She admitted to researcher Anthony Summers that she identified him more from his name. After watching film of Oswald she concluded '. . . the man on the film is not like the man I saw here in Mexico City.'

Could it be that Silvia Duran was, all the time, a CIA agent? She is suspected of being so.

The entire Mexico City episode appears at first to be a complete muddle. It is only with hindsight and after much further research carried out by the House Select Committee on Assassinations, which included the notable work of Edwin Lopez, and the labours of other dedicated individuals, that we can piece together what really happened and why.

The first important question to be resolved was whether Lee Harvey Oswald ever went to Mexico at all, and it would be easy to believe he didn't. Those he spoke to on the buses he travelled on to Mexico City have more than satisfactorily confirmed that he did, however. The identifications of the Australian girls he conversed with about hotels in Mexico City and the English doctor, for instance, seem entirely reliable. His knowledge of the hotels tends to confirm that he had been to Mexico City before, although CIA agents are well primed for what they are to appear to be. Those who would like this to prove that he went to Mexico City on 18 September, supporting the 'pay-off' story, can only be disappointed that, had he flown there and back in one day, he would have had no opportunity to learn about hotels. Lee Harvey Oswald did travel to Mexico on 26 September because his real CIA masters had sent him. From the 'renegades' point of view this was quite acceptable because it added substantiation to the stories of his visits to the Cuban and Russian embassies. It would also be useful to have him there for any signatures required or for personal details that might be required.

The big question is why other people purported to be him at the embassies. This, at first, does not make sense, especially because Oswald was already in Mexico City, but a closer look at exactly what happened reveals an important achievement on the part of those who impersonated him. **He did not get his visa to Cuba**. He was probably told that other agents would make the applications in his stead because of their skill at handling embassy staff and securing visas. As we have seen, the impersonators deliberately caused trouble and made sure they did not obtain his visa to enter Cuba. It also seems to me that there were two people impersonating Oswald, one whose Russian was atrocious but who, at least, looked like him, and another, whose Russian was also very poor and who was small and well built. The mission Oswald had been given by the CIA appears to have been to enter Cuba and to go on to do further work in Russia. He was required by the 'renegades' to return to Dallas to become the fall-guy in the murder of the President, however, and the fact that they could tell him he would be flown out to Cuba, which I believe was the case, allowed him to accept this as an alternative to securing his visa. Since it appears that an important part of the conspiracy to kill President Kennedy was to lay a trail which led to Cuba and Fidel Castro, the last segment of the plan, it would seem, was to whisk the 'assassin' out by plane immediately after the killing of the President.

But this is where it all went wrong . . .

---

[1] Quoted from another source in my book, *JFK: The Second Plot*, in 1992.

[2] Oleg M Nechiporenko, *Passport to Assassination*, Birch Lane Press, New York. 1993

CHAPTER TWENTY

. . . Now You Don't

AT ABOUT THE TIME OSWALD travelled to Mexico City, on 26 or 27 September, three men visited Silvia Odio, who lived in Dallas. Silvia Odio, whose father was in a Cuban jail, lived with her sister Annie, and was active in anti-Castro politics. She had helped to form the Cuban Revolutionary Junta before coming to Dallas, and when her guests said they wanted her help to raise funds for their revolutionary work, she was interested. She asked them in and they introduced themselves to her, Leopoldo and Angelo, who were Mexicans or Cubans, and Leon Oswald, an American, who looked dirty and unkempt. Leopoldo and Angelo did the talking: Leon hardly opened his mouth. They knew about her father and were well-versed in Cuban affairs. They talked, but the conversation led nowhere. Silvia Odio was uncomfortable. She felt there was something odd about the men. But they soon left.

No one was more surprised than she to receive a phone call the following day from Leopoldo. 'What do you think about the American?' he asked her. She was surprised at the question and expressed no opinion. He continued:

> Well, you know, he's a Marine, an ex-Marine, and an expert marksman. He would be a tremendous asset to anyone, except that you never know how to take him . . . He could go either way. You know our idea is to introduce him to the underground in Cuba, because he is great, he is kind of nuts. The American says we Cubans don't have any guts. He says we should have shot President Kennedy after the Bay of Pigs. He says we should do something like that.

Silvia Odio was somewhat bewildered. She had felt uncomfortable about the men's visit and now she could not make any sense of the phone-call she received from Leopoldo. What was its purpose?

She found out when President Kennedy was assassinated. The whole thing seemed to be a plan to impress upon her that the Cubans were behind the murder of the President, and that Leon Oswald – unmistakably intended to represent Lee Harvey Oswald, whom she recognised at once from newspaper photographs – was the marksman. The Warren Commission agreed that the man Silvia Odio saw could not have been Lee Harvey Oswald. Silvia Odio was most cooperative with the Commissioners who, faced with this and several other instances of Oswald being impersonated in or around Dallas, did not seem to grasp the implications of the visit of Leopoldo, Angelo and Leon, or was it that they did not want to?

Another incident which involved two men, one perhaps a Cuban, with 'Lee Harvey Oswald' was on the outskirts of Dallas, where Mrs Lovell Penn found them firing a rifle on her land. Mrs Penn despatched them promptly and then reported the matter to the authorities. They came and investigated, finding – significantly – a spent 6.5 Mannlicher-Carcano cartridge case on the ground. At approximately the same time as the shooting was taking place on Mrs Penn's property, 'Lee Harvey Oswald' was visiting a radio station at Alice, Texas, with his wife and daughter. The station manager of KPOY said they stayed about twenty-five minutes, so it was not a hit-and-run visit. Alice was about 350 miles from Dallas and the question arises of how 'Oswald' and family got there. They travelled in a 1954 car, the station manager said. Lee Harvey Oswald had no car and he could not drive. Neither could he be in two places at once.

During the next few weeks, 'Oswald' was seen buying ammunition at Morgan's Gunshop in Fort Worth, enquiring about a gun part in Irving – he brought his wife, his daughter and two-week-old baby here – and the Irving Sports Shop, to which 'Oswald' brought a rifle and asked for holes to be drilled for the mounting of a telescopic sight. At about the same time, he turned up at the Southland Hotel in Dallas, seeking a job as a parking attendant and asking how high the hotel was and what kind of view of Dallas could be had from it. The manager recalled writing the name down as Lee Harvey Osborne and being corrected: it was Lee Harvey Oswald.

'Oswald', this time in the company of a teenage boy, paid a visit to a hairdresser in Irving. The hairdresser remembered hearing them pass leftist comments. He noticed that when they left they headed for a grocery store, where 'Oswald' asked the manager, Leonard Hutchinson, to cash a cheque for $189. Hutchinson, who recalled the cheque was made out to 'Harvey Oswald', refused. He claimed to have seen 'Oswald' in his shop before, in the company of two women. The Lincoln-Mercury car salesman, Albert G. Bogard, who took 'Oswald' for a test drive in a red two-door hard-top Caliente Mercury Comet, said he drove very fast along the Stemmons Freeway. He told the dealer afterwards he could not afford the down payment and commented to a colleague of the salesman that he would do better going back to Russia 'where they treat workers like men'. He spoke of coming into some money in the next few weeks, Bogard recalled.

From then on, almost every night until the day of the assassination, 'Oswald' was seen at the Sports Drome Rifle Range at Dallas or at a range at Irving, shooting an ancient 6.5 Italian carbine with a telescopic sight affixed. He made a thorough nuisance of himself so that people remembered him. He fired at other people's targets, for instance, and generally behaved in an obnoxious manner. It was noted how expert his shooting was, however, even though his weapon emitted a 'ball of fire' from the barrel when it was fired.

The Warren Commission made a point of having these 'sightings' investigated, and found that, in every case, Oswald was somewhere else. It was not Oswald who had been seen, but someone impersonating him. The reason became obvious after the assassination, though the Warren Commission seemed oblivious to the implications. 'Oswald' bought ammunition, had a telescopic sight fixed to his rifle and was a brilliant shot, even with his old Italian carbine. He was obnoxious, he made leftist remarks, he received cheques for (in those days) quite large sums which were not salary cheques, and was expecting to come into money so that he could buy an expensive car. It was a classic case of being 'set up', though not so classic that errors weren't made. The 6.5 cartridge case from the Mannlicher-Carcano fired on Mrs Penn's land was examined by the FBI. It had not come from the Mannlicher-Carcano in Oswald's possession. The 'Oswald' who had holes drilled for fitting a telescopic sight had three holes drilled. Oswald's rifle sight mounting had only two. When Oswald's rifle was examined, he had not had the gun part replaced which he asked for in the Irving shop. The 'Oswald' who practised every night on a rifle-range with an elderly Italian carbine also made an error. One of the spectators there had a close look at the weapon which was not a Mannlicher-Carcano at all. It was noted that this 'Oswald' curiously picked up every one of his spent shells. And of course the greatest blunder was the number of times 'Oswald' drove a car. He had no car, neither could he drive.

Albert G. Bogard, the car salesman who accompanied 'Oswald' for a test drive in the smart red car, submitted to a lie-detector test for the FBI. The results were consistent with truthful statements. Bogard was severely beaten up after giving his testimony and had to be taken to hospital. Later he left town suddenly and some time after this was discovered dead in a fume-filled car parked in a cemetery. The Warren Commission never asked the FBI to find out who was behind all the incriminating Oswald impersonations. Perhaps the Commissioners were afraid of what they might find.

If I am right in saying that a quick flight to Cuba for Lee Harvey Oswald was intended to be the last part of the conspiracy to kill President Kennedy, then it can be seen that the impersonations of Oswald were not expected to be scrutinised in the way they were. The blunders and imperfections would not have been likely to come to light if the President's 'killer' had fled to the protection of Fidel Castro. There would have been no need to make a close investigation of what would have looked like a political assassination. In the mood of the day it would have come as no surprise if Castro had been found to be behind the murder of Kennedy in retaliation for the number of attempts the CIA had made on his life. The likelihood would have been that a war would have started, in which other countries would have joined, notably Soviet Russia and probably the United Kingdom. Oswald, of course, would likely have been shot on sight landing in Cuba as Castro attempted to avert disaster, and the nitty-gritty of the investigation of details would never have taken place. But, if I am right in my assessment of the assassination conspiracy, thankfully for the people of America and Cuba, and possibly for the rest of the world, Oswald never made it to the airport to fly out, as he thought, on his new mission.

The series of Oswald impersonations was unlikely to be the work of one person or even two. Even allowing for the blunders, they were carefully planned and thought out and carried out with proficiency. There were no faults with the execution of the plan. The question arises: who was most likely responsible for such a campaign of deception? It springs to mind that the organisation most adept at lies, deceit, deception and disinformation was the CIA. Though most of this is the stock-in-trade of that organisation, I am here not thinking in terms of the CIA per se being behind the impersonations or involved in the assassination. I am thinking of that band of disaffected agents which, I believe, was involved in the assassination, took control of Oswald and 'ran' him to be the patsy.

CHAPTER TWENTY-ONE

Final Touches

WHEN OSWALD RETURNED TO DALLAS, Marina and June were living with Ruth Paine in Irving. Marina was heavily pregnant with her second daughter, Audrey. Oswald took a room in a boarding house at 1026 North Beckley Avenue and, in view of the expected arrival of a new baby, Ruth Paine was anxious to help Oswald into work. She is said to have heard from a neighbour that work might be available at the Texas School Book Depository on Elm Street, and arranged for Oswald to be interviewed by Roy Truly, the manager. The consequence of all this was that he started work the following day as an order filler.

I find it hard to believe that it was merely an incredible coincidence that Ruth Paine just happened to hear of a job going at the Texas School Book Depository, however. It was vital to the conspirators' plans that Oswald should work there at that time. The conspirators had gone to a great deal of trouble to make sure he returned to Dallas to take this job instead of starting a new mission for the CIA in Cuba, then in the USSR. I feel there is no doubt we see again the work of the CIA 'renegades' in making sure he applied for this particular job and in making sure he got it. Many believe Mrs Paine to have been part of the 'arrangements' for getting Oswald into place and this may well be so. Her husband, Michael, was known to have CIA associations.

At the place of his work, Oswald, as always, got on well with those around him. One friend, Wesley Frazier, drove him out to Irving at weekends. On the Thursday night before the assassination Oswald had, unusually, asked for a lift out to Irving and Frazier drove him into work next morning. Frazier said he carried a brown paper package which contained, Oswald said, curtain rods for the room

FIGURE 33

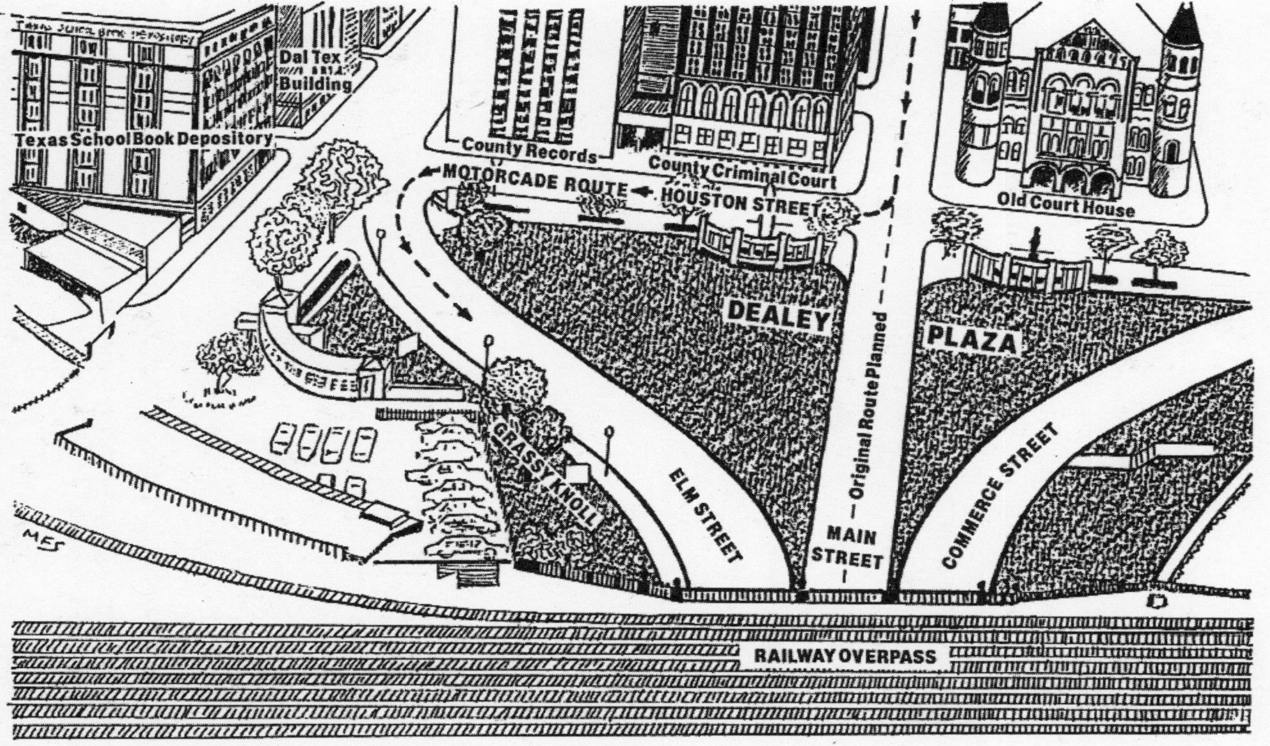

The Dealey Plaza

he had taken at North Beckley, although Oswald, when later questioned, was evasive about this. Both Frazier and his sister, who also saw the package, insisted it was not long enough to contain a rifle, even if disassembled. They said he had tucked one end under his arm and held the other end, arm extended vertically downwards, with his cupped hand. This was not a little out of the reckoning for the Manlicher-Carcano he is said to have carried into work that morning; it was some eight inches out. When questioned Oswald said it had contained his lunch. 'Oh, I don't recall. It may have been a small sack or a large sack. You don't always find one that just fits your sandwiches.'

We know that on the morning of 22 November, Oswald worked on the sixth floor of the School Book Depository, from where the Warren Commission said he shot and killed President Kennedy, but not a single workmate placed him there during the lunchbreak period which led up to the time of the assassination. Bonnie Ray Williams, who had been laying plywood flooring on the sixth, said that as he went down in the elevator at lunchtime he heard Oswald calling from the fifth or sixth floor for the elevator to be returned to him. Williams then went back to the sixth to eat his lunch and watch the motorcade, but when no one had joined him by about 12.20 p.m. he left, throwing the remains of his lunch on the floor. It would appear that the lunch remains were those said by the Warren Commission to have been left by Oswald. On his way downstairs, Williams saw two of his workmates, Harold Norman and James Jarman, on the fifth floor, and he joined them to watch the motorcade from that floor.

Norman and Jarman said they ate lunch in the first-floor 'domino' room. Oswald said he had been sitting in there, also, and that he had seen two other people there. The two people he described were clearly Norman and Jarman, although they could not say for sure who was in the room at the time. Another employee, Eddie Piper, told the Warren Commission he spoke to Oswald on the first-floor[1] at 12 noon. 'I'm going up to eat,' he told Piper. Oswald wanted to go up to the second-floor lunchroom to eat because the Coke machine was there. Carolyn Arnold was the vice president's secretary and she knew Oswald because he came into her office at times for change. She said:

> About a quarter of an hour before the assassination . . . about 12.15 p.m., it may have been later . . . I went to the lunchroom on the second-floor for a moment . . . Oswald was sitting in one of the booth seats on the right-hand side of the room as you go in. He was alone as usual and appeared to be having lunch. I did not speak to him but I recognised him clearly.

Immediately after the President was shot, a police officer, Marrion Baker, dropped his motorcycle at the kerb and raced into the Texas School Book Depository. He ran to the elevator shaft because he thought there might be a sniper on the roof of the building. Intercepted by Roy Truly, a manager, together they tried to bring one of the two elevators down. Obviously the gates had been left open and there was no response. The elevators were both stationed on the fifth floor. The two men took to the stairs and when they reached the next floor, the second, Baker saw, through a window on the landing, a man walking away with a bottle of Coke, and approached him with gun drawn. It was Lee Harvey Oswald. He was near the lunchroom. Baker asked Truly if the man was a member of staff and Truly said he was. Baker then was not interested and ran off upstairs to the roof. Baker had spoken to Lee Harvey Oswald one and a half minutes after the assassination.

Oswald was seen by the clerical supervisor of the Texas School Book Depository, Coke bottle in hand, after she heard the shots and returned to her second-floor office. She told him, as she passed him, that someone had fired at the President. He made a reply but a conversation did not ensue. An important point usually neglected is that the motorcade was running late. It was due to arrive at the Trade Mart for the President's luncheon appointment at 12.30 p.m. but had only reached Elm Street by that time. Had Oswald been the assassin he would have been in his place by 12.15 p.m., expecting the motorcade at 12.25 p.m. or before, not on lunch break in the second-floor lunchroom.

Oswald heard a foreman saying that there would be no more work that day and then left, walking out of the front door, to make his way home to North Beckley. I do not believe Oswald was 'fleeing' the scene of his infamy, and I also find it hard to believe he was not interested in what had gone on in Elm Street, when he strode off almost before the sound of the gunfire had died away. He behaved like a man who had firm commitments that afternoon. Making no progress on the bus, which was bogged down in traffic, he went home by taxi, something he never did, and clearly indicating a sense of purpose. Reaching the apartment house where he lived, he did not settle down to enjoy some extra time off, but donned a dark jacket and left almost immediately. Oswald had a schedule to keep and it is my belief he had been instructed to stay in place at the Book Depository until the President's motorcade had passed, then to make his way to Red Bird airfield. It is my contention that this was where he was to board a small aircraft which would take him to Cuba on his new mission. When he left the School Book Depository he was travelling in a straight line for Red Bird airfield when he called in at his lodgings and then went to meet Officer Tippit, whom, I am convinced, he believed would take him to Red Bird airfield.

Two days before the assassination, on Wednesday, 20 November, Wayne January was in his office when a car drew up in front of his window. Wayne January was a partner in a small aircraft company operating out of Red Bird, and his office was at the front of the administration block. The car was only a few feet from where he was sitting, and caught his attention. It was a 1947 four-door, black Dodge, identical to one he owned himself and still used to carry tools around. He was interested in it, and as he looked across at it two of the three occupants of the car, a man and a woman, knocked on his door and came into the office. They asked if he could arrange for them to charter a light aircraft to take them to Yucatan. They asked intricate questions of the kind that were unusual for people planning a vacation. They asked about fuel consumption, the number of hours in the air, the total distance and whether the aircraft would be capable of flying to a further location under certain wind conditions. Wayne January eyed them up. They did not look the types who could afford the charter they were asking for and he wondered whether, in fact, they were headed for Cuba rather than Yucatan and whether, if they asked him to pilot the plane, he would ever come back again.

January said they should look elsewhere and, distinctly irritated, the man and the woman left and made their way back to the car. Interested in the car, he escorted them and had a look at it. He also had a look at the young man sitting in the passenger's seat, as he wondered why he hadn't joined them and whether he was dressed any better than the two he had talked to. Two days afterwards he recognised the man said to have killed the President as the man who had been sitting in the car. It was Lee Harvey Oswald. It would appear that the man and the woman with him were CIA agents who were given the task of organising his flight to Cuba. They were successful in this, it seems. A small aircraft was standing by the perimeter fence at Red Bird airfield on the afternoon of Friday, 22 November, all ready to go, its engines revving up. But Oswald never made it. The revving went on so long that people living close to the perimeter fence phoned in a complaint to the police. The local television station, devoted exclusively to news of the assassination that afternoon, mentioned the complaint reported by the police. One account of the revved-up plane said that FBI agents came to the airfield and impounded it.

I was able to show Wayne January an FBI report of his 29 November statement about his sighting of Oswald (see Figure 34A) which I had dug out from the hundreds of documents obtained under the Freedom of Information Act by veteran researcher Harold Weisberg. Wayne January had never seen a copy of the report before and he was astounded to see they had recorded the date of the Oswald visit as July 1963, several months before the assassination. 'However

FIGURE 34A

DL 89-43
KBJ:JVA:cv
1

The following interview was conducted by SA's KENNETH B. JACKSON and JOHN V. ALMON on November 29, 1963:

AT DALLAS, TEXAS

DALLAS, TEXAS

WAYNE JANUARY, owner, American Aviation Company, Room 101, Terminal Building, Red Bird Airport, advised that from February through April, 1963, he, together with several friends, on occasion frequented the Carousel Club, Dallas, Texas, which he understands is owned by one JACK RUBY. JANUARY stated that during February, 1963, he received an anonymous telephone call from a man who offered him the sum of $5,000.00 to fly to Laredo, Texas, and back with no questions asked. JANUARY said that he surmised that this individual planned to transport narcotics to Dallas and for this reason he declined the offer. JANUARY further stated that during March, 1963, he received a second anonymouse telephone call from a man who wanted him to fly $12,000,000.00 worth of gold dust to Mexico City where he was to pick up the currency and return with it to Dallas. He stated that this individual offered him $400,000.00 to make this flight which he also declined.

JANUARY stated that during the latter part of July, 1963, a man and woman whom he had never seen before contacted him at his office at which time they inquired about chartering a plane for a trip to "Old Mexico". JANUARY stated that when he asked this man questions essential to such a flight he was definitely evasive in his answers. JANUARY explained that this individual did not appear to know exactly where he desired to go in Mexico but said something about the West Coast. Furthermore, he did not appear to know when he desired to return or exactly how many passengers could be expected on the flight. JANUARY said that this man, after stating that he did not wish to make the flight for a couple of months, stated that he would consider the information which JANUARY had given him and let him know at a later date. He said that when the couple left he observed a third man who had been waiting in their automobile during the entire conversation, and after observing a photograph of LEE HARVEY OSWALD on television it now seems to him that this man somewhat resembled OSWALD although he was not definitely sure in this respect. JANUARY was unable to offer any additional information which might be of assistance in identifying the man and woman who inquired about the flight to Mexico. He said

FBI report which was dug out of Harold Weisberg's mass of documents obtained under the Freedom of Information Act. Wayne January was stunned when I showed it to him. It asserted those whom he said sought a small aircraft to fly them out on Friday 22 November, the day the President died – with Oswald waiting for them in a car – had really called four months before the assassination. 'It was the Wednesday before the assassination,' said January. (*Continued*).

FIGURE 34A (CONTD.)

DL 89-43
KBJ:JTA:cv/cah
2

that they did not appear to him to be persons of sufficient financial means to charter a trip such as the one discussed.

JANUARY reiterated the fact that the man, accompanied by the unidentified woman, who made inquiries concerning a chartered flight to Mexico, was not LEE HARVEY OSWALD and said that he has no records or any other method of identifying the persons who contacted him during the latter part of July, 1963.

JANUARY further commented that he never visited the Carousel Club when he did not observe several plainclothes officers, and when a friend of his attempted to date one of the performers, KATHY KAY, she informed this friend that she had to go with another man, whom she identified as a plainclothes officer.

JANUARY concluded with the opinion that JACK RUBY was not the type individual who would have killed, or attempted to kill, anyone charged with the assassination of the President. He said that he does not think that RUBY would care that much, even about his own mother.

'How would I have been able to remember a face for that long to compare it with Oswald's face which I saw on television the day of the assassination?' he asked. Was this the FBI's way of discrediting January's testimony? No one would give it a second thought as they wrote it up.

would I have recognised him after all that time,' he said to me. 'He came on the Wednesday before the assassination.' One has to wonder whether a change of date, backwards four months, was not an FBI device to 'bury' the January statement. Certainly no one would credit a recognition made from a casual sighting four months previously.

I asked Wayne January a lot of questions about his visit from Oswald, and tried to sort out with him the time of day he had been there. As far as I could detect, it seems that Oswald was there in the early morning, which fits with waitress Mary Dowling's testimony. Mary Dowling worked at Dobbs Restaurant on North Beckley and she knew Oswald as a regular customer who called in for breakfast every morning between 7 a.m. and 7.30 a.m. Not on Wednesday the 20th, however. Oswald didn't reach Dobbs for breakfast until 10 a.m. that morning. That was the morning he made a great fuss about his eggs. They were not cooked the way he wanted them and he swore, Mary said. She also remembered there was a police officer in the restaurant at that time who heard the commotion. The police officer was J.D. Tippit. Since Oswald and Tippit had never met, was this the prearranged way of Oswald identifying himself?

When Oswald saw Officer Tippit killed, he fled. He carried out what was a standard procedure of an agent in difficulty: he went to the nearest theatre cinema where he would expect to be joined by his handler. This did not happen, however, and Oswald was arrested, first charged with the murder of Officer Tippit and later with the murder of the President of the United States. During twelve hours of questioning we were at first led to believe that, apart from superficials, not a word was taken down or recorded. Captain Will Fritz, who interviewed Oswald, knew better than that. An old hand at police procedures, Fritz knew that every word uttered by the prisoner had to be either written down or recorded. It is my belief that this record was made and still exists, and one day it will come to light. The 'Fritz' notes which were released by the Assassination Records Review Board in 1997 (see Chapter Twenty-six) told us little and don't get anywhere near representing twelve hours of questioning. They will turn up one day, but until then we can but guess what he told Fritz.

I would say that he deemed it necessary to identify himself as a CIA agent and described how he had been 'set up', and he would, no doubt, ask to make contact with a senior agent who could tell the police who he was and vouch for him. This would account for the number on a scrap of paper rescued from a waste bin by Mrs Troon. Mrs Troon was a telephone operator at Police Headquarters in Dallas and she confessed to being very curious about any calls which Lee Harvey Oswald would make. The day after he was arrested, the Saturday, predictably, Oswald rang Mrs Paine's number twice and spoke about obtaining legal representation. Later on, however, he asked for another number but was apparently unsuccessful in getting through. Two men arrived, showed their identification and were directed to a room next to the switchboard room. Presumably they were there to monitor any calls Oswald might make. Mrs Swinney, another operator, took another number he requested later that night, with Mrs Troon listening in. She later told how Mrs Swinney first consulted the two men in the next room and then told Oswald his number didn't answer. Mrs Troon was appalled and later retrieved the scrap of paper Mrs Swinney tore off her pad and threw in the waste bin. She told how Oswald had been trying to call a man named Hurt in the 919 area. In 1963 the 919 area code related to Raleigh in North Carolina. An investigation by the House Select Committee revealed that there were two Mr Hurts living in that area at the time, both of whom denied knowing Oswald. But one Mr Hurt had been in Military Intelligence during the war, and other research shows it was from Nag's Head in North Carolina that a programme of infiltration to countries behind the Iron

Curtain was run by the Office of Naval Intelligence. Was Oswald trying to reach someone who would identify him as an intelligence agent? When the CIA was, much later, asked if Oswald was an agent they said he was neither an informant nor an agent. But then we know the intelligence agencies disowned their people when they got into trouble. And we know that the CIA, in any case, said whatever it liked to suit the circumstances. He would not get any help from his CIA masters.

---

[1] For British readers – the 'first floor' is the ground floor in the USA, and the floor above is the first floor.

CHAPTER TWENTY-TWO

Double Vision

WHEN WE RECALL HOW THE 7.65 Mauser was found on the sixth floor of the Texas School Book Depository, it will be remembered that Deputies Luke Mooney and Seymour Weitzman were persuaded to change the affidavits they had already drawn up identifying the rifle, to say that, effectively, they were wrong and in fact, the rifle they found was a 6.5 Mannlicher-Carcano. It is decidedly odd that two experienced police officers could make the same mistake, and get as far as writing up an affidavit before realising their mistake. It is odder still that such a thing could happen with Captain Will Fritz looking on. As we said earlier, the German rifle had 'Mauser' stamped on the barrel whereas the Italian Carbine bore the legend 'Made in Italy' on the butt. Deputy Sheriff Roger Craig saw the Mauser and he was the only one who refused to change his identification.

Craig also witnessed a man running from the back door of the School Book Depository. He ran down the slope to Elm Street where he was picked up by a green Rambler station-wagon which quickly made off. When he saw Lee Harvey Oswald in Captain Fritz's office for interrogation, he instantly identified him as the man he had seen, raising all kinds of questions. Craig recounted:

> I looked through the open door [of Fritz's office] . . . and identified the man I saw running down the grassy knoll and enter the Rambler station-wagon – it was Lee Harvey Oswald. Fritz and I entered his private office together. He told Oswald, 'This man (pointing to me) saw you leave,' at which time the suspect replied, 'I told you people I did.' . . . Fritz again: 'What about the car?' Oswald replied, leaning forward on

> Fritz's desk, 'That station wagon belongs to Mrs Paine, don't try to drag her into this.'

Two Oswalds, one leaving the front door and one leaving the back? A green Rambler station-wagon? 'Don't try to drag [Mrs Paine] into this?' One can only assume the lookalike Oswald was to provide a temporary trail for the police so that the real Oswald could quietly drive off unimpeded with Tippit to Red Bird airfield and make his way to Cuba. Time then to raise the hue and cry. The involvement of the green station-wagon and Mrs Paine is obscure, but there is a hint that Oswald knew about it and believed she was innocent of any knowledge of a plot to kill the President. The fact that there was no investigation of these events is another indication of the reluctance of the Warren Commission to involve itself in anything which suggested conspiracy. Remarkably, Roger Craig was present at the questioning of another man whom he identified as the driver of the station-wagon. He was wasting his time, however. They released the driver without charge.

Craig had received four promotions and had been named 'Officer of the Year' before the time of the assassination. He received no more promotions afterwards. Captain Will Fritz tried to discredit him by saying he had never been in his private office during the time Oswald was being interrogated. When Police Chief Jesse Curry published a book about the assasination, however, he included a picture of Fritz's office clearly showing Roger Craig to be present. (See second picture section.) Craig was admonished and instructed not to talk to reporters about what he had seen. When, as late as 1967, he did, he was fired. He later spoke of feeling that he was being followed and complained of being fired at by an unknown assailant. The bullet grazed his head. In 1973 his car was run off a mountain road, causing him a back injury with which he lived for the rest of his life. He reported that his car was bombed and in 1973 his marriage broke up as a consequence of the ongoing harassment. Two years later he was shot at and wounded by an unknown gunman and, at the age of 39, Craig was found at his father's home in a pool of blood. He had taken his own life, they said.

CHAPTER TWENTY-THREE

Shadows in Mexico

CIA AGENT L. F. BARKER sent a hair-raising message from Mexico City to Washington four days after President Kennedy was assassinated. It described how one Gilberto Nolasco Alvarado Ugarte, a Nicaraguan, heard and saw discussions taking place in the Cuban consulate office between Lee Harvey Oswald and two others who were planning the assassination. The CIA message gave, word for word, Alvarado's description of the three, plus that of another man who joined them briefly.

> While standing near bathroom door Subj (Alvarado) saw group of three persons conversing in patio few feet away. One was tall, thin, negro with reddish hair, obviously dyed, prominent cheekbones, noticeable scar on lower right side of chin. Rapid speaker, Cuban accent, spoke some English. Another was white person Subj had seen carrying Canadian passport in waiting room. Blondish hair, 'existialist' hairdo with pompadour, dark eyeglasses of type with mirror like reflection on outer surface. Third person was Lee Harvey Oswald. Subj completely convinced from published photos that this was Oswald, not shadow of doubt in his mind. Oswald was wearing black sport coat, buttoned up white shirt with short collar tabs, no tie, dark gray pants. Clear eyeglasses . . . Subj saw tall Cuban join group momentarily and pass American currency to negro. This man unidentified Cuban apparently came out of Azcue office into patio. Described as tall, solidly built Mulatto, curly hair. Brown suit. Red striped tie, about 37 years old. Subj never saw this man after 18 Sep . . .

> Subj overheard following conversation between negro and Oswald: Negro (in English): I want to kill the man. Oswald: You're not man enough. I can do it. Negro (in Spanish): I can't go with you. I have a lot to do. Oswald: The people are waiting for me back there. Negro gave Oswald six thousand five hundred dollars in large denomination US bills, saying this isn't much of sum, one thousand five hundred was for extra expenses. Also gave him about 200 Mexican pesos . . .

The director of the CIA sent another message on this subject to Washington on 28 November 1963:

> Odenvy [Code for FBI] says their follow-up investigation of Oswald's activities has produced 'reliable indications' that he was in New Orleans on 19 September 1963. Repeat 19 September 1963. This coupled with earlier evidence that he was in New Orleans applying for unemployment insurance on 17 September 1963, means Oswald would have had to fly to Mexico and back between 17 and 19 September in order to be at the Cuban embassy getting his pay off, as Alvarado claims, on 18 Sep . . . With this added info, believe next can confidently regard Alvarado as fabricator and tailor interrogation accordingly. Perhaps he might respond to the suggestion that he has been having delusions and needs psychiatric treatment . . .

On 30 November 1963 a CIA cable gave the results of an interrogation of Alvarado by the Mexican authorities. It ran:

> Our Station in Mexico City has just advised us that at 1230 Washington time today 30 September 1963, Gilbert Alvarado, Nicaraguan, admitted to Mexican security official in writing that his whole story of having seen Lee Oswald receive money in the Cuban embassy in Mexico City to assassinate President Kennedy was false. He admitted he had not seen Lee Oswald at all and that he had not seen anybody paid money in the Cuban embassy. He also admitted he had not tried repeatedly to phone a warning about this to the US embassy in Mexico City on 20 September as he had previously claimed. Instead he had first contacted the US embassy, in person, on 25 November . . . Alvarado said that his motive in telling this false story of seeing Oswald paid money in the Cuban embassy was to help himself get to the United States so that he could participate in action against Fidel Castro. He says he hates Castro and thought that

> his story about Oswald, if believed, would help cause the USA to take action against Castro.

At first sight this appears to be a classic example of opportunism: a young Nicaraguan who, having read of the assassination, jumped on the bandwagon for his own gain. Looking more closely at it, however, it bears all the hallmarks of a disinformation ploy. How was it the Nicaraguan knew Oswald had been to Mexico City shortly before the assassination? How was it he knew Oswald had visited the Cuban embassy? Knowing, as we do, it was unlikely the real Oswald was ever at the embassy, what inspired the man to weave his story around the consulate? Why did he choose 18 September as the date for his story? That was the only 'slot' in which it was literally possible for Oswald to have flown to Mexico City and back, although, as we have seen, the idea was so tenuous that it was even dismissed by the FBI, an organisation which was not exactly Oswald-friendly. Alvarado failed a lie-detector test administered by the Mexican authorities, though lie-detectors are not always reliable and are sometimes rigged. Why did he not argue this? Why did he crumble so quickly under interrogation when there was no way his story could have been broken? The answers may lie in the direction of the intelligence services.

Alvarado admitted to being a Nicaraguan agent and it is believed the Nicaraguan Secret Service was at that time controlled by the CIA. It would seem the 'renegade' agents into whose hands Oswald had fallen had, as part of their plan, enlisted Alvarado to carry out this service for them. It could have had far-reaching consequences, especially if their plan to fly Oswald into Cuba had been successful. It would likely have led to war with Cuba, which was exactly what the conspirators were seeking. Fortunately, Alvarado caved in. It may have been that he was beaten or abused with drugs. Or it might have been that it was enough to sow the seeds of doubt.

CHAPTER TWENTY-FOUR

The Cuban Pilot

AT THE SAME TIME AS Lee Harvey Oswald was seen at Red Bird airfield by Wayne January, another airfield employee was, without knowing it, heavily involved with the men who killed the President. Hank Gordon had worked at Red Bird before this time, though he had moved on to live in Phoenix, Arizona. He was asked to return to work for a few days at Red Bird airfield again by Woburn Inc., a contractor who operated out of Red Bird. Woburn was winding down after a two-year stint of working out a contract flying planes on a government experiment they were carrying out. The planes they had bought for the government contract were big by Red Bird standards and they had no problem disposing of them after the contract was done. That is, they sold all of them except one, a Douglas DC-3, which was slow in the market, although it was eventually acquired by a telephone buyer who said he would call in person to handle the paperwork. And so it was that the last of the extra aircraft was sold. The buyer wanted the plane made ready for the transaction, which meant it had to be checked and serviced from stem to stern before the sale was complete. This was why Hank Gordon, who was very knowledgeable about Douglas aircraft, was called in.

Gordon was happy about returning to Dallas to service the DC-3 when the sale came up. He was there when the buyer arrived to settle the purchase. He brought his pilot with him, for it was normal that a representative of the buyer, and the seller's mechanic, Hank Gordon in this case, should thoroughly check the aircraft through, working together on the service and make-ready. Gordon saw the buyer only briefly. He was smart and well dressed with the appearance of a military man. The pilot was a younger man in his late thirties. Well built and muscular, the pilot had short and neat brown hair and was physically trim, being of medium weight and height. Working at close quarters, as they did, Hank Gordon and the pilot got on well together and they chatted freely as they worked. They swapped stories of close shaves they had had in their flying careers, as fliers are prone to. The pilot told Gordon he was born in Cuba, though he spoke with no trace of an accent. An intelligent man, the conversations between the two broadened to a variety of subjects. Gordon was curious about his boss. He asked if he was a flier. 'Oh, yes,' came the reply. 'He is an Air Force colonel who deals with planes of this category.'

As time went by the relationship between the two men cemented and their discussions became more and more relaxed. It was clear the pilot knew the Douglas DC-3 well; he had no difficulty coping with its intricacies. Gordon asked him where he had acquired this experience and, to his surprise, the man told him he had been a pilot in Castro's air force and had risen to high rank. The pilot was an interesting man. The conversations continued. Hank Gordon was puzzled that the pilot's boss did not appear from time to time to check on progress and make sure everything was to his satisfaction. He did not appear at all after the first day. Surely he was not holed up in some hotel somewhere all this time? It was Thursday now, 21 November. Was the colonel visiting some friend in the area? The work was scheduled to be completed by Thursday night. Gordon and the pilot did a check on what remained to be done and it was clear they were behind with things. They would not be able to complete by that night even if they worked late. They would do well to finish by Friday lunchtime.

But other things had begun to bother Gordon by then. He realised that the pilot never accepted any invitations to join him for lunch at the airport restaurant. He relied on Hank bringing sandwiches from the restaurant for them both each day. It was not a reluctance to spend money, he noted, for the pilot would happily have paid the cost of the food for them both if he had been allowed to. On that Thursday when they sat down to eat lunch, it was between 12.30 p.m. and 1.00 p.m., and as they leaned against the wheels of the plane the mood in the conversation changed. 'Hank, they are going to kill your President.' This was no idle chatter. Hank looked across at him. 'What do you mean?' he asked. The pilot repeated what he had said, 'They are going to kill your President.' Hank Gordon was embarrassed. He did not know how to handle such a dreadful statement from an otherwise amiable man. He certainly was not joking. 'You mean President Kennedy?' The pilot nodded his head. 'But what makes you say that? Why would anybody want to do a thing like that?' asked Hank, hardly able to grasp the implications of the sombre change in the conversation. It may have been that the pilot felt he owed a debt of gratitude to the man who had become such a good friend to him at Red Bird airfield. Warm-hearted Hank had made him welcome and had fed him and looked after his well-being during his time there. Perhaps he reasoned he owed it to him to tell him what was afoot.

> Hank, I tell you. I was a mercenary pilot, hired by the CIA. I was involved in the Bay of Pigs planning strategy which was operated by the CIA. I was there involved with many of my friends when they died, when Robert Kennedy talked John Kennedy out of sending in the air cover which he'd agreed to send. He cancelled the air cover after the invasion was launched. Many, many died. Far more than was told. I don't know all that was going on but I do know that there was an indescribable amount of hurt, anger and embarrassment on the part of those who were involved in the operation.

Hank Gordon was at first silenced by what he had heard, then he asked 'Is that why you think they will kill the President?' The pilot had finished eating. He stood up and dropped his sandwhich wrapping into the bin they had for rubbish. He met Hank's stare. 'They are not only going to kill the President, they are going to kill Robert Kennedy and any other Kennedy who gets into that position.' Hank was squirming by now. His embarrassment was acute. Could he tell his new friend he was crazy? Could he pretend he had never said what he had said? Could he nod sagely and make some inane remark? The situation did not allow for him to have been mistaken about it all. Hank decided he would be above board. He said, feeling his way, 'To be honest with you – and with myself – I have to take what you have just told me with a grain of salt, not meaning to insult you, or hurt you in any way.' Hank squirmed some more. He was not doing well.

> It's just too far fetched for me to believe. If I went and told anybody what you have just told me my reputation as a man of business would be up the creek: they would laugh at me and, more important than that, they would say I was a nut and never let me fly a plane again. You can't have crazy people flying airplanes, you know.

The pilot had listened patiently and simply murmured, in a matter-of-fact way, 'You will see.' By this time they were both hard at work again. Time was of the essence if they were to deal with what yet had to be done. The conversation changed, but what had been said had made a deep impression on Hank. Inevitably, the subject came up again. 'They want Robert Kennedy real bad,' the pilot said, pensively. Hank felt a bit rattled. 'But what for?' he asked. The pilot did not want to get into the subject on Hank's terms. 'Never mind,' he said. 'You don't need to know.' Then, 'Let's get this job done, time is running out. My boss wants to return to Florida and I thought we'd be through today. I told him we'd be through tomorrow, by early afternoon.' Hank Gordon, along with the Cuban pilot, worked late that night.

On Friday morning the jobs still left were promptly dealt with, odds and ends like buttoning-up inspection plates and latching the engine cowling. By lunch-time there was only one vital job left to do. The plane needed fuelling before it was ready for take-off. There was some kind of disturbance at the terminal building and Hank set off to find out what was happening. As he went he saw a friend of his, a Texas Ranger, setting off at speed in his car, which surprised him. Another friend driving up slowed down as he passed Hank. 'Have you heard?' he asked. 'Heard what?' replied Hank. The answer stunned him.

'The President has been shot.' Hank somehow got over to the terminal building and sat by a radio. He heard the news announced that the President was dead. Whatever he really looked like, Hank Gordon felt grey. In his mind he calculated that the pilot could not have been involved in the actual shooting of the President. He had never left the airfield. Hank had a strong desire to find out what his reaction would be to the news of President Kennedy's death, and he made his way to the Douglas. The pilot was loading baggage onto the plane and needed help with a few cases of oil. Hank asked him if he had heard what had happened and he said he had been told by the driver of the fuel truck. There was a long silence. It was a heavy, poignant silence broken by the Cuban pilot. 'It's all going to happen just like I told you,' he said. Sickened, Hank shook the pilot's hand; it was merely a formality to indicate his departure. He did not feel like doing any more work that day. He asked when they were leaving. 'Whenever the boss is ready,' replied the pilot. It was early afternoon: the plane was ready for departure. During make-ready, the twenty-five seats which had been removed to accommodate Woburn's technical equipment had been reinstalled in the aircraft. Hank left to find a television set to sit beside. A deep sense of foreboding settled like a cloud on his heart and mind. Totally unwittingly, Hank Gordon had, it would seem, prepared for the conspirators the aircraft which would whisk out of Dallas, during Friday afternoon, the team of marksmen who had actually killed the President.

Hank Gordon returned to Phoenix. When he had sorted out what was in his mind, he was appalled. He felt he should tell someone what he knew, but as time went by he heard of first one, and then another, of those who had some inside knowledge of the assassination having unaccountable accidents or otherwise meeting violent deaths. He got to thinking about his wife and family, and his own safety. The memory of what had happened hung over him like a pall but he decided he would say nothing. And he said nothing.

In 1991 I was in Dallas and district, talking to people and putting together material for my first book on the Kennedy assassination, *JFK: The Second Plot.* I had met Wayne January and his charming wife, Sylvia, and had learned what had happened on the day Lee Harvey Oswald visited Red Bird airfield when those with him were seeking to charter a small aircraft. Little did I know that news of my talks with Wayne January would reach Hank Gordon. I suppose Hank visited Dallas from time to time and news travels fast. Wayne had, apparently, flatteringly, said that he had found me reliable, and a person of integrity, and it seems that this had filtered back to Hank, who was impressed. It was more than a year after this time that I received a telephone call from Phoenix. Hank Gordon said he wanted to offload the burden he had been carrying for thirty years and asked how could he communicate with me in total privacy. I told him I had no plans at that time for a visit to the United States, but if he wrote down what he wanted to tell me he could motor to the next town and fax the sheets to me from a drugstore totally anonymously. He decided he would do this and I, therefore, received the above account of Hank and the Cuban pilot exclusively, with the intention it should be published.

In all the essentials this evidence is just as I received it from Hank Gordon save for one thing: I have withheld the real name of Hank. He made it a condition of giving me his story that I would not reveal his real name. He still feared for his life and for that of his wife. I agreed with this, but explained if I could not publish his name, I would have to take certain steps which would provide a guarantee that the story was genuine and not something I had concocted. He therefore agreed to my divulging his name to that esteemed researcher, Mary Ferrell, and he also agreed, much to my relief, that he would journey to Dallas to meet Mrs Ferrell and tell his story all over again to her. She afterwards telephoned me to tell me she had complete confidence in what he had said. A Christian man, she had found him reliable and trustworthy and she agreed I could accept what he had told me. She told me on another occasion she had questioned him at the time of the assassination because she thought he knew something, but he would not talk. There was some satisfaction that after all this time the man I call Hank Gordon found he could tell his story. Mary had been right. He knew a great deal. Among other things he knew, for instance, that CIA agents were involved in the assassination and he also knew how they flew their team of assassins out of Red Bird airfield after the President had been killed.

There was still a great deal of work to be done after receiving Hank's story, before I could put it into print. There were a lot of points which could be checked, and I enlisted the help of Wayne January, since he knew Red Bird airfield, as well as how to check out information with the aircraft authorities. I am indebted to him for a great deal of the information I obtained about the Douglas DC-3 and other data. My checks revealed that there certainly were Douglas DC-3s used in 1962 and 1963 by the aircraft company concerned.

Hank Gordon had told me he remembered the number of the plane he had worked on, and I asked Wayne January to check this out with the Aircraft Owners and Pilots Association. I wanted to know if it had changed hands in November 1963 and, if so, who had bought it. The AOPA told January there was no such plane. The number quoted was given to a small aircraft. No DC-3 bore the number. I went back to Hank Gordon and told him what I had been told and he exploded. He said he had made no mistake and that number was on the Douglas DC-3 bought at Red Bird airfield. 'Tell them they're wrong,' he said. Wayne January did exactly that and an argument ensued. 'To check what is in the books we'll have to go back into files long since bundled up and put into long-term storage,' they said. 'It'll cost you.' Wayne said we would pay the fee and they went back into the archives. Phone call followed phone call, but sheer persistence won the day. They, at last, told Wayne January that Gordon was right! **The number he had quoted had originally belonged to a Douglas DC-3 but after the date it was sold at Red Bird airfield, the number had been changed and the original number given to a small aircraft.**

This was an incredible development and I telephoned Colonel Fletcher Prouty for advice. Prouty had been liaison between the Air Force and the CIA before his retirement and he was extremely knowledgeable about the workings of the CIA. He told me that aircraft numbers were normally never changed. The only time he had known of them being changed was when the CIA did it. This told me all I wanted to know on the subject. As for the name of the person who had bought the aircraft, this also proved tricky. It seems that aircraft are not re-registered at once after purchase, because tax became payable on the transaction upon registration of purchase. Wayne persevered for me, however, and the transfer of ownership data was finally obtained: the plane was bought by the Houston Air Center.

The Houston Air Center occupied premises in the Houston's affluent Airport Boulevard. This was dug out for me by a highly reputable investigator in that city – an ex-CIA man – who told me that the airport nearby was used by the CIA and the Houston Air Center was a front for the Agency. We now had confirmation that the Douglas DC-3 had been bought at Red Bird airfield by agents of the CIA. I also discovered when the company was formed and by whom, and that it was dissolved in 1969.

I also researched the details of planes taking off from Red Bird airfield on the afternoon of 22 November, but was wasting my time. CIA planes, it seems, are not logged out of airports. There was one interesting small aircraft which took off in the afternoon and went in the opposite direction from that which the pilot had said it would be going when he gave details to the airport authorities. It returned to Red Bird later on in the day but, oddly, it had taken off with three passengers and returned with two, though nothing suspicious was found in this. One strange echo of the account given by the Cuban pilot regarding the Bay of Pigs débâcle was later recognised in the background attributed to David Ferrie. Ferrie was a CIA man who worked with Guy Banister in New Orleans and knew Lee Harvey Oswald when he worked out of Banister's office. Ferrie was a long-experienced aircraft pilot and was said to have served the CIA as a flier at the Bay of Pigs. On the day of the assassination he braved a terrific thunderstorm to motor to Houston where, he said, he went ice skating. It has been argued he went there to pilot the team of assassins to safety, and it might well be the case that the Douglas DC-3 flew first to what would become its home base at Houston, then was piloted to a safe haven by Ferrie, well experienced in flying to nearby countries, including Cuba. **When sought, Ferrie was 'away' for some days after the assassination**. But we will return to Ferrie in the next chapter.

I wanted to put a name to the Cuban pilot who had befriended Hank Gordon and I discussed this long and deeply with Hank. He looked at pictures I sent him and considered names, but nothing registered. He was anxious not to put the wrong name to the man, and he really could not remember it. I respected this. It was another of those things which recommended Hank as a man of integrity. The pictures drew a blank.

Pictures of men who might have been the Air Force colonel were also sent without response at the time. Quite recently, Hank said to me that one picture I had sent just might have been the man he saw. The picture was of a lt. colonel who was a pilot at the Bay of Pigs. He saw the Air Force colonel on one occasion only, however, and he would not put it any stronger than 'just might'. His sighting of the CIA colonel and the time he spent with the Cuban pilot were burnished into his brain after the events of 22 November, but names were not vital to him then. Hank recounted what he knew with clarity and conviction. Without knowing it, he had had a first-hand brush with some of those involved in the assassination of the President. It raises the question of how many others may have had experiences of one kind or another which still have not yet come to light. The Cuban pilot must have slept somewhere those few nights, and, for that matter, every one of the team of marksmen and their aides were likely to have occupied beds the night before the assassination. Yet, so far, no one has come forward to tell of a stranger or strangers who might have belonged to the murder team.

CHAPTER TWENTY-FIVE

The Jolly Green Giant

ON 1 MARCH 1967, Jim Garrison, New Orleans District Attorney, had Clay Shaw, a well-known and respected businessman, arrested. He was charged that he did wilfully and unlawfully conspire . . . to murder John F. Kennedy.

Garrison, as a young man, had enlisted in the US Army before Pearl Harbor and was promoted to the rank of lieutenant. After the war he entered the legal profession and went to work for the FBI. He first served as Assistant DA in New Orleans, and in 1962 ran for the District Attorney's office, succeeding in beating his boss.

On the day of the assassination, the six-foot-six Garrison, known as the 'Jolly Green Giant', heard of accusations being made by Jack Martin, a private detective who worked for Guy Banister, about local people being involved. Banister had attacked Martin over some missing files and this had led to his hospitalisation. Perhaps from pique, Martin, among other things, had said that David Ferrie had gone to Texas to fly the assassins out, and Garrison decided to find Ferrie and face him with it. Ferrie was nowhere to be found, which, on the face of it, lent support to Martin's claim, but he turned himself in to Garrison on the Monday following the assassination. Ferrie was claimed to have driven to Galveston the evening after the assassination and had then returned to New Orleans the next morning. Ferrie denied any connection with the assassination of the President, and since the FBI had expressed interest in him, Garrison handed Ferrie over to them for further interrogation. The FBI reports that were generated were classified top secret, he found, but the Bureau promptly ordered Ferrie's release.

Ferrie was a strange man. Suffering from alopecia, he grew no bodily hair. He was totally bald but wore a red wig, which drew unnecessary attention to himself, as did the eyebrows he painted on. A clown in everyday clothes, he had been a senior pilot for Eastern Airlines, losing his job when his homosexual orientation was discovered. A one-time candidate for the Roman Catholic priesthood, he reportedly later founded his own church.

Ferrie said he had gone to Houston on the day of the assassination and had spent his time at the Winterland ice skating rink. It later proved he had motored, with two young friends, through one of the worst thunderstorms in years to get to Houston, and had indeed gone to the ice rink, but had spent his time using the public telephone there. He also deposited a large sum of money – seven thousand dollars, a fortune in 1963 – in the bank at about that time. When Garrison later opened his investigation and decided to arrest Ferrie, he was too late. Ferrie was found dead at his home, naked and with all the obvious signs of having committed suicide. When his death was investigated, however, suicide appeared doubtful. Men contemplating suicide, for instance, do not usually leave *two* suicide notes, neither do they *type* them and *type the signatures*. Remarkably, the coroner recorded death from natural causes.

Garrison discovered that one of the medicine bottles lying beside Ferrie's bed, had contained Proloid, which increases bodily metabolism. Ferrie did not need such a medicine, however, for he suffered from high blood pressure. Garrison went on to find out what the effect of someone like Ferrie taking Proloid would be and was told either a 'heart storm' or a brain aneurism – the explosion of a blood vessel. In ruling the cause of Ferrie's death as natural causes, the coroner had specified a ruptured blood vessel in the brain. Who had provided the Proloid? And was it administered by Ferrie or someone else? A few hours after Ferrie's death, his associate, Eladio del Valle, met with a particularly violent death. He had been shot and had had his skull split open. Del Valle was also on Garrison's list for questioning.

Garrison, who had assumed that the Warren Report would be a reliable record of a thorough investigation, was appalled when he began to examine it. He wrote:

> I had expected to find a thorough and professional investigation. I found nothing of the sort . . . The number of leads that were never followed up offended my professional sensibility. And, perhaps worst of all, the conclusions in the report seemed to be based on an appallingly selective reading of the evidence, ignoring credible testimony from literally dozens of witnesses.

Garrison's interest was aroused and he began to gather to himself a hand-picked team. His investigation started at home, in New Orleans, where he pulled together data on Lee Harvey Oswald and his connections during his time there. He discovered Oswald's links to 544 Camp Street and Guy Banister, his forays into Cuban politics and his involvement with the intelligence agencies. Ferrie had said he did not know Lee Harvey Oswald but there was eyewitness evidence to the contrary. There was also the fact that Oswald was a member of the Civil Air Patrol in Dallas at the same time as Ferrie was an instructor, and a library card in Ferrie's name was said to have been found among Oswald's possessions.

Ferrie tried hard to find out what had happened to that library card, calling on people at places where Oswald had lived in New Orleans, asking questions within hours of the assassination, before he set off on his 350-mile drive to Houston. Although the library card was not officially listed among Oswald's possessions – interesting in itself – the Secret Service made a point of asking Ferrie about it. He, of course, denied lending it to Oswald, but then, David Ferrie denied everything.

Banister, Martin, Ferrie and Oswald were all working out of 544 Camp Street during the summer of 1963. They all worked for intelligence agencies, and Banister and Ferrie were involved in supplying arms to Cuban insurgents. To this group Jack Ruby may be added for his part in gun-smuggling to Cuba. Another name associated with them was that of Clay Bertrand. Dean Andrews, a lawyer known to the New Orleans group, told Garrison he had received a telephone call the day after the assassination from a client he had never met, Clay Bertrand, commissioning him to go to Dallas to represent Lee Harvey Oswald. Garrison made it his business to find out who Clay Bertrand was. His investigations showed that 'Clay Bertrand' was a name used by the distinguished New Orleans businessman Clay Shaw in his relationship to the homosexual community of the city. Shaw was the founder of the New Orleans Trade Mart and had connections in many countries across the world.

Garrison's best chance of securing a conviction in a prosecution resulting from his investigation would have been to put Guy Banister on trial. Banister, however, had died before Garrison's case was opened. He had suffered a heart attack in 1964 and died in 1966, presumably from his heart condition. With Banister and Ferrie both dead, Garrison concentrated on Clay Shaw. Garrison sent his investigators to Dallas and they spent time at Red Bird airfield asking questions. The stalwart District Attorney would have made great capital out of the Hank Gordon evidence if it had been made available to him but, alas, it was not. Garrison, like Mary Ferrell, drew a blank at Red Bird. In his other enquiries he found the government his biggest obstacle. As time progressed he found he himself was under scrutiny for the public money he was spending on the Kennedy investigation.

The trial was something of a disaster, He failed to prove that Clay Shaw was working for the CIA. But Shaw had worked for the OSS as a liaison officer to Winston Churchill during the war and his connections with intelligence had probably continued after that. Another 'nugget' unearthed by Garrison was that Guy Banister sent Maurice Brooks Gatlin, who was the legal representative of Banister's Anti-Communist League of the Carribean, to Paris with an estimated $200,000 – a vast fortune for those days – for the outlawed Secret Army Organisation, OAS.[1]

With the greatest difficulty, Garrison obtained the Zapruder film to show in the courtroom. The owners of the film, *Time-Life*, did not want Garrison to have the film, and even when subpoenaed fought against letting it go until the Supreme Court ordered it should do so. When the film was shown, the effect was electrifying. Up to this time the people of the United States had not been permitted to see the film. The best they had had was an account of it rendered by famed television newscaster Dan Rather, who told them of the President's head being propelled 'forward with considerable violence' – the opposite to what really happened – as the fatal bullet struck. CBS rewarded Rather for this episode by promoting him to White House Correspondent and he later became their chief anchorman. Now those in the courtroom could see for themselves what the film showed and they were astounded. With or without Garrison's knowledge – it is not known – bootleg copies began to circulate among researchers after the courtroom showing. It would not be until 1975, twelve years after the assassination, that it would be shown on television for the nation to see.

Clay Shaw was intimately involved with an organisation called Permindex, which stood for Permanent Industrial Expositions. A few years before the time of the assassination, the Italian press spotlighted both Permindex and its Italian-based parent company, Centro Mondiale Commerciale. It seems that a member of the CMC board had strong links to the former Mussolini regime while his son's wife had connections running into the wartime Nazi government and other interesting places. The founder and chairman of Permindex was Canadian-born Major Louis Bloomfield, who had a strong background in intelligence. First with British intelligence, he moved, during the Second World War, to the OSS and became friends with J. Edgar Hoover. His intelligence work continued while he was with Permindex.

Both CMC and Permindex were thrown out of Italy in 1962 for subversive activities. Such was the organisation with which Clay Shaw, with his own background in intelligence, had strong connections. Probes into the banking arrangements for this international mish-mash also produced a link with Mafia boss Meyer Lansky.

Garrison's investigation was bitterly attacked by the media. This was a time when people trusted their government, and if the government said that a lone nut called Oswald had killed the President, then that is what happened. It was unpatriotic to say that the government was mistaken, and unthinkable to say it was lying, and here was a district attorney, of all people, a public servant, challenging the findings of a presidential investigation. But Garrison suspected there was more to it than the protective stance adopted by the media towards the Warren Report. He believed he was under attack at the behest of the government itself, and he quoted incident after incident in support of his belief that government agencies were determined to undermine his investigation. He discovered his investigatory team had been infiltrated by a federal government agent named Boxley, and was appalled to think they would go to such lengths to prevent him from digging out the truth. Garrison, however, was lucky to escape from a 'set-up' in which he would have been branded a sexual pervert, a 'set-up' he realised could only have been arranged by Boxley. When he was finally identified, the agent contacted newspapers with a story that Garrison was a drug addict. The stakes had risen: the fight was now dirty.

Garrison, to those who saw the Oliver Stone movie, *JFK*,[2] was personified as a laid-back Kevin Costner. This was not so. Garrison was something of a flamboyant showman. He played to the gallery. He knew how to manipulate the press. But this did not prevent him from being an honest and effective district attorney. It did, however, attract criticism and made many people uncertain of his motives. In the case of his investigation into the Kennedy assassination, however, he was 'straight up'. Convinced there had been a conspiracy to murder President Kennedy, and realising much jiggery-pokery had gone on right where he was in New Orleans, he was determined to show to the world what had happened, hence the case against Clay Shaw. The trial against Shaw finally began on 29 January 1969, but after his years of investigation the case Garrison had against Shaw was slipping away. Ferrie had died and vital witnesses had moved to other states, where the authorities refused to allow their extradition. Garrison produced several witnesses to the fact that Ferrie, Lee Harvey Oswald, and a man answering Shaw's description, were seen together. Perry Russo, an insurance salesman, testified not only that he had seen Ferrie and Shaw together, but also that he had heard them discuss murdering President Kennedy. Importantly, Russo also testified Shaw had been introduced to him as 'Clem' Bertrand, which neatly linked him to the claim lawyer Dean Andrews had made about a telephone call in which he was approached to represent Lee Harvey Oswald by a client, Clay Bertrand.

Witness Vernon Bundy introduced a theatrical touch to the proceedings when he asked Clay Shaw to walk from the back of the courtroom to the front. There, for everyone to see, was the almost imperceptible limp which Bundy said identified Shaw to him. He said that in June 1963 he had seen Shaw talking to Lee Harvey Oswald on a seawall at Lake Pontchartrain, the site of a training camp for anti-Castro Cuban exiles.

But a setback came in the evidence given by Dean Andrews when he took the stand. The lawyer brazenly denied receiving a telephone call from a Clay Bertrand asking him to defend Oswald immediately after the assassination. He claimed the name Clay Bertrand was merely a 'figment of [his] imagination', and went on to deny ever knowing Clay Shaw. These blatant lies were later challenged by Garrison in a perjury charge and Andrews was convicted, but this came long after his denials had had the desired effect on the jury.

Fighting back, Garrison produced postman James Hardiman, who told how he had delivered mail addressed to Clay Bertrand to a forwarding address for Clay Shaw, and the case for identifying Shaw as Bertrand was momentarily shored up. Garrison's star witness on this subject would be the policeman, Aloysius J. Habighorst, who had filled out the form with Clay Shaw when he was first arrested. During this procedure, Shaw was routinely asked by Habighorst if he used any alias. Shaw had replied, 'Clay Bertrand', and this had been recorded on the card. This would prove conclusively that Shaw was also Bertrand.

But the trial judge, Judge Edward A. Haggerty, refused to allow the jail card to be used in evidence since Shaw had not had his lawyer present when he gave the details for it. Garrison knew it was not necessary for a prisoner to have a lawyer present for this routine, but he did not argue. He called Aloysius J. Habighorst to the stand. Unbelievably, Judge Haggerty sent the jury members out of the courtroom before the officer could take the stand, and instructed the prosecuting attorneys he would not allow him to testify on the same grounds, namely that a lawyer had not been present when Shaw gave details for the jail card, so the alias story appeared to violate his rights.

Garrison was dumbfounded. Judge Haggerty said, 'Even if [Shaw] did [admit the alias], it is not admissible. If Officer Habighorst is telling the truth – and I seriously doubt it.' An incredulous Assistant District Attorney James Alcock swung in at once with, 'Are you passing on the credibility of a state witness in front of the press and the whole world?' Haggerty replied, 'It's outside the presence of the jury. I do not care. The whole world can hear that I do not believe Officer Habighorst. I do not believe Officer Habighorst.' A move for mistrial was denied by Judge Haggerty, and the case against Shaw was in shreds.

Clay Shaw took the stand and denied knowing Oswald, Ferrie or Jack Ruby. He told the jury he had not been part of a conspiracy to assassinate President Kennedy and the jury believed him. While Garrison had failed to convict Clay Shaw, he had succeeded admirably, however, in persuading the jury that a conspiracy had taken place. Questioned after the trial – permitted in Louisiana – the jurors told of being convinced that a conspiracy had existed.

Garrison was accused of accepting pay-offs from pinball machine operators. He was arrested, and in the two years before his case came to trial his reputation was badly tarnished. The trial was something of a shambles, where operator after operator appearing for the prosecution had to admit he had made no payments to Garrison. The main protagonist was a man who had claimed Garrison's friendship from many years before this time. Pershing Gervais made the claim he had paid his old friend $150,000 in pay-offs. When cross-examined, however, Gervais admitted he had made a statement previously to a media reporter that he had been compelled by the Justice Department to tell lies about Garrison and incriminate him in the pinball scandal. He said it was '. . . a total, complete political frame-up, absolutely'. A tape recording used in evidence by the prosecution was found, by an expert witness, to have been spliced together from comments made at different times. The case was dismissed. While all this was going on the campaign for the elections to the District Attorney's office was in full swing, but Garrison had little time for electioneering. Not surprisingly, he lost.

To add insult to injury, the Internal Revenue authorities came at the beleaguered Garrison for unpaid taxes on the pinball pay-offs. By the time he had obtained clearance from these accusations his career as a swashbuckling lawman was over. The controversial New Orleans District Attorney ended his career as a distinguished Judge of the Louisiana Court of Appeal.

Experts are still divided over the investigations Garrison conducted. Some see Garrison as having drawn attention from the Mafia, the true culprits in the assassination, whilst others saw his work on the assassination as grandstanding, hoping his national exposure would lead to high office. In the eyes of many, Garrison's besetting weakness was that, in spite of the highly successful campaign he conducted against vice and crime in New Orleans, he conspicuously ignored the clubs operated by Mafia boss Carlos Marcello. It was as though the Mafia did not exist in New Orleans. At the end of the day, however, Garrison is acknowledged as having served assassination researchers well, drawing attention to a number of important issues.

In my own opinion Garrison saw a loose thread in the fabric of the conspiracy to kill the President and he pulled it for all he was worth. Perhaps his weakness was in attributing roles too great for his players. I see Shaw, Banister and Ferrie as much smaller fry than he did, primarily concerned with 'making ready' the patsy, Lee Harvey Oswald. Nevertheless I believe Garrison served the overall investigation into the conspiracy surrounding the assassination of President Kennedy well.

In a foreword to distinguished researcher Harold Weisberg's book, *Oswald in New Orleans*, Jim Garrison passionately wrote:

> The American people have suffered two tragedies. In addition to the assassination of the President by dishonorable men, our national integrity is now being assassinated by honorable men. It does not matter what the rationale is – whether to calm the public or to protect our image – the fact remains that the truth is being concealed.
>
> The United States Constitution . . . does not give anyone the power to rewrite history. The fact that this has happened should be evidence enough that it is far later than any of us have dreamed.
>
> The question now is whether we have the courage to come face to face with ourselves and admit that something is wrong, whether we have the will to insist on an end to deception and concealment with regard to the execution of John Kennedy – or whether we will let the official fairy tale be told and retold until the truth itself fades into a vagrant rumor and finally dies forever.
>
> If we will not fight for the truth now – when our President has been shot down in the streets and his murderers remain untouched by justice – it is not likely that we will ever have another chance.

Clay Shaw died in 1974 amid a further mystery. Neighbours saw what appeared to be a body being carried into Shaw's house on a stretcher and it was not until afterwards the death of Clay Shaw – at home alone – was reported. The neighbours alerted the authorities of what they had seen, but when investigators arrived at the house they found it empty. The body of Shaw, who was said to have died from lung cancer, was quickly buried, so quickly that the coroner decided he wanted an exhumation. Memories of the Garrison trial of Shaw were, however, raised, and the coroner's office decided discretion was the better part of valour. There was no exhumation.

There is an ironic tailpiece to this chapter concerning Clay Shaw, however. As we have seen, it might have tipped the scales in favour of Garrison in his quest to unmask Shaw if he had been able to prove he had connections with the CIA. In 1975, Victor Marchetti, at one time a high-ranker at CIA headquarters, wrote an article for *True* magazine, in which he revealed the Agency's concern at the time of the Clay Shaw trial. 'Are we giving them all the help they need?' he quoted CIA Director, Richard Helms, as asking. Others, he said, asked, '. . . is everything going all right down there . . . ?' In a trial held in 1979 Richard Helms was asked, under oath, if he knew Clay Shaw and he responded, 'The only recollection I have of Clay Shaw and the Agency is that I believe that at one time as a businessman he was one of the part-time contacts of the Domestic Contact Division, the people that talk to businessmen, professors and so forth, and who travelled in and out of the country.' At last Helms told the truth. Shaw *was* working for the Agency. He later admitted he had earlier publicly denied this.

Jim Garrison made an astute remark to the press which is worth remembering: '. . . the answer is through the looking glass. Black is white and white is black.'

---

[1] In 1962 French intelligence said that approximately $200,000 was sent to a Permindex bank account in France. The money was used by OAS to finance several attempts on the life of President Charles de Gaulle.

[2] In the film *JFK*, Garrison played the part of Earl Warren.

CHAPTER TWENTY-SIX

In Not So Many Words . . .

CONSIDERING THAT LEE HARVEY OSWALD was accused of committing one of the most ignominious murders of all time, he had little to say for himself. That is, if we believe what we are told. Yet it is interesting to examine what he did say after his arrest, and consider what he did not say.

At the time of his arrest the only words recorded at that time were, 'I am not resisting arrest,' and 'Well, it's all over now.' The first sentence is interesting because it is the kind of thing a well-informed person might say in such circumstances. If he feared the police might shoot him, for some reason, those words were an excellent defence. With a cinema audience watching and listening, even the most aggressive police officers would have found it difficult to abuse a prisoner hearing him cry, 'I am not resisting arrest.' It could be believed that Oswald had been trained how to react in such circumstances. The second sentence was even more interesting. 'Well, it's all over now' might mean many things, especially to a man in his circumstances, though it might well indicate he knew at that point that the CIA mission, which he believed he was about to start, had just come to an abrupt end.

Oswald was questioned for twelve hours of the short time he was in custody. The early researchers no doubt looked for volumes of notes taken down by Captain Fritz or perhaps a stenographer, or otherwise a series of tape recordings made of the proceedings. In 1963 the police offered nothing. They said notes had not been taken during the interviews and this was recognised for the outright lie it was. Notes are taken of the interviews of all prisoners, even those arrested on the most trivial charges. Where notes are not taken, a sound recording is made. This is standard practice in most, if not all, countries of the world. It is ludicrous to tell the people that the man accused of killing the President of the United States was questioned for twelve hours without notes being taken.

We knew, then, from the outset that notes existed somewhere and I expressed the belief in my earlier book on the subject of the assassination, *JFK: The Second Plot*, that they would appear one day. They did, such as they were, but first we should look at a set of notes first made available to us by the FBI, which were frustrating for what they did not contain. They ran as follows:

> Lee Harvey Oswald was interviewed by Captain J.W. Fritz, Homicide and Robbery Bureau, Dallas Police Department. Oswald was advised of the identity of SA James W. Bookhout, and his capacity as a Special Agent of the Federal Bureau of Investigation (whose report this is). He was informed of his right to a attorney, that any statement he might make could be used against him in a court of law, and that any statement which he might make must be free and voluntary. He furnished the following information in the presence of T.J. Kelley, US Secret Service; David B. Grant, Secret Service; Robert I. Nash, United States Marshall; and detectives Billy L. Senkel and Fay M. Turner of the Homicide and Robbery Bureau, Dallas Police Department.
>
> Following his departure from the Texas School Book Depository, he boarded a city bus to his residence and obtained transfer upon departure from the bus. He stated that officers at the time of his arrest took the transfer out of his pocket.
>
> Oswald advised that he had only one post office box which was at Dallas, Texas. He denied bringing any package to work on the morning of November 22 1963. He stated that he was not in the process of fixing up his apartment and he denied telling Wesley Frazier that the purpose of his visit to Irving, Texas, on the night of November 21 1963, was to obtain some curtain rods from Mrs Ruth Paine.
>
> Oswald said that it was not exactly true as recently stated by him that he rode a bus from his place of employment to his residence on November 22 1963. He stated actually he did board a city bus at his place of employment but that after about a block or two, due to traffic congestion, he left the bus and rode a city cab to his apartment on North Beckley. He recalled that at the time, some lady looked in and asked the driver to call her a cab. He stated that he might have made some remarks to the cab driver merely for the purpose of passing the time of day at that time. He recalled that his fare was approximately 85 cents. He stated that after arriving at his apartment, he

changed his shirt and trousers because they were dirty. He described his dirty clothes as being reddish colored, long-sleeved, shirt with a button-down collar and gray colored trousers. He indicated that he had placed these articles of clothing in the lower drawer of his dresser.

Oswald stated that on November 22 1963, he had eaten lunch in the lunchroom at the Texas School Book Depository alone, but recalled possibly two black employees walking through the room during this period. He stated possibly one of these employees was called 'Junior' and the other was a short individual whose name he could not recall but whom he would be able to recognise. He stated that his lunch had consisted of a cheese sandwich and an apple which he had obtained at Mrs Ruth Paine's residence in Irving, Texas, upon his leaving for work that morning.

Oswald stated that Mrs Paine receives no pay for keeping his wife and children at her residence. He stated that their presence in Mrs Paine's residence is a good arrangement for her because of her language interest, indicating that his wife speaks Russian and Mrs Paine is interested in the Russian language.

Oswald denied having kept a rifle in Mrs Paine's garage at Irving, Texas, but stated that he did have certain articles stored in her garage, consisting of two sea bags, a couple of suitcases, and several boxes of kitchen articles and also kept his clothes at Mrs Paine's residence. He stated that all the articles in Mrs Paine's garage had been brought there about September 1963, from New Orleans, Louisiana.

Oswald stated that he has had no visitors at his apartment on North Beckley.

Oswald stated that he has no receipts for purchase of any guns and has never ordered any guns and does not own a rifle nor has he ever possessed a rifle.

Oswald denied that he is a member of the Communist Party.

Oswald stated that he purchased a pistol, which was taken off him by police officers on November 22 1963, about six months ago. He declined to state where he had purchased it.

Oswald stated that he arrived about July, 1962, from USSR and was interviewed by the FBI at Fort Worth, Texas. He stated that he felt they overstepped their bounds and had used various tactics in interviewing him.

He further complained that on interview of Ruth Paine by the FBI regarding his wife, that he felt that his wife was intimidated.

Oswald stated that he desired to contact Attorney Abt, New York City,

NY, indicating that Abt was the attorney who had defended the Smith Act case about 1949–1950. He stated that he does not know Attorney Abt personally.

Captain Fritz advised Oswald that arrangements would be immediately made whereby he could call Attorney Abt.

Oswald stated that prior to coming to Dallas from New Orleans he had resided at a furnished apartment at 4706 Magazine Street, New Orleans, Louisiana. While in New Orleans he had been employed by William B. Riley Company, 640 Magazine Street, New Orleans.

Oswald stated that he had nothing against President John F. Kennedy personally, however in view of the present charges against him he did not desire to discuss this phase further.

Oswald stated that he could[1] not agree to take a polygraph examination without the advice of counsel. He added that in the past he had refused to take polygraph examinations.

Oswald stated that he is a member of the American Civil Liberties Union and added that Mrs Ruth Paine was also a member of same.

With regard to the Selective Service card in the possession of Oswald bearing a photograph of Oswald and the name of Alek James Hidell, Oswald admitted that he carried this Selective Service card but declined to state that he wrote the signature of Alek J. Hidell appearing on same. He further declined to state the purpose of carrying same or any use he has made of same.

Oswald stated that an address book in his possession contains the names of various Russian immigrants residing in Dallas, Texas, whom he has visited with.

Oswald denied shooting President John F. Kennedy on November 22 1963, and added that he did not know that Governor John Connally had been shot and denied any knowledge concerning this incident.

This is the total, verbatim, of the construction of the questioning which came from the files of the FBI. It deals mainly with what I consider to be superficials and does not get down to hard questioning at all. It is also noted that whilst Oswald was accused of the murder of Officer Tippit there is nowhere any reference to it here.

It was not until 20 November 1997 that the Assassination Records Review Board,[2] published in a news release what it called the 'Dallas Police Homicide Chief's Handwritten Notes on Oswald's Interrogation'. That august body said in its covering statement:

FIGURE 35

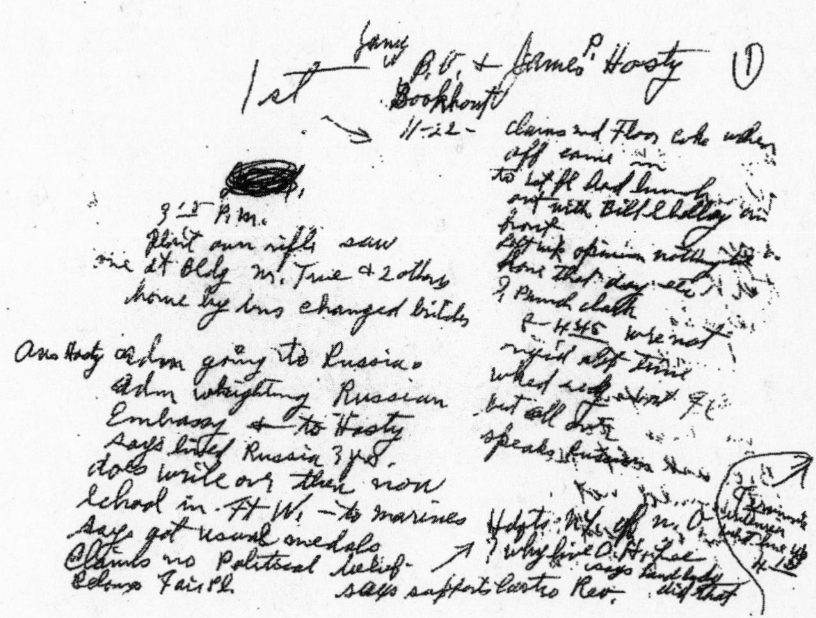

1st — P.O. + James P. Hosty
Bookhout
11-22-

claims 2nd Floor coke when off came
to 1st fl had lunch
out with Bill Shelley in front

Russian Embassy + to Hosty
says lived Russia 3 yrs.
school in Ft W. — to marines
says got usual medals
claims no political belief
belongs Fair Pl.
says supports Castro Rev.

A page from the notes made by Captain Will Fritz when he interviewed Oswald. They tell us nothing we did not already know.

Fritz told the Warren Commission in 1964 that he took no notes during the Oswald interrogations, but indicated that he later typed a report based on 'rough notes' that were made 'several days later'. These notes are believed to be the ones acquired by the Review Board. They chronicle all of the key points of the Oswald interrogation, including his denials that he shot President Kennedy or owned a rifle, that he said nothing against the President and claimed that a photo of him holding a rifle was a forgery, with his head superimposed on someone else's body. The notes end abruptly, showing the time of the last interrogation session on Sunday morning, 24 November as '10-11:1'. Oswald was shot by Ruby a few minutes later.

Nowhere does the Review Board indicate that there must be a great deal more to come if Lee Harvey Oswald was interrogated for twelve hours, however, neither do they question Fritz's statement that he did not take notes. This, to me, is puzzling, since the Board was aware of this and aware also that there was no stenographer present, nor a recording machine operating. Dr Henry F. Graff, a member of the Review Board, actually pointed this out in a statement made on the release of Fritz's notes. He said:

> Captain Fritz's original notes on the Oswald interrogations add depth to the primary record of what went on during the hours following the shooting of the President while Oswald was in custody. The notes are important because a stenographer was not present and no audio recording was made during the interrogation sessions.

I suggest they add little more than the FBI notes already quoted in this chapter which have been available for many years. Uncannily so, in fact. It could certainly be believed they were used as a guide so that a selective Fritz did not reveal any more than had already been revealed. No one seems to challenge the absence of sound recording or a stenographer or, indeed, Fritz's claim that he made no notes while the interrogations took place. Surprisingly, the ARRB appears to accept the scant notes it publishes as a complete record of the interrogations. Particularly for the benefit of students and those who wish to make specific comparisons, I now show, in full and verbatim, the Fritz notes:

> (1)
> 1st 11-22 B.O. + James P. Hosty James W. Bookout 3.15 p.m.
> Didn't own rifle saw one at Bldg M. True + 2 others home by bus changed britches
> Ans Hosty adm going to Russia adm wrighting Russian Embassy + to Hosty says lived Russia 3 yrs. Does write over then now school in Ft W. – to Marines says got usual medals claims no political belief belongs Fair Pl Hdqts NY off N.O. says supports Castro Rev. claims 2nd floor Coke when off came in to 1st floor had lunch out with Bill Shelley in front lft wk opinion nothing be done that day etc.
> ? punch clock 8-4:45 wre not rigid abt time wked reg 1st Fl but all over speaks
> Russian
> ?Why live O>H>Lee says landlady did that
> Terminate interview with line up 4:15

(2)

4 man left to right as #2

Time of filing 11:26 pm Johnson Pres 22nd Precinct 2 F154

Received evidence 1st then filed

2nd Interview 23rd Present 10:35 – 11:34 T.J. Kelly Robt Nash Grant??

B.O + myself Boyd + Hall

Says 11 – 22 – 63 rode bus got trans same out of pocket says 1 p.o. box deniedbringing package to wk. Denied telling Frazier purpose of going to Irving – denied curtain rods – got off bus after seeing jam got cab etc .85 fare told you wrong before at apt. Changed shirts + tr. Put in dirty clothes – long sleeve red sh + gray tr.

(3)

morning 23rd. says 11 – 21 – 63 say two negr came in on Jr. + short negro

- ask? for lunch says cheese sandwiches + apple says doesn't pay cash for wife staying with Mrs. Payne denies owning rifle in garage or elsewhere admits other things these

Came there 63 – N.O. Says no visitors at apt. Claims never order owns ???? for gun denies belonging to Com party says bgt gun 7 mo Ft W. didn't know what Place. ams to grest ant questioning Arv. July 62 from U.S.S.R. Int by F.B.I. Ft W says Hard + Soft meth etc Buddy says on interview of Payne by F.B.I. He thought she was intimidated

(4)

Desires to talk to Mr. Abt. I ask who says Smith act att.

Says did live N.O. 4706 Magazine St. Frem Apt. Wkd Wm B. Riley Co 640 says nothing against Pres does not want to talk further – No Pahy at time in past had refused Oswald A.C.L.U. member he says says Mrs. Payne was too. I ask aby organisation he says to pay lawyer fees when needed B.O. asks about Heidel selective s. Card – adm having would not admit signature – wouldn't say why he had it. Says add. Book has names of Russian Emigrants he visits – denies shooting

Pres says didn't know Gov. shot

(5)

3rd 11 – 23 – 6:35

Shows photo of gun. Would not discuss photo denies buying gun from Kleins. Comp of wanting jacket for line up. Says I made picture super

> imposed arr 10 – 11:15 4th. 11 – 24 Insp Holmes – Sorrels – Kelley et al Chief

Here, as in the FBI notes, there is no indication of in-depth questioning. There was certainly more questioning about the card bearing the name 'Hidell' which was never noted. A tired Oswald retorted at one point – and this was reported – 'I've told you all I'm going to about that card. **You took notes, just read them for yourself if you want to refresh your memory**.' Here Oswald clearly draws attention to the fact that Fritz was taking notes. The Warren Commission apparently missed this for they did not challenge Fritz when he said he did not take notes. And the ARRB accepted that he made no notes when they released the above, which they said he constructed later.

The interruption when Deputy Sheriff Roger Craig identifies Oswald is not entered in either set of notes, neither his response, as reported by Craig, 'Everybody will know who I am now.' Perhaps they thought this remark would take some explaining away. I find it fascinating in the context. It says to me that whilst his earlier comment, on his arrest ('Well, it's all over now') related to what he believed was his new mission, 'Everybody will know who I am now.' marked the point where he acknowledged his cover was well and truly blown, and even when he proved his innocence his career with the CIA was ended. Craig made an interesting observation on what was happening in the interview room. He said it looked as though Oswald was in charge.

But nowhere in the notes is any suggestion that Oswald was working for the CIA and the FBI. It was, in my view, likely that he would tell them who he really was, after the point where he realised there was nothing left to gain by keeping quiet about it. We pointed out earlier that he had tried to make contact with the headquarters in North Carolina from which his mission to the Russia had been run. This was, more than likely, however, after CIA Headquarters at Langley had disowned him. There was, of course, every reason to take Oswald seriously in his claim to be an intelligence agent, in view of the tell-tale items discovered among his possessions – four cameras including a Minox, the 'spy' camera,[3] a telescope, two pairs of binoculars and a pedometer. It has to be wondered how Fritz accounted for these items being in Oswald's possession without at least considering the possibility of him being an intelligence agent. Yet nowhere in the notes available is there any reference to these items or any questions about them.

An interrogation neglected by the Warren Commission was carried out by Secret Service Agent Forrest Sorrels in the early evening of Friday, 22 November, and with Sorrels was Winston Lawson of the White House Secret Service detail. The comments made by these two appears to illustrate well how the attitude of the questioner is reflected in the account they give of the questioning later. Sorrels testified that Oswald 'was arrogant and had a belligerent attitude about him', and that after he had answered a number of questions he said he didn't care to answer any more. Lawson, however, had a completely different recollection of the questioning session. He said, 'Oswald just answered questions as asked to him. He didn't volunteer any information. He sat there quite stoically . . . he didn't seem to be belligerent at all.' Lawson also said that he didn't believe that Oswald particularly resented the interrogation and that he believed that Oswald had answered all the questions put to him. But, again, where is there any record of what questions were asked and how Oswald answered?

It was not until 7.10 p.m. that Oswald was charged with the murder of Officer Tippit, and not until 1.30 a.m. Saturday morning that he was charged that he 'did voluntarily and with malice aforethought kill John F. Kennedy by shooting him with a gun'. His reponse to Judge David Johnston, who read the charge, and Police Chief Jesse Curry, who was present, was, 'I don't know what you're talking about. What's the idea of this?' and 'What are you doing this for?' He could not conceal his contempt for this development. 'I guess this is the trial,' he said. Oswald denied all the charges made against him.

When he was asked about the curtain rods, which Wesley Frazier said he had told him he was carrying in a brown paper wrapper, Oswald tried to fob off his questioners saying a container he had brought contained his lunch, which brought more questions about the size of his package. 'Oh, I don't recall,' he said. 'It may have been a small sack or a large sack. You don't always find one that just fits your sandwiches.' But Frazier knew better than this. He also knew it could not have been a rifle which Oswald brought to work that morning. He saw him cup his hand under the bottom of the package which he had tucked underneath his arm. The Mannlicher-Carcano, even when disassembled, was too long to have been carried that way. However, it does raise questions about what Oswald did carry in to work that morning and why.

Had the CIA rogues into whose hands he had fallen conspired to create another piece of 'evidence' against him? Had they instructed him to carry something they thought might incriminate him? Perhaps they intended it should resemble a package containing a rifle. Somewhat remarkably, two weeks after the assassination, a package addressed to 'Lee Oswald' was found in the dead-letter section of a Dallas post office. Wrongly addressed, it contained a heavy brown paper bag open at each end. Since the name on the package would have drawn attention to it after the assassination, it was presumably sent before the President was killed. Did the rogue agents actually provide an incriminating bag for Oswald to wrap whatever it was they wanted him to carry into the School Book

Depository that morning? And because it didn't turn up did he improvise? The heavy brown bag might have spoken reams to forensic experts, but when it came to light Warren simply ignored its existence.

When Oswald was arrested he raised his arms and showed off the handcuffs they had placed on his wrists. Twice he was told he could hide his face if he wanted to but he replied, 'Why should I hide my face? I haven't done anything to be ashamed of.' When pressed by reporters for a comment he called out, 'I'm just a patsy.' Later that night, at midnight, he was allowed to speak to the gathered press. When he was asked, 'Did you kill the President?' he replied, 'No, Sir. I didn't kill anybody.' At that same time he spoke out about legal representation. 'I do request someone to come forward to give me legal assistance,' he asked, and it was probably this plea which brought a visit from H. Louis Nichols of the Dallas Bar Association. Oswald said to him, '. . . if I can find a lawyer here who believes in anything I believe in, and believes as I believe, and believes in my innocence as much as he can, I might let him represent me.'

Others who had enquired about the protection of his legal rights were representatives of the American Civil Liberties Union, of which Oswald was a member, who were quick off the mark and were asking about him in the early evening of the day of the assassination. They were told by the police that Oswald was informed of his rights and was free to seek a lawyer, but when it came to the subject of a visit, so that they might talk to Oswald himself, the representatives were dissuaded. They later regretted their willingness to comply with the wishes of the police.

Oswald never knew what was planned for him when it came to legal representation. Lawyer Dean Andrews had been commissioned to represent him by Clay Bertrand, whom we now know was Clay Shaw. It was only because Andrews was too ill that he did not race to Dallas to represent his client. He did get round to asking a colleague to deputise for him, but by that time Oswald was dead. It was clear that the CIA 'renegades' in New Orleans, who had skilfully set Oswald up as the 'patsy', were making sure he stayed the 'patsy' by providing their own man to 'take care' of him.

The attempt to bring in Dean Andrews has an interesting backwash effect on another theory that some have proposed, that Ruby was part of the conspiracy from the beginning, with the task of silencing Oswald. I have never subscribed to this. I don't think the conspirators expected Oswald to be arrested. He was intended at least to take off for Cuba from Red Bird airfield, as I see it. The role of Ruby? It seems to me the plan to send in Dean Andrews to rescue the plan which had gone wrong was thought too risky by Shaw's superiors, who ordered the even riskier execution.

On Saturday, 23 November, Oswald's family were allowed to see him. Marina and Marguerite, his mother, were there, and his brother Robert. Robert told him the evidence stacked up against him was overwhelming. 'Do not form any opinion on the so-called evidence,' Oswald said. Robert later recorded in his diary, 'All the time we were talking I searched his eyes for any sign of guilt. There was nothing there – no guilt, no shame, no nothing. Lee, finally aware of my looking into his eyes, stated, "You will find nothing there".'

---

[1] The words in the FBI document appeared to have been partially obliterated and it could have been 'would'.

[2] The ARRB was established by the JFK Act, signed into law by President George Bush. The law gives the Review Board the mandate and the authority to identify, secure and make available all records related to the assassination of President Kennedy.

[3] The authorities kept quiet about this. We did not learn a Minox was among Oswald's possessions for many years afterwards.

CHAPTER TWENTY-SEVEN

You Can Get More Out of Me

JACK RUBY WAS QUESTIONED by the Warren Commission in jail. At the end of one such session, Ruby appeared anxious his questioners should not leave. The three-hour session had been singularly unproductive, but Jack had something very pressing on his mind. He said, 'You can get more out of me. Let's not break up too soon.'

Gerald Ford, later to become President, settled down to question Ruby on topics related to his visits to Cuba in 1959, but then Earl Warren cut in and changed the subject. Joe Tonahill, who represented Ruby, was present and later commented, 'Warren blocked Ford out on it. That was very impressive.' Ford responded with a hard stare, but the questioning was abandoned.

> 'Is there any way you can get me to Washington?' Ruby asked Warren.
>
> 'I beg your pardon,' replied the astonished Warren.
>
> 'Is there any way of getting me to Washington?' repeated Ruby. 'Gentlemen, my life is in danger here . . . I may not live tomorrow to give any further testimony . . . . the only thing I want to get out to the public, and I can't say it here, is with authenticity, with sincerity of the truth of everything and why my act was committed, but it can't be said here . . . Chairman Warren, if you felt that your life was in danger at the moment, how would you feel? Wouldn't you be reluctant to go on speaking, even though you request me to do so?'

Chief Justice Warren then made a most remarkable statement in reply:

> I think I might have some reluctance if I were in your position; yes, I think I would. I think I would figure it out very carefully as to whether it would endanger me or not. If you think that anything that I am doing or anything that I am asking you is endangering you in any way, shape, or form, I want you to feel absolutely free to say that the interview is over.

Unbelievable. The chairman of the Commission given the job of investigating the assassination of the President of the United States was, effectively, inviting a key witness to refuse to testify.

On numerous occasions Ruby asked to be taken to Washington where he would talk.

> 'Is there any way of getting me to Washington?'
>
> 'I don't know of any,' replied Warren. 'I will be glad to talk to your counsel about what the situation is, Mr Ruby, when we get an opportunity to talk.'
>
> 'I would like to request that I go to Washington and take all the tests that I have to take. It is very important . . . my life is in danger . . . [My] whole family is in jeopardy.'

Warren stonewalled:

> We have no place for you to be safe when we take you out, and we are not law enforcement officers, and it isn't our responsibility to go into anything of that kind. And certainly it couldn't be done on a moment's notice this way.

Ruby persisted:

> 'Gentlemen, unless you get me to Washington, you can't get a fair shake out of me . . . and I am not a crackpot, I have all my senses – I don't want to avoid any crime I am guilty of. If you understand my way of talking, you have got to get me to Washington to get the tests . . . Gentlemen, if you want to hear any further testimony, you will have to get me to Washington soon, because it has something to do with you, Chief Warren . . . When are you going back to Washington?'
>
> 'I am going back very shortly after we finish this hearing – I am going to have some lunch,' replied Warren.

> Ruby: 'Can I make a statement?'
>
> Warren: 'Yes.'
>
> 'If you requested me to go back to Washington with you right now, that couldn't be done, could it?'
>
> Earl Warren replied, 'No, it couldn't be done.' He reiterated, 'It could not be done. There are a good many things involved in that, Mr Ruby.'
>
> Ruby: 'Gentlemen, my life is in danger here . . . You said you have the power to do what you want to do, is that correct?'
>
> Warren: 'Exactly.'
>
> Ruby: 'Without any limitations?'
>
> Warren answered, 'Within the purview of the Executive Order which established the Commission. We have the right to take testimony of anyone we want in this whole situation, and we have the right, if we so choose to do it, to verify that statement in any way that we wish to do it.'
>
> 'But you don't have a right to take a prisoner back with you when you want to?' quizzed Ruby.
>
> 'No; we have the power to subpoena witnesses to Washington if we want to do it, but we have taken the testimony of 200 or 300 people, I would imagine, here in Dallas without going to Washington,' said Warren.
>
> 'Yes; but those people aren't Jack Ruby . . . Maybe something can be saved, something can be done. What have you got to answer to that, Chief Justice Warren? I want to tell the truth, and I can't tell it here. I can't tell it here. Now maybe certain people don't want to know the truth that may come out of me. Is that plausible?'

From these conversations it would appear the Chief Justice was first in line to prefer that Jack Ruby kept his mouth shut. He was unwilling to accommodate him in a move to Washington on the reasonable grounds that what he had to say would endanger his life in Dallas, and at the end of the day his advice was to say nothing if it was dangerous for him to speak. But then it seems Earl Warren had his eye on being able to support a statement which would later appear in the Commission's Report

'Ruby's background and activities,' it said, 'yielded no evidence that Ruby conspired with anyone in planning or executing the killing of Lee Harvey Oswald.'

And when he asked, 'Is that plausible?' Jack Ruby had in mind those others who were anxious he kept his mouth shut, the 'listeners' who would be monitoring every word he said.

> If you don't take me back to Washington tonight to give me a chance to prove to the President that I am not guilty, then you will see the most tragic thing that will ever happen. And if you don't have the power to take me back, I won't be around to prove my innocence or guilt . . . All I know is that maybe something can be saved. Because right now, I want to tell you this. I am used as a scapegoat . . . Now maybe something can be saved. It may not be too late, whatever happens, if our President, Lyndon Johnson, knew the truth from me. But if I am eliminated, there won't be any way of knowing.

Ruby was beginning to be desperate. Perhaps here was where he began to contemplate the unthinkable: Warren had no intention of taking him to Washington. He was to be left, surrounded by his demons, to whatever would befall him in Dallas.

> Well, you won't ever see me again. I tell you that . . . A whole new form of government is going to take over the country, and I know I won't live to see you another time.

Ruby was right. He died.

Author and researcher Anthony Summers found a piece of videotape which added to what Jack Ruby had to say. The tape ran during a recess in one of his court appearances, and Ruby said to reporters:

> 'The only thing I can say is – everything pertaining to what's happened has never come to the surface. The world will never know the true facts of what occurred – my motive, in other words. I am the only person in the background to know the truth pertaining to everything relating to my circunstances.'
>
> A reporter chipped in, 'Do you think the truth will ever come out, Jack?'
>
> 'No,' said Jack. 'Because unfortunately these people, who have so much to gain and have such an ulterior motive to put me in the position I'm in, will never let the true facts come aboveboard to the world.'
>
> 'Are these people in high places?' pressed the newsman.
>
> 'Yes,' he answered.

Ruby had more to say to those who saw him in prison. When a psychiatrist, Dr Werner Teuter, visited him, he reported Ruby saying that the assassination was

'. . . an act of overthrowing the government'. Ruby told him he knew 'who had President Kennedy killed', and that he had been 'framed into killing Oswald . . . They got what the wanted on me.' Dorothy Kilgallen, the celebrated broadcaster and writer, was granted the special privilege by Judge Joe B. Brown of having time alone with Jack Ruby in an office behind the Judge's bench, said by Lee Israel, friend and biographer of Kilgallen to be the 'only safe house Ruby had occupied since his arrest'. For once Ruby did not have the four guardian deputies with him and, whatever she got, Dorothy Kilgallen went back to her home telling her friends, 'I'm going to break the real story and have the biggest scoop of the century.' But before she told what she knew she died suddenly. At first it was said it was the result of a heart attack and later this was changed to suicide. Later on, the cause of death stated it was from 'circumstances undetermined'. Dorothy's friend, Mrs Earl Smith, in whom she may have confided, also died suddenly within forty-eight hours of Dorothy.

Jack Ruby wrote two letters which we know of from jail. One was acquired after authentication by distinguished researcher, Penn Jones Jnr. It ran:

> First, you must realise that the people here want everyone to think I am crazy, so if what I know is actually [sic], and then no one will believe me, because of my supposed insanity. Now, I know that my time is running out . . . they plan on doing away with [me] . . . As soon as you get out you must read *Texan looks at Lyndon*[1] and it might open your eyes to a lot of things. This man [Johnson] is a Nazi in the worst order. For over a year now they have been doing away with my people . . . don't believe the Warren report, that was only put out to make me look innocent in that it would throw the Americans and all the European country's [sic] off guard . . . There are so many things that have been played with success that it would take all nite to write them out . . . There wouldn't be any purpose in my writing you all of this unless you were convinced of how much I loved my country . . . I am going to die a horrible death anyway, so what would I have to gain by writing all this. So you must believe me . . . Johnson is going to try to have an all-out war with Russia and when that happens, Johnson and his cohorts will be on the side-lines where they won't get hurt, while the Americans may get wiped out. The only way this can be avoided is that if Russia would be informed as to [who] the real enemies are, and in that way they won't be tricked into starting a war with the US . . . One more thing, isn't it strange that Oswald who hasn't worked a lick most of his life, should be fortunate enough to get a job at the Book Bldg. two wks. before the president himself didn't know

> as to when he was to visit Dallas. Only one person could have had that information, and that man was Johnson who knew weeks in advance as to what was going to happen because he is the one who was going to arrange the trip for the president, this had been planned long before president himself knew about [it], so you figure that one out. The only one who gained by the shooting of the president was Johnson, and he was in a car in the rear and safe when the shooting took place. What would the Russians, Castro or anyone else have to gain by eliminating the president. If Johnson was so heartbroken over Kennedy, why didn't he do something for Robert Kennedy? All he did was snub him.

This letter was written to another prisoner who took it with him when he was released. The second letter was smuggled out of jail for Ruby, and was later acquired by author and researcher J. Gary Shaw. It said:

> . . . they found some very clever means and ways to trick me and which will be used later as evidence to show the American people that I was part of the conspiracy in the assassination of [the] president, and I was used to silence Oswald. ..They alone planned the killing, by they I mean Johnson and others . . . read the book *Texas Looks At Lyndon* and you may learn quite a bit about Johnson and how he has fooled everyone . . . In all the history of the US never has a president been elected that has the background of Johnson. Believe me, compared to him I am a Saint.

The first letter may well indicate that, when it was written, Ruby was breaking under the strain. He talks of Johnson taking the American people into an all-out war with the Soviet Union, for instance, which on the face of it seems to suggest Ruby had lost touch with reality. On the other hand, read for 'Russia', 'Communism' and for 'Communism', 'Vietnam' and he might be said to have had impressive insight into Johnson's intentions. John F. Kennedy had been watching the Vietnam situation and had signed an order bringing back home US personnel ('observers'), the first batch of which actually arrived in the US during December 1963. Two days after Kennedy was shot on Friday, 22 November – he was not yet buried – Lyndon B. Johnson attended a meeting at which Kennedy's order was rescinded and therefrom, with Johnson's approval, America was thrust into an escalating war in Vietnam.

Ruby's assessment of the ruthlessness of Lyndon Johnson in Texan affairs, and his hair-raising political career, would be agreed by many who knew the details of the background to Johnson's rise to prominence. It might also be recalled that he stood at the brink of personal ignominy and, indeed, political extinction on the very day John F. Kennedy was murdered. When he was sworn in with unseemly haste on Air Force One, standing at Love Field, with the body of President Kennedy aboard ready for the flight to Washington, he might well have been sending signals to those who had been on the point of destroying him. It was certainly unnecessary to be sworn in to assume the mantle of the presidency: as Vice-President he became President the moment John F. Kennedy died. His personal and political misdemeanours became history at that moment, also.

Ruby's lawyers won a new trial for him, and also an application for the new trial to be heard at Witchita Falls, away from Dallas. They were confident he would win his retrial and be released. It was at this point, however, that Jack Ruby was moved to hospital, where he died of cancer in January 1967. Many people recalled the fears he expressed for his safety and, indeed, his life if he remained in Dallas. In 1982, Deputy Sheriff Al Maddox, who had been one of Ruby's jailers, said:

> We had a phony doctor come into [the jail] from Chicago, just as phony . . . as a three-dollar bill. And he worked his way in through – I don't know, whoever supplied the county with doctors . . . you could tell he was Ruby's doctor. He spent half his time up there talking with Ruby. And one day I went in and Ruby told me, he said, 'Well they injected me for a cold.' He said it was cancer cells. That's what he told me, Ruby did. I said you don't believe that shit. He said, 'I damn sure do!' I never said anything to Decker or anybody . . . [Then] one day when I started to leave, Ruby shook hands with me and I could feel a piece of paper in his palm . . . [On it] he said it was a conspiracy and he said . . . if you will keep your eyes open and your mouth shut, you're gonna learn a lot. And that was the last letter I ever got from him.

Al Maddox was not alone in his suspicions about Ruby's death. Police Officer Tom Tilson said:

> It was the opinion of a number of other Dallas police officers that Ruby had received injections of cancer while he was incarcerated in the Dallas County Jail . . .

Jack Ruby failed to convince anyone in authority that President Johnson should be investigated, just as he had previously failed to convince Earl Warren that he should be taken to Washington because his life was in danger. Of all the statements he made to those representing the Warren Commission there is one which ranks above all others for its irony in the light of what we have learnt about the assassination and the Warren Commission. He said to those present, 'I am as innocent regarding any conspiracy as any of you gentlemen in the room . . .'

Quite so.

---

[1] J. Evetts Haley: A *Texan Looks at Lyndon: A Study in Illigitimate Power*, Palo Duro Press, 1964

CHAPTER TWENTY-EIGHT

The Evidence Before You . . .

IN THE EYES OF THE Warren Commissioners, one of the most damning pieces of evidence against Lee Harvey Oswald was provided by a photograph of the accused holding in one hand the rifle which they said killed President Kennedy, and in the other, Communist literature. In a holster at his side there was also the gun reputed to have killed Officer Tippit. The photograph was said to have been found in Oswald's possessions after he was arrested. What more damning evidence could be imagined? Marina Oswald was questioned about this picture and she told the hearing she had taken it in the backyard. This, for Warren, sewed it up. It said everything he wanted said about her husband.

Marina, as we have already seen, was terrified of being deported to the Soviet Union, and was anxious to tell the Commission what it wanted to hear. She needed the support the government could, if it wished, give her. At one time or another she lied, changed her statements and was evasive in some of her answers. In the case of the photograph it seems her anxiety caught her out. Her testimony related to one photograph, when there were, in fact, two taken. She did not appear to know about the second. They were not copies of the same photograph. The second was taken at a different distance and was a different pose. Much later, a third pose would turn up. (See second picture section.)

An examination of these photographs has caused much concern among researchers. In each case, the shadow of the nose followed the direction a noon-day sun would have produced, where the body shadow was at an angle suggesting it was taken much later in the day, perhaps the evening. How could this be? It appeared that Oswald's head had been added to someone else's body.

Then there was something else about the head. Though the first two pictures available were taken at different distances, the heads on both were identical in size. The grass and tree foliage also betrayed the date of 31 March attached to the taking of the photograph; grass and foliage do not normally appear in Dallas until late April. Much controversy followed these revelations, although the Warren Commission did not budge on the issue. The photographs were of Oswald, they said, and the evidence told strongly against him. In the '70s, the House Assassinations Committee also supported the Warren Commission in this.

But many people scrutinised the pictures carefully and continued to declare them forgeries. The BBC became interested and commissioned a British forensic photography expert, Detective Inspector Malcolm Thompson, to examine them. Thompson reported that the photos had been retouched, a sure sign of tampering. The retouching had not been carried out carefully enough, he said:

> . . . there has been retouching done in the chin area which is what one would expect if my conclusion is correct, that this face has been added to the chin . . . The head itself, I have seen photographs of Oswald and his chin is not square. He has a rounded chin. Having said that, the subject in this picture has a square chin but again it doesn't take any stretch of the imagination to appreciate that from the upper lip to the top of the head is Oswald and one can only conclude that Oswald's head has been stuck on to a chin not being Oswald's chin.

Thompson was not happy with the shadow purported to be produced by the rifle butt. To be compatible with the body shadow the butt shadow, if it were genuine, would not have protruded at such an acute angle. And Thompson was not the only specialist to declare the backyard photographs forgeries. An expert from the Canadian Department of Defense reached the same conclusion.

During the time the investigation by the House Assassinations Committee was in session, George de Mohrenschildt died of a shotgun blast to his mouth. It was said to be suicide, though his wife disputed this. She thought he had been killed. He died just at the point where the Committee required him to testify, which naturally aroused suspicions. Out of George's possessions came another copy of a backyard photograph, as though on cue, to persuade the unconverted. This copy bore the legend, 'To my dear friend George from Lee'. And then, as though to press home that it was no other Lee, it was signed 'Lee Harvey Oswald'. In Russian Cyrillic script it also said 'Hunter of the fascists Ha-ha-ha!!!' Handwriting experts declared the writing Oswald's and no importance was paid to the timing of the appearance of the photograph, neither the fact that George de Mohrenschildt could not now comment on it. Jeanne de Mohrenschildt, George's wife, said neither George nor she had seen the photograph until it turned up in the storage items they recovered on their return to Dallas. Jeanne has said she believes it was 'planted'.

Unbelievably, another copy of a backyard photograph turned up some years later. It was found among the possessions of Roscoe White, who had been a Dallas police officer. It would almost seem copies were passed around as souvenirs. Prior to serving in the Dallas force, White had worked for the CIA. After his death, his son tried to promote what he called his father's diary, which 'revealed' he had been one of the assassins who shot the President. Whilst these were not authenticated, and they are generally regarded as forgeries, there remains a lingering doubt that Roscoe White could have been the man who shot Officer Tippit. He fitted the description well and the 'diary' implicates him.

Today few researchers give any credence to the backyard photographs. They are generally relegated to the status of false evidence created for the specific purpose of incriminating Lee Harvey Oswald. When Captain Fritz showed a backyard photograph to Oswald he instantly declared it a fake and told Fritz he knew how it had been done. His time at Jaggars, the printers whose extremely sophisticated techniques he had encountered some months before, had not been wasted.

Perhaps the most incriminating evidence of all was the Mannlicher-Carcano rifle which Oswald was said to have bought by mail order from Klein's of Chicago. It was bought under the name of 'A. Hidell' for delivery to 'PO Box 2915, Dallas, Texas', which was Oswald's box number. The money order, dated 12 March 1963, and bought from Dallas GPO, could have been obtained by anyone, and the Hidell signature did not have to be added by Oswald. The rifle was established as belonging to Oswald in view of an identity card bearing the name, 'Alek James Hidell', which turned up among Oswald's belongings. No mention was made of the identity card on the day Oswald was arrested. The FBI claimed that the Hidell identity card was the only one found on him, but the arresting officer, Officer Bentley, reporting that Oswald at first refused to give his name, said that he had to examine his belongings to find out who he was. Bentley said nothing about not being sure whether he was Oswald or Hidell. It was the following day – the Saturday – that the Hidell identity card came into the picture, leading to suspicions that it had been produced – from wherever it had been – especially to link Oswald with the rifle. Police Chief Jesse Curry still did not appear to know about the Hidell card the day after the assassination, when he appeared on television. He told his audience about the rifle bought by Hidell but when his interviewer asked him if that was an alias used by Lee Harvey Oswald, the Chief replied, 'I do not know.'

There seems little doubt that this was a name Oswald used in relation to his intelligence work. We have already mentioned the fact that, even though the name Hidell was never breathed by anyone on the day Oswald was arrested, military personnel reporting back details of the assassination straight after the event, to the 112th Military Intelligence Group, said that A.J. Hidell had been arrested, and staff from that same 112th Military Intelligence Group later admitted they had had – until 1973 – a file on Oswald under the name A.J. Hidell, which they 'routinely' destroyed.

When asked about the Hidell identity card, Oswald refused to tell Fritz he had signed it. I have already suggested elsewhere that the card may have been signed for him by a senior CIA agent and that the same agent may have placed the order for the weapon. One might imagine that anything turning up in his PO box addressed to Hidell would be accepted without question as having been supplied by his CIA superiors, and that he would await instructions as to its purpose. In the first place, however, it must be asked how a package addressed to 'Hidell' was accepted for a box rented to 'Oswald'?

Harry D. Holmes, Dallas Postal Inspector, was called by the Warren Commission to explain the regulations about PO boxes. A few days after the assassination Holmes had been quoted in the *New York Times* as saying that '. . . no person other than Oswald was authorized to receive mail . . .' in his box at Dallas. Now he told the Commission he could not say that the name Hidell had been entered as a recipient of mail at Oswald's box, neither could he say it hadn't. It all hinged on what had been entered on Part Three of the registration form, and Part Three had been duly thrown away in accordance with regulations when Oswald closed his box in May 1963. Too bad.

A quick look at Post Office Regulations – which the Warren Commission failed to take – tell a different story, however. They state unequivocally that, '. . . the third portion of box rental applications, identifying persons other than the applicant authorized to receive mail, must be retained for two years after the box is closed.' Besides all this, if the third portion of Oswald's application was destroyed in May 1963, how was it Harry Holmes could write as he did in the *New York Times*? The Warren Commission failed to enquire into that, either. The whole thing was a muddle, with the Commission being given – and accepting without question – wrong information. In fact, therefore, the chain of evidence was broken and it was never proved that Lee Harvey Oswald received the Mannlicher-Carcano said by the Commission to have been the murder weapon.[1]

Lee Harvey Oswald was never seen by anyone with the rifle in question. No fingerprint belonging to Oswald was ever lifted from it, and the palm print reputed to have been belatedly lifted was ever questionable. Lt. J.C. Day, who said he lifted it, refused to sign a document confirming this to the Warren Commission. Since it is impossible to fire a rifle without traces of nitrates transferring to the cheek, a paraffin test was carried out on Oswald's face. It proved negative and, remarkably, the police carried out no tests to prove that the rifle, they said he used, had been fired on the day of the assassination.

As far as the Mannlicher-Carcano in question was concerned, an official from the Aberdeen Proving Ground, who was making a detailed examination of it, introduced another problem for the Warren Commission. He said that on close examination of the scope and its mounting, it appeared to have been adjusted for a left-handed man. Since Oswald was right-handed, the Commission did not pursue this point. It could have produced a serious challenge to the purchase and ownership of the rifle. In a court of law it would have. The Warren Commission quietly buried it. The Warren Commission also kept quiet about the shims which army experts were obliged to place under the telescopic sight before the accuracy of the rifle could be tested.

Three shell cases were said to be recovered from the sixth floor of the Texas School Book Depository, at the site where the Warren Commission asserted Oswald fired his rifle at the President. There was no hard evidence that they belonged to shells which had been fired from the Mannlicher-Carcano said to belong to Lee Harvey Oswald, though Warren accepted they had did. Only two cases were sent on immediately to the FBI in Washington. Captain Will Fritz was said to have retained the third for a few days before sending it on to Washington, which constitutes another breach of the chain of evidence.

A 6.5 bullet was found at Parkland Hospital. It rolled off a stretcher and, tagged by the Warren Commission as exhibit CE 399, became, for them, the bullet which passed through President Kennedy's body, passed through Governor Connally's body, his wrist, and finally caused a wound in the Governor's left thigh. This was, they said, what became known as the 'magic bullet'. We now have evidence from the Smith–Vidit study to show that no bullet ever did what the 'magic bullet' was supposed to do, though most researchers did not need a computer study to convince them of this. To add to the absurdity of the Warren claim, bullet CE 399 was in pristine condition. Adding together the weight of the exhibit and the fragments of metal produced from Governor Connally's wounds, the total exceeded the weight of an unused bullet. And to add further absurdity, the stretcher from which the bullet rolled was, a member of the hospital staff confirmed, never used by either President Kennedy or Governor Connally. The bullet was clearly planted there.

The revolver Oswald was said to have bought also produced problems. To begin with, there is no evidence to show that Oswald received the .38 pistol said to have been obtained by him via Railway Express. Elsewhere, we have recounted the anomalies relating to the shell cases found at the site of the Tippit shooting, which left Dallas police with yet another break in the chain of evidence, and no link between the shell cases and Oswald's gun. In view of this, it was astounding that the Warren Commission could still say that Oswald was Tippit's killer.

The evidence against Oswald was not as strong as it was made to look. The Warren Commission constituted a massive prosecution team with no provision for a defence for Lee Harvey Oswald. In a courtroom they would not have got away with the tenuous and doubtful evidence, the imaginative treatment of testimony, the highly selective, indeed loaded, choice of witnesses, and a general attitude to the procedure which suggested that the end result had been decided before the beginning of the investigation. Had he survived to appear in court, Lee Harvey Oswald, with a good lawyer, would have disposed of the government's case hands down. And he may also have left some reputations in tatters.

---

[1] Holmes later stated that the practice relating to PO boxes in Dallas was that if a package bearing an unregistered name was received a notice was placed in the box which, if taken by the person having access to the box to the window, the package would be handed over. PO Regulations stated that such mail should be endorsed 'addressee unknown' and returned to sender where possible.

CHAPTER TWENTY-NINE

Sounds That Drive Against the Wind

THE HOUSE SELECT COMMITTEE ON ASSASSINATIONS received four mandates. The first: who killed President Kennedy? The second: did the killer(s) receive any assistance? The third: did US Government agencies adequately collect and share information prior to the assassination, protect the President properly, and conduct a thorough investigation into the assassination? And four: should new legislation on these matters be enacted by Congress? The Committee's brief was extended to include an investigation into the murders of Senator Robert F. Kennedy and Dr Martin Luther King, and the shooting of Governor George Wallace.

The Committee began its work in 1976 and produced its report in 1979. Taking out of that period the protracted time it took at the beginning to set itself up, its procedures and its investigatory machinery, and the time it required to write and produce its report at the end, there was actually only six months in the middle for its real work. Not surprisingly, in the time available for real investigation it was unable to achieve all it had been given to do. In fact, it concentrated on the assassination of President Kennedy and the murder of Martin Luther King.

The first six months in the life of the Committee were spent fighting for survival: it did not represent a popular cause in the House. First, Representative Thomas N. Downing of Virginia was named as chairman, but he was shortly to retire. Congressman Henry Gonzalez of Texas became chairman next, miffed because he was not the first chosen. There was much infighting between Gonzalez and Richard A. Sprague, who had been appointed chief counsel, and there were indications that an organised opposition to the existence of the Committee was trying to dispose of it. Gonzalez eventually resigned saying 'it was an exercise in futility . . . Strong organized forces have combined to stop the enquiry at all costs.'

The chairmanship then passed to Representative Louis Stokes, who allied himself to Richard Sprague. Sprague, however, by now had had enough and resigned. He was replaced by Professor G. Robert Blakey, director of the Notre Dame Institute on Organised Crime. Where Sprague had advocated openness in the work of the Committee, Blakey was entirely the opposite. Secrecy became the keynote, along with the muzzling of the staff, rigid control of the findings, and access to the material produced. It was discovered, all too late, that Blakey was accommodating to the CIA and FBI, and, once again, the investigation of the assassination of President Kennedy came to be controlled by the very agencies the Committee might profitably have investigated.

The House Assassinations Committee spent most of its time reinvestigating what the Warren Commission had investigated. There was little doubt that it saw its task as that of shoring up the Warren Commission, the influence and integrity of which was steadily being undermined from about the time the Zapruder film was first seen on television by the American public in 1975. The sterling efforts of the early researchers such as Harold Weisberg, Sylvia Meagher, Penn Jones Jr, Mark Lane and Bernard J. Fensterwald had also had their effect, and fewer and fewer people believed what the Warren Report told them. Furthermore, a crop of vigorous new researchers had joined the ranks of the 'pioneer' critics of the Warren Report. They were not going to go away, and confidence in the work of the Warren Commission was being steadily eroded. People trusted the government less and less, and those who ran it, less still. A new investigation into the death of President Kennedy was needed, and it merited the stature of a committee of the Senate itself. But it had made a very bad start.

Unhappily, as we have said, the Assassinations Committee did not appear to want to restore people's confidence in government by providing a truly fresh investigation, dedicated to finding out all the things the Warren Commission had not found out, and revealing what really had happened when Kennedy was killed. It seems it wanted to tread the same paths as Warren had and, reaching the same conclusions, reassure the public that Warren had been right in the first place. But then the Committee had reckoned without the new evidence which was dramatically thrust upon it. This was evidence obtained from the police dictabelt which had been recovered from the obscurity in which it had lain since the time of the assassination.

The discovery of the dictabelt was the work of researchers Mary Ferrell and

Gary Mack. The suggestion that tape recordings made in the Dealey Plaza at the time of the assassination might yield evidence had occurred to the Warren Commission. They considered the idea that the recordings made by the police at the time could be valuable, but the dictabelt on which such recordings were made was found to be so worn that the project was dropped. It was due to the efforts of Mary Ferrell and Gary Mack that the dictabelt was eventually found, in the possession of Paul McCaghren, the Director of Dallas Police Intelligence Division. It had lain for six years in a file at Police Headquarters before Paul McCaghren took personal control of it, such as it was. In a battered condition, it was as worn as when the Warren Commission rejected it, and it was now many years older. Nevertheless it was, at last, to be examined for the evidence it might contain. Gary Mack at first obtained a poor copy of the police recordings and found he could identify rifleshots from among the sounds. He next obtained a better copy, and improved the clarity of the recordings.

Finally the dictabelt, retrieved from the home of Paul McCaghren, was placed in the hands of Bolt, Beranek and Newman (BBN), acoustics experts, for their analysis and appraisal. The sounds were converted into digitised waveforms, and BBN's chief scientist, Dr James Barger, suggested at first the presence of six shots on the tape, which he later reduced to four. He then wanted tests carried out in the Dealey Plaza to develop his findings. The tests in the Dealey Plaza produced even more spectacular results. One of the shots had come from a different general direction from the others – from the direction of the grassy knoll! Furthermore, the timing of the shots heard on the tape revealed that one shot came only 1.6 seconds after a previous shot, and it was impossible they had both come from the Mannlicher-Carcano, which required, minimally, 2.3 seconds between shots. Here was clear evidence that there had been more than one gunman.

Barger's results constituted the proverbial bombshell for the Assassinations Committee. This was exactly what it didn't want; new evidence which lay outside the control of the intelligence agencies. It was then decided that the dictabelt recordings should now be passed to two brilliant acoustics scientists at Queen's College of the City University of New York, Professor Mark Weiss and Dr Ernest Aschkenasy. If Professor Blakey hoped a different set of analysts would throw out BBN's findings he was doomed to disappointment. They carried out more sophisticated tests in the Dealey Plaza, creating computerised graphic images for comparison with the dictabelt recordings. Their results confirmed six shots, one of which was from the grassy knoll and two of which came from directions other than the grassy knoll or the School Book Depository.

The source of the recordings was identified as the microphone on a motorcycle ridden by Patrolman H.B. McLain, who had reported his microphone being stuck in the 'open' position. He said he had had trouble with it before: it often got stuck. He testified to the Assassinations Committee that he was in the right place to transmit the sound of the shots. Patrolman McLain reflected on what he had testified, however, and it appears he was unhappy with his transmissions creating such disturbing new evidence. Immediately after the Committee was wound up, he challenged the acoustics evidence on the grounds that his microphone, after all, couldn't have transmitted the sounds in question. He had accompanied the Lincoln to Parkland Hospital, he said, with siren blaring, and there was no siren on the tape. Whatever Patrolman McLain was up to in attempting to reverse his testimony, and discredit the acoustics evidence, he did not succeed. One of the many photographs taken in the Dealey Plaza after the President's limousine had sped off to Parkland showed McLain still in Elm Street.

Time after time there have been attempts to discredit the acoustics evidence. The FBI entered the arena with a report which attempted to scotch the new findings, declaring them invalid. This drew a stinging response from Chief Counsel Blakey, who spoke of the FBI work as a 'sophomoric analysis . . . superficial, shoddy, and shot full of holes'. Next it was the Justice Department itself which asked the National Science Foundation to fund a new study. A National Academy of Sciences panel undertook the work and said the grassy knoll shot had not been proven in the recordings, nor had the presence of a second gunman. Effectively, they threw out the acoustics evidence.

The results of this expensive piece of work – it cost $23,360 – were quickly attacked by Gary Mack, who had conducted the original work on the tapes. The panel had based its studies on problems involving the Automatic Gain Control on police Channel 1, and Gary Mack pointed out to them that Dallas police had no such refinement on their radios at the time of the assassination. Furthermore, the study had been carried out in the belief that the police operated an AM system. In fact it was an FM system. How could the panel's findings be valid?

The final word on the arguments surrounding the acoustics evidence came early in the year 2001, from a study published in the *Journal of the US Forensic Science Society*. Donald B. Thomas reanalysed the dictabelt recordings and looked at the data the National Academy of Sciences panel had been examining. **He confirmed that the data they had used was inaccurate and their findings, therefore were not valid.** This constituted another nasty shock to rock the US Government. Donald Thomas made the necessary adjustments to the data and his results showed that the submissions to the House Committee on Assassinations were right in the first place. The fatal shot – the shot which actually killed the President – came from behind the picket fence on the grassy knoll.

The tapes contained two distinct 'recording hums' indicating two recordings. When the National Academy of Sciences panel completed its work, it suggested the two be identified and separated. It would have made better sense if they had done this before they started. Dr James Barger had suggested the same thing long before this, when he made his original study of the tapes.

At one point an argument arose over the authenticity of the tapes themselves. It was found they had been acquired for a few days, shortly after the assassination, by the FBI, and it was thought that body may have tampered with them. There is no doubt this constituted a break in the chain of ownership which might or might not be significant. The tapes which were examined were not the originals; that also has been determined.

It is reassuring that, regardless of the attempts to undermine this evidence and possible interference with the tapes, the work of BBN and Weiss and Aschkenasy in identifying the shots has been revalidated and upheld. The evidence of the Dallas police tapes made its mark. Researchers recognised in it what they had known from the beginning; there had been more than one assassin and shots came from the grassy knoll area. The public at large also felt it confirmed what they had long since suspected, and any amount of trying to shoot it down was unlikely to succeed. To those who ponder on such things, it is odd, to say the least, that it was the Justice Department, the very body which should have been most anxious to obtain the truth about President Kennedy's death, which was hacking at the roots of the Assassinations Committee's work.

Earlier in the proceedings the Committee had delved into the medical evidence, although, far from shedding light on the questions concerning the President's wounds, it managed to create even further problems. It seems that the President's back wound kept changing position, and the massive head wound, caused by the bullet which had actually killed the President, disappeared altogether. The forensic panel consisted of nine members, three of whom had seen the X-rays and photographs before and six who hadn't. Those who were expecting a fresh view of the autopsy results were disappointed, however. In their deliberations they proceeded to reach, identically, wound by wound, the same conclusions reached by the Warren Commission.

The photographs and X-rays provided for the panel caused many problems. Those who had been present at the autopsy could not reconcile their recollections of what they had seen then with what they saw now. The huge opening in the rear of the President's head had become, according to the photographs the panel had before it, a neatly drilled hole higher up on the head in the cowlick area. Dr Pierre A. Finck, who had been one of the original autopsists, objected to what he saw, and pointed out that the observations of the autopsy pathologists were more valid than those considering the wounds at a later date. He was simply told that he and his colleagues had made a mistake, and they were ignored. One member of the panel, Dr Cyril H. Wecht, a former president of the American Academy of Forensic Sciences, found himself so at odds with the others on the panel that a footnote to their report was agreed:

> In many of its conclusions, the forensic pathology panel voted 8–1, with the dissenting vote being consistently that of Cyril H. Wecht, MD, Coroner of Allegheny County, PA. In all references to conclusions of the panel, unless it is specifically stated that it was unanimous, it should be assumed that Dr Wecht dissented.

Something was clearly wrong with the autopsy photographs being examined by the panel. Photographic expert Robert Groden, who was adviser on photography to the Committee, complained he was not given access to the photographs in question until just before the Committee disbanded, and well after the panel had reached their decisions. When he did see them he identified two as distinct fakes. The authenticity of the photographs and X-rays was challenged. The means by which they had been authenticated for the panel were closely examined and found defective. The items involved had no identifications which, by themselves, could vouch for their authenticity. A lot could have been done to prove – or disprove – authenticity if the cameras and lenses used to take them had been available, but these could not be found. Talk ensued on techniques used to fake the contents of photographs and how near-perfect results could be obtained. Critics of the Assassinations Committee gave up on them and dismissed them as forgeries.

The House Assassinations Committee, in spite of its problems and the fact that it spent so little time doing the things it was there to do, did, nonetheless, achieve a number of extremely creditworthy things. It highlighted the failure of the Secret Service to protect the President, the failure of the CIA to obtain and share with the Warren Commission information relevant to the assassination, and the failure of the FBI to properly investigate the possibility of a conspiracy to kill the President, although it then absolved them all of having any part in the assassination.

The CIA might be said to have displayed outright contempt for the House Assassinations Committee in the affair of the burgled safe. One of the Committee's safes was broken into and a top-secret photograph torn from its file.

The investigation which followed produced fingerprints which matched those of CIA Agent Regis Blahut. At the conclusion of the investigation, it appears the reason accepted by the Committee for the break-in, unbelievably, amounted to no more than Regis Blahut's curiosity. The agent was fired and the matter dropped.

The Committee also determined that when Jack Ruby slew Lee Harvey Oswald, he was not acting spontaneously, although it might be said that anyone reading the account of his pleas to Earl Warren to be taken to Washington for questioning would have drawn this conclusion anyway. But then it further determined that Ruby probably had assistance in slipping into his position in the basement car park when he shot Oswald, and that the police were less than forthcoming on this question. This was an extremely valuable contribution.

There is no doubt, however, that the House Assassinations Committee's most valuable achievement was in recognising the importance of the acoustics evidence, even though it was reluctant to do so. It said there were at least four shots[1] – which alone scuppered the Warren findings – one of which had come from the direction of the grassy knoll. It acknowledged that there had been more than one gunman and conceded that a conspiracy had 'probably' taken place. In this it was finally sailing against the prevailing wind.

The acoustics evidence was put before the Assassinations Committee long before it 'accepted' it. The Committee left it until the very end, demonstrating its reluctance to accept such evidence and the implications involved. Perhaps it did not want to accept it earlier because it would have been expected then to investigate the conspiracy, which it never did. At its close, however – in 1979 – it passed the buck elsewhere. It officially recommended that the Justice Department take up the investigation into the conspiracy to assassinate President Kennedy. For this, we are still waiting.

It would seem that no department or organ of the United States government wants to find out who killed President Kennedy. In spite of the findings of the Assassinations Committee, which might be said to have stood the Warren Report on its head, the official position of the United States government on the assassination of President Kennedy is still represented by the findings of the Warren Commission; one shooter – Lee Harvey Oswald – and no shots from anywhere but the Texas School Book Depository.

---

[1] It is claimed Professor Blakey privately admitted he believed six shots were on the tape.

CHAPTER THIRTY

Silent Witnesses

THERE WAS AN AMAZING number of people associated one way or another with the assassination of President Kennedy, who died suddenly, violently, or mysteriously. Brought to the attention of the House Assassinations Committee, investigator Donovan Gay was delegated to look into what they termed 'the mysterious deaths project'. This work was soon taken over by Jacqueline Hess, who was the Committee's Chief of Research and who, at the end of her investigation, reached the conclusion that 'the available evidence does not establish anything about the nature of these deaths which would indicate that the deaths were in some manner, either direct or peripheral, caused by the assassination of President Kennedy or by any aspect of the subsequent investigation.'

This reflected a somewhat high-handed position to adopt in view of the many deaths under review, a second group of deaths coinciding with the Garrison investigation, and yet another distinct group linked to the timing of the House Select Committee on Assassinations.

Activities leading to violent deaths started even before the assassination itself. Karen Kupcinet, whose father was a TV host, picked up her phone two days before the assassination took place, asked for the long-distance operator, and screamed hysterically that President Kennedy was to be killed. Two days after the assassination, 23-year-old Karen was found dead in her apartment. No one was charged with her murder.

Karen Kupcinet was not the only one to give advance warning that the President was to be killed. Melba Christine Marcades, otherwise known as Rose Cheramie, said she had worked at one time for Jack Ruby at the Carousel Club.

Thrown out of a car and suffering from minor injuries, she was picked up by Lt. Francis Fruge of Louisiana State Police, who had been called out to look into the incident. He took her to hospital in Jackson, Louisiana, talking to her as he drove. She appeared to be under the influence of some drug or other, but this did not stop her giving the officer an account of what had happened. She told him that she had been travelling from Florida to Dallas with two men; Latin types, she said. Fruge wanted to know what her intentions were when she reached Dallas, and she said, '. . . number one, pick up some money, pick up baby and . . . kill Kennedy.' She told him she had heard the two men discussing a plot to assassinate President Kennedy. This, also, was two days before the assassination.

At hospital she repeated to doctors that Kennedy was to be killed in Dallas. Details sent to the Assassinations Committee showed she was lucid and 'without psychosis'. She said that this knowledge had came from 'word in the underworld'. On the day of the assassination Rose Cheramie was taken into custody by Lt. Fruge and further questioning took place. The two men she had previously mentioned were on their way to Dallas to kill President Kennedy. For her part she was to receive $48,000, and she was also to travel to Houston with the two men, who would complete a drug deal there, and she would pick up her young son. Rose gave Lt. Fruge the name of a seaman involved in the drug deal and the name of a ship. Fruge verified her information through US Customs.

Lt. Fruge made contact with Captain Will Fritz, who ran the Dallas police investigation into the President's death, and repeated the incredible information he had obtained from Rose Cheramie. **Fritz told him he wasn't interested**, and Fruge, no doubt both puzzled and frustrated, found he could take his own investigation little further. He did, however, speak to the owner of the brothel where Rose and her companions had stayed, who linked her with a Cuban exile, Sergio Arcacha Smith. Smith, in turn, was linked to David Ferrie, who was linked to Rose's old boss, Jack Ruby.

Rose Cheramie made another attempt to pass information to the FBI in August 1965. A few weeks later she was found, yet again, by the side of a road, but this time she was dead. The road was near Big Sandy, Texas, and the indications were she had, again, been thrown from a car. A man who gave a Tyler, Texas, address reported to the police that, although he tried to avoid her in the roadway, he ran over her head. The police later found he had given an address which didn't exist.

William Whaley was the cab driver who drove Oswald home after his bus got bogged down in traffic. Present at a line-up, he was forthright when testifying to the Warren Commission about what happened:

> . . . me and this other taxi driver who was with me, sir,[William Scoggins, Tippit murder witness] we sat in the room awhile and directly they brought in six men, young teenagers, and they were all handcuffed together . . . you could have picked [Oswald] out without identifying him by just listening to him because he was bawling out the policeman, telling them it wasn't right to put him in line with these teenagers . . . He showed no respect for the policemen, he told them what he thought about them . . . they were trying to railroad him and he wanted his lawyer . . . Anybody who wasn't sure could have picked out the right one just for that . . .

Whaley died as a result of a traffic accident in December 1965. It was an extremely rare event for a Dallas cab driver to die from an accident. It very seldom happened.

Rose Cheramie was not the only former Carousel Club showgirl to die following the assassination. In early 1964, Nancy Jane Mooney, also known as Betty MacDonald, gave an alibi to Darrell Wayne Garner who stood accused of shooting Warren Reynolds. Reynolds had seen a man – not Lee Harvey Oswald – fleeing the scene of the Tippit killing. Garner obtained his release as a consequence of Nancy Jane Mooney's testimony. Mooney, however, was picked up for a minor offence and found herself in jail. About an hour after being put in a cell, she was found hanged. Garner died of an overdose in 1970.

Carousel girl Marilyn Magyar, who was also known as Marilyn Moore Walle, Marilyn April Walle, Marilyn Magyar Moor and 'Delilah', was murdered in 1964. Her husband was chief suspect and ultimately convicted of killing her. Afterwards it was discovered she had been planning to write a book about the assassination. Yet another of Ruby's girls, Karen Bennett Carlin, who was also known as Teresa Norton and Little Lynn, was shot and killed in a hotel room in Houston in 1964.

Heart attacks figured prominently in the deaths of a number of people linked one way or another to the assassination. Earlene Roberts, who ran the boarding house Oswald lived at in North Beckley, died of a heart attack. She was elderly, it is true, but it seemed strange that this lady, who had rubbed shoulders with Oswald right until the time of the assassination, should die so dramatically. Tom Howard, Jack Ruby's first lawyer, also died of a heart attack. Howard was said to have been at Ruby's side in the basement of Police Headquarters before he shot Oswald. Bill Chesher was a Dallas businessman who said he knew of a link between Ruby and Oswald. He also died of a heart attack.

We have mentioned celebrated broadcaster and journalist Dorothy Kilgallen earlier in this book. She died a few days after interviewing Jack Ruby in prison.

She was said at first to have died from a heart attack but later this was changed to suicide. Her close friend, Mrs Earl T. Smith, with whom she had talked after the interview, was found dead two days later. Another suicide they said. Judge Joe Brown, who tried Jack Ruby and who permitted the interview of Ruby by Dorothy Kilgallen, making special provisions for privacy, died of a heart attack in 1966, the year following the Kilgallen interview.

Others who were said to have taken their own lives included Roger Craig, the deputy sheriff who was present when the Mauser rifle was found in the Texas School Book Depository and refused to change his affidavit. He also witnessed someone running from the Texas School Book Depository, someone who was picked up in a green Rambler car. Craig was warned not to talk to newsmen about these things, and when he was caught out doing so, he was fired. He was at later times shot at more than once and had his car run off the road. His wife left him and his life lay in ruins. He was found dead and was declared a suicide.

Gary Underhill was a CIA agent who said he had inside knowledge of the assassination of President Kennedy and the involvement of the CIA. Underhill was found dead with a bullet in his head and was another declared suicide. Albert Guy Bogard was the car salesman at the Lincoln-Mercury dealership to which a man purporting to be Lee Harvey Oswald went looking for a car. The man, whoever he was, left saying he could not afford the car and that in Russia they treated their workers better. He was clearly there to advertise left-wing sentiments which would attach to Oswald. Bogard was found in a car parked in a cemetery. A hose pipe leading to the car had been attached to the exhaust with fatal results. Another suicide?

James Worrell saw a man, who was not Oswald, running from the rear of the School Book Depository. He described the man, who was wearing a dark sports coat and who slowed to a walk and went off on Houston Street. Worrell died in a road accident in November 1966. Thomas H. Killam, known as Hank, whose wife worked for Jack Ruby, was said to know of a link between Ruby and Oswald. Killam reportedly said in a conversation with his brother, 'I am a dead man, but I have run as far as I am running.' In March 1964 he was found dead in an alley with his throat cut.

Bill Hunter and Jim Keothe were journalists who interviewed Ruby's lawyer, Tom Howard, together. Hunter was shot and killed in a shooting mishap in a police station at Long Beach, California, while Keothe was killed by a karate chop to the throat by an assassin waiting for him to step out of his shower. Harold Russell also died a strange, perhaps similar, death. He witnessed the escape of the man who murdered Tippit. One night, at a party in a bar, Russell became hysterical and told his friends he was going to be killed. They called the police and when they came, some kind of brawl ensued. One of the police officers struck Russell, who died of head injuries soon afterwards.

Lee Bowers Jnr. was an important witness who worked at the railroad yard adjacent to the School Book Depository. He was located on the second level of the control tower in the yard, beyond the car park and prominent in many photographs taken at the time of the assassination. Bowers said that after the police closed off the car park 'anyone moving around could actually be observed'. He gave an account of three cars which entered the car park within half hour before the assassination took place. The first was a 1959 blue and white Oldsmobile station-wagon, bespattered with red mud, which showed a 'Goldwater for President' sticker. The driver of this car combed the area in front of the control tower as though checking it out or looking for another exit. He left the same way as he had entered. The second car to appear was a 1957 black Ford. Bowers spoke of the driver of this car holding something to his mouth, perhaps a microphone. This car probed further into the area, said Bowers, and left after three or four minutes. The third car was a Chevrolet, also bearing a Goldwater sticker and bespattered with red mud. This car spent longer in the area, driving up quite close to the control tower and pausing at the assassination spot before leaving. It was there just 'seven to nine minutes before the shooting', said Bowers.

Bowers also told the Warren Commission that he had seen two men near the picket fence just before the President was killed. One was thick-set and middle-aged, while the other was in his mid-twenties. The younger man, he said, wore a plaid shirt, or perhaps it was a plaid coat or jacket. The two were there when the shots were fired and they were the only strangers thereabouts, he said.

Another important piece of testimony related to what might have been a flash from a rifle. Giving evidence, Bowers said that '. . . something occurred in this particular spot which was out of the ordinary, which attracted my eye for some reason, which I could not identify.' He was then about to develop what he had said when he was cut off by Counsel, who changed the subject. It would seem the Commission had no wish to know what Bowers had seen. Interviewed later by Mark Lane, who wrote *Rush to Judgment* and *Plausible Denial*, he added:

> At the time of the shooting, in the vicinity of where the two men I have described were, there was a flash of light or, as far as I am concerned, something I could not identify . . . some unusual occurrence – a flash of light or smoke or something which caused me to feel like something out of the ordinary had occurred there.

When out driving, Bowers's car left the road and he was killed. When doctors examined his body, they said he appeared to have been in a state of 'strange shock' at the time the accident occurred. Bowers was forty-one years old when he died.

Eddy Benavides was shot to death. He looked much like his brother, Domingo, who was a witness to the Tippit killing. Domingo had steadfastly refused to identify Oswald as Tippit's killer until his brother was shot. He suspected the shot was meant for him and he then became more 'compliant' with the authorities.

When it came to the Garrison investigation, there was a fresh crop of deaths. Guy Banister was the first to die of a heart attack. Dave Ferrie died in strange circumstances and was declared a suicide, and Eladio del Valle, Ferrie's friend and associate, died an extremely violent death. He was shot and an axe was taken to his head. Clay Shaw also died in mysterious circumstances which we recounted earlier. Shaw was found dead, alone in his home a few hours after a neighbour had reported a stretcher being carried into his house from an ambulance, a figure covered by a sheet reposing on the stretcher. Shaw was certified as having died from cancer. There was no autopsy. Garrison's potential bombshell witnesses had died before they could give evidence, and now the man he suspected of leading the group was dead. He did obtain testimony from the Rev. Clyde Johnson who was later shot to death, but when it came to the husband of Nancy Perrin Rich, Robert Perrin, he was too late. He died from arsenic poisoning. Nancy Perrin Rich, a mine of information about the background of Jack Ruby, had testified before the Warren Commission.

Dr Mary Sherman, who worked with Ferrie on cancer research, was another of Garrison's potential witnesses who died violently. She was shot dead and had her bed set alight. Dr Nicholas Chatta, Coroner of New Orleans, who conducted the autopsies on Ferrie, Perrin and Sherman, died of a heart attack, and his assistant and brother-in-law, Dr Henry Delaune, was murdered a few months later.

Unbelievably there were even more deaths from the time the House Select Committee on Assassinations began its work in 1976. We mentioned earlier the death of CIA agent George de Mohrenschildt, a supposed suicide. His wife, Jeanne, did not believe he killed himself. A sufferer from bronchitis, de Mohrenschildt had had a particularly bad attack and, because he had a distrust of hospitals, he accepted the advice of a friend and sought the help of a new doctor in Dallas, Dr Charles Mendoza. His bronchitis soon cleared up but he began displaying symptoms of having a nervous breakdown. Jeanne became very worried and began to suspect the 'treatment' Mendoza was giving her husband was inducing the condition. Investigations carried out much later revealed that Dr

Mendoza first appeared and registered with the Dallas County Medical Society in April 1976, only weeks before de Mohrenschildt went to him, and about the time the Assassinations Committee was setting up. Mendoza disappeared from Dallas just as mysteriously some months after Jeanne de Mohrenschildt insisted her husband stop seeing him. The damage had been done, however: her husband never recovered from the unbalanced mental condition from which he suffered. He was eventually compelled to go to Parkland Hospital for electroshock therapy. It was no doubt because of de Mohrenschildt's condition that it was easy for a coroner's jury to declare him a suicide.

Earlier on the day of his death, however, he had given an interview to author Edward Jay Epstein, which hardly indicated a severely depressed state. Epstein showed him a document which told him he might have to return to Parkland for more treatment. That may have brought on a fit of depression, but was it really enough to make him want to kill himself? Jeanne thought not. She said to gathered newsmen after his death:

> If George's death was engineered, it is because you focused such attention on my husband that the real conspirators decided to eliminate him just in case George actually knew something, just like so many others in the assassination.

There were two things which may have had a bearing on the timing of the death of George de Mohrenschildt. The first was that he had just finished writing a book before he died. It was entitled, *I am a Patsy! I am a Patsy!* which was enough to reveal what he believed about Oswald's role in the assassination, and George was in a position to know. It was never published. The second was that he received a visit that final day from an Assassinations Committee investigator to sort out a date for him to testify.

The Senate Intelligence Committee was established the year before the Assassinations Committee, and had the brief to examine US intelligence agencies in relation to the assassination of President Kennedy. Chicago-based Mafia boss, Sam Giancana, was required to give evidence before it.Giancana was said to have had connections with the Kennedys for some time. The mobster claimed he was responsible for rigging the vote in Cook County which effectively put JFK into the White House. This is hard to believe since Mayor Daley was reputed to always deliver the Chicago vote for the Democrats.

But of more immediate interest to the Senate Intelligence Committee was that Giancana and his associate, Johnny Rosselli, had gone into partnership with the CIA to kill Fidel Castro. This scandalous relationship between the Mafia and the CIA came to light by accident, and the media went to town on the story with headlines such as 'GIANCANA HIRED TO KILL CASTRO'. The partnership, in fact, achieved nothing but bring enormous discredit to the Agency. The mobsters, of course, were as anxious to get rid of Castro as were the US Government; there were all their gambling assets in Havana to be recovered if the Castro regime could be dislodged.

The House Assassinations Committee's interest in Giancana lay in another direction, however. They were exploring the theory that because the mob had been unsuccessful in killing Castro, the plan had been rejigged with President Kennedy as its target. The argument was that, not only would the death of Kennedy bring a more 'enlightened' administration, more likely to wage war on Castro, it would carry the huge bonus of getting Robert Kennedy off their backs. Robert Kennedy, as Attorney General, had been fighting a very successful campaign against the Mafia, and had been producing the kind of results never before seen. The statistics in regard to successful prosecutions were spectacular. Robert Kennedy was a considerable threat to the Mafia.

But the Committee's plans to question Giancana were thwarted. He was found dead at home, shot once in the back of the head and six times in his face, the bullets forming a circle around his mouth. On the face of it, Sam's mobster friends had decided to make sure he didn't talk to the Committee about their partnership with the CIA. Doubts arose about this, however. It could have been that the murder was carried out in this way by others who wanted to give that impression. There is no doubt that the Assassinations Committee would have had Giancana high on the list of those they wanted to question.

Hit man Johnny Rosselli was the next to die. He had made one appearance before the Senate Intelligence Committee and was due to appear again. He never made it. He disappeared, and ten days afterwards his body was found in an oil drum in Florida's Dumfoundling Bay. No doubt he, also, would have been on the list to give evidence to the Assassinations Committee, formed only a few months after his death. Rosselli had been garrotted and stabbed to death. His body was dismembered and rammed into the drum, which was weighted to prevent it from surfacing. He had already told the Intelligence Committee enough to spark off considerable interest in the theory that Castro had had Kennedy killed in retaliation for the attempts on his own life. The House Assassinations Committee was, however, extremely distrustful of Rosselli's evidence. It would have been interesting to see what the Assassinations Committee could have obtained from him, but that was not to be.

Another Mafia associate of Giancana, Charles Nicoletti, was also shot and killed. His body was found in a car which had been torched.

Six FBI officials died within a six-month period in 1977. The six included William Sullivan, Head of Division Five and Director Hoover's right-hand man. Sullivan, who was much involved with the investigation of the assassination of President Kennedy, was required to testify to the Assassinations Committee, but he died as a result of an early-morning shooting accident before he could do so.

To the above list the name of Lee Harvey Oswald should be added, and possibly that of Jack Ruby.

Jacqueline Hess's 'final conclusion', '. . . that the available evidence does not establish anything about the nature of these deaths which would indicate that the deaths were in some manner, either direct or peripheral, caused by the assassination of President Kennedy or by any aspect of the subsequent investigation', in this author's opinion, leaves much to be desired.

CHAPTER THIRTY-ONE

Letters and Other Documents

AN ASSORTMENT OF LETTERS and documents of one kind or another have contributed, in some ways, to the clarification of aspects of the investigation into President John F. Kennedy's murder, and in other ways they have created puzzles which we are still trying to resolve. The letter said to have been left behind by Lee Harvey Oswald when he went to shoot Major General Edwin Anderson Walker is one of the latter. The letter – or list of instructions – known as the 'If I am Caught' letter, was written in Russian for the benefit of his wife and ran:

> (1) This is the key to the mailbox which is located in the main post office in the city on Ervay Street. This is the same street where the drugstore, in which you always waited is located. You will find the mailbox in the post office which is located four blocks from the drugstore on that street. I paid for the box last month so don't worry about it.
> (2) Send the information as to what has happened to me to the Embassy and include newspaper clippings (should there be anything about me in the newspapers). I believe that the Embassy will come quickly to your assistance on learning everything.
> (3) I paid the house rent on the 2nd so don't worry about it.
> (4) Recently I also paid for water and gas.
> (5) The money from work will possibly be coming. The money will be sent to our post office box. Go to the bank and cash the check.
> (6) You can either throw out or give my clothing, etc., away. Do not keep

these. However I prefer that you hold on to my personal papers (military, civil, etc.).

(7) Certain of my documents are in the small blue valise.

(8) The address book can be found on my table in the study should need same.

(9) We have friends here. The Red Cross [written in English] also will help you.

(10) I left you as much money as I could, $60 on the second of the month. You and the baby can live for another two months using $10 per week.

(11) If I am alive and taken prisoner, the city jail is located at the end of the bridge through which we always passed on going to the city (right in the beginning of the city after crossing the bridge).

The first reason this letter is interesting is that he never did go out to shoot General Walker. He was accused of taking a shot at him by the Warren Commission, but hard evidence that he did so is non-existent. Even a cursory reading of the letter would indicate that there was no connection between the shooting and the instructions contained. The very last item creates the problems. This is the 'if I am caught' instruction which suggests he is getting into something which involves the risk of being arrested. Perhaps oddly, it is the disposal of his clothes which bothers me in looking at item (11). If there was the risk of being jailed, he would need his clothing sooner or later, unless he was going to jail for a very long time.

The shooting of a retired general would hardly be an action which would obtain the support of 'the Embassy' – presumably the Russian embassy – for Marina and the family, neither would it be likely to attract support from friends or, for that matter, the Red Cross. But if the letter did not pertain to the consequences of shooting General Walker, what other circumstances would fit such a list of instructions?

Clearly the tenor of the letter suggests Oswald was leaving the country for a long time and that his mission, whatever it was, would attract the support of the Soviets. While his clothes could go, his documents could not, which suggests he would eventually need them again. The letter would entirely fit the mission on which he believed he was embarking at the time the President was killed, except for item (11), although this might be accounted for if he had begun to smell a rat and suspected he was being involved in something of which he had not been told. It might also be accounted for if it was added to cause confusion. Just a thought. But then the whole letter may have been concocted by person or persons unknown to cause confusion and create doubts.

There are one or two other things that are of interest in the letter. It refers to Marina and the baby. Which baby? His first daughter was born shortly before they returned to the United States from Russia, so there was a baby to be considered at that time. They had another child in the summer of 1963, but if this was the baby to which Oswald referred, what about June, the older child? Why did he not make provision for her?

There is also the quality of the language in this letter, which is quite good, much superior to other of Oswald's writings. This was written entirely in Russian except for the name 'Red Cross', ostensibly because Marina could cope with her own language more easily. This, again, might suggest it was – if genuine – an early letter, because she began to understand English better as time went by. We must here assume the translator was meticulous in representing in English what was written in the note. If the translator made changes to grammar and spelling, however, it raises the question of whether he or she made other changes, and whether the English version really said what Oswald had written. Assuming the translator simply translated, we have a piece here without misspellings or difficulties with language construction. Oswald's command of the English language was actually quite good, though his somewhat scrawled hand and the way he used capitals for his diary, for example, suggested otherwise. Though he did misspell words, there were no misspellings here. In this note, however, the use of commas and full stops where they follow, for instance 'etc.', are extremely precise and not quite what one would expect. It would be hard to believe that his Russian grammar was superior to his use of English, though even if it was, his use of punctuation would almost certainly remain unchanged. There is much to learn about this letter. What we have discussed here may only indicate Oswald did not write it at all.

Earlier, in a footnote, I referred to a telegraph message received which warned that Kennedy might be killed on his visit to Dallas, and even indicated the date. William S. Walters, the FBI agent on duty in the New Orleans office when the TWX message was received, made a copy of it which, verbatim, read:

> INFO HAS BEEN RECEIVED BY THE BUREAU DETERMINED THAT A MILITANT REVOLUTIONARY GROUP MAY ATTEMPT TO ASSINATED PRESIDENT KENNEDY ON HIS PROPOSED TRIP TO DALLAS TEXAS NOVEMBER TWENTYYWO DASH TWENTYTHREE NINETEEN SICTYTHREE.
>
> ALL RECEIVING OFFICE SHOULS IMMEDIATELY CONTACT ALL CIS; PCIS LOGICAL RACIAL AND HATE GROPUP INFORMANTS AND DETERMINE IF ANY BASIS FOR

> THREAT. BHRGEU SHOULS BE KEPT ADVISED OF ALL DEVELOPMENTS BY TELETYPE.
> SUBMIY FD THREE ZERO TWOS AND LHM
> OTHER HOFFICE HAVE BEEN ADVISED
> END AND ACK PLS

The message arrived on 17 November, five days before the assassination, and came from the FBI Director marked 'Urgent'. But later, when questioned about it, the FBI disclaimed any knowledge of this message, and when Walters went back to the file in which it had been put, it had disappeared. 'They had a system established to make damn sure there was no record of some of those sensitive matters, especially when it became an embarrassing situation,' said Walters. But Walters, having read the message, had made a copy of it. Regardless of the errors, which may be copying errors, the message was clear; there was risk of the President being killed, a risk which was known of in advance. If Hoover had the message transmitted to field stations, why was it not acted upon?

Recalling that Walters worked in the FBI New Orleans office, it is interesting that he claimed also to have seen documents which showed that Lee Harvey Oswald worked for the FBI, which they always denied.

In 1999, in a gesture made by President Boris Yeltsin to President Clinton, about eighty pages of documents relative to the assassination of President Kennedy were handed over on the occasion of their meeting in the United States. I examined them all and, whilst they were all interesting one way or another, they mostly dealt with two broad subjects. One was the responses made by various departments of the Soviet government to the news of the assassination and the implications thereof. The second was the sorrow expressed to the American nation and to the Kennedy family. This latter included accounts given by those who attended the funeral on behalf of the Soviet government. Three of the documents included, diverse in content, are interesting for different reasons.

The first is an extract from an example of how the Russian press treated the news of President Kennedy's death:

> In the past few days the world has witnessed a monstrous crime. The US President, John Fitzgerald Kennedy, has died at the hand of an assassin. This heinous crime has evoked the rightful indignation of all decent people, all those interested in preserving and strengthening peace. The assassin's bullet cut down President Kennedy at a moment when there were visible prospects in the world for a reduction in international tension, and trust had begun to appear in relations between states. It is

> well known how fiercely the late president of the US was attacked for his steps aimed at resolving international disputes by reaching agreement between countries, particularly the USSR and the US.
>
> Finally, it is no accident that certain groups are now attempting to cover up their tracks and conceal the real perpetrators of this foul crime. The more that events connected with the assassination of President Kennedy unfold, the easier it is to discern the identity of those who directed the assassin's hand. Now that Lee Harvey Oswald, accused of murdering the President, has himself been killed under mysterious circumstances, one can see even more clearly the absurdity and malice of the slanderous fabrications . . . using the fact that he spent some time in the Soviet Union as the basis for their insinuations. [There follows at this point an account of Oswald's stay in Russia].
>
> Hardly anyone gave credence to those fabrications even when the first reports came out regarding the circumstances of President Kennedy's assassination. But now that a new shot has been fired in Dallas, aimed this time at a person accused of murdering the U.S. president, such fabrications cannot but elicit a bitter smile and understandable indignation not only outside the United States but among all decent Americans, who have the right to expect that justice will be meted out to the real murderers and organizers of this shameful crime. Who does not realize that the physical destruction of Oswald is an additional link in the chain of crimes leading to the real masterminds of President Kennedy's assassination, who stop at nothing in their efforts to mislead the investigation and put it on a false trail?

This article was written less than a week after President Kennedy's death. In the batch of documents I also discovered a letter addressed to Chairman Krushchev, the original of which was written entirely in the hand of Jacqueline Kennedy – a sign of respect for President Krushchev – less than a month after her husband had died. It was a secret letter. Whilst President Johnson knew Mrs Kennedy was writing a letter he had no knowledge of what was in it. Neither had Secretary of State Dean Rusk. It ran:

> White House, December 1 1963
> Dear Mr Chairman-President:
>
> I would like to thank you for sending Mr Mikoyan as your representative to my husband's funeral.

He looked so upset when he approached me, and I was very touched by this.

I tried that day to tell you some things through him, but it was such a horrible day for me that I do not know if my words were received as I wanted them to be.

Therefore now, on one of the last nights I will spend in the White House, in one of the last letters I will write on this White House stationery, I would like to write my message to you.

I am sending it only because I know how much my husband was concerned about peace [translator's note: the Russian word 'mir' used here can mean either 'peace' or 'the world' but the context seems to indicate that she meant 'peace'] and how important the relations between you and him were to him in this concern. He often cited your words in his speeches: 'In the next war the survivors will envy the dead.'

You and he were adversaries, but you were also allies in your determination not to let the world be blown up. You respected each other and could have dealings with each other. I know that President Johnson will make every effort to establish the same relations with you.

The danger troubling my husband was that war could be started not so much by major figures as by minor ones.

Whereas major figures understand the need for self-control and restraint, minor ones are sometimes moved rather by fear and pride. If only in the future major figures could still force minor ones to sit down at the negotiating table before they begin to fight!

I know that President Johnson will continue the policy my husband believed in so deeply – the policy of self-control and restraint – and he will need your help.

I am sending you this letter because I am so deeply mindful of the importance of the relations that existed between you and my husband, and also because you and Mrs Krushchev were so kind in Vienna.

I read that she had tears in her eyes as she was coming out of the American Embassy in Moscow after signing the book of condolences. Please tell her 'thank you' for this.

Sincerely,

Jacqueline Kennedy

There was a warm reponse from Chairman Krushchev, who suggested Mrs Kennedy be unofficially invited for a holiday with the children on the Black Sea. Jackie's simple letter shows her confidence that the Soviets were not behind her

FIGURE 36

Commemoration postage stamp. It was approved by Jackie Kennedy but criticism arose from the fact that the top of Kennedy's head was not shown.

husband's death and how much she trusted them to realise this, even though all around her were suspicious. It has to be wondered whether this letter did not achieve more at a time of crisis than all the politicians put together.

The third document I found specially interesting referred to a letter purported to be sent by Lee Harvey Oswald to the Russian embassy in Washington shortly before the assassination. Marked 'Top Secret', it appeared to be a memo to be sent on to the Soviet Ambassador in Washington. It said:

> You may send Rusk photocopies of the correspondence between the embassy and Oswald, including his letter of November 9, but without waiting for a request by the US authorities. When sending the photocopies, say that the letter of November 9 was not received by the embassy until November 18, obviously it had been held up somewhere. The embassy had suspicions about this letter the moment it arrived; either it was a forgery or was sent as a deliberate provocation. The embassy left Oswald's letter unanswered.

The letter of 9 November was published in the Warren Report, an extract of which ran:

> I was unable to remain in Mexico indefinitely because of my mexican [sic] visa restrictions which was [sic] for 15 days only. I could not take a

> chance on requesting a new visa unless I used my real name, so I returned to the United States.

The letter is interesting for a number of reasons. Posted to the Soviet embassy, it suggested Oswald had been in Mexico on business for the Russians, and we know that was not so. The reference to using his 'real name' is also a mystery. Some thought that if Lee Harvey Oswald was not his real name, it was because the man who returned from Russia was not Oswald at all, but a Russian substitute. Michael Eddowes, a British researcher who had been suspicious of just such a duplication, tried and tried again to have the body of Oswald exhumed so that he could find out for sure who had returned from Russia. He did not succeed until 1981, when four forensic pathologists examined the corpse. After four hours the team of pathologists declared without doubt the body they had examined was that of Lee Harvey Oswald.

The letter of 9 November to the Soviet embassy was, to all appearances, a forgery. It appears that it was sent – probably by those who had manipulated Oswald in Mexico City – for the sole purpose of creating the impression that Oswald was a Russian spy. The events of 22 November would, retrospectively, suggest that, after writing the letter, his next assignment was the assassination of President Kennedy. The Soviets were astute enough to understand they were being 'set up', but the Warren Commission did not quite view it that way. They attributed the letter to Oswald.

It should be asked why the Kremlin included this particular memo in the eighty documents handed over to President Clinton. It certainly advertised the willingness of the Soviets to help at the time of the assassination, but perhaps it was there to say more than that. It is hard to say what the reason is for its inclusion, although when I reread the letter in question, I am happy enough to hear a small voice saying, 'we didn't believe Oswald wrote this letter, in which case there is still someone out there who did.'

Two other notes deserve close attention. One was written by Lee Harvey Oswald when he called at the FBI office in Dallas to see Agent James P. Hosty. Hosty, whose name, address, phone number and car licence plate number were later found in Oswald's notebook, indicated, it seems, that he had some kind of relationship with Oswald, though he never admitted it. When he was told that Hosty was not in the office, Oswald wrote his note and left it with the receptionist, Nannie Lee Fenner, saying brusquely, 'Get this to him.' This happened only ten days before the assassination.

The fact that a note had been left by Oswald did not come to light until 1975, shortly before the House Select Committee on Assassinations came into being.

Another indication that Oswald worked for the FBI was that he asked Nannie Lee Fenner for 'SA [Special Agent] Hosty', a term with which the general public would be unlikely to be familiar. Where is this important note, and what did it say? The answer to the first question is that the note was destroyed soon after the assassination took place, another prime example of a government department destroying evidence, and to the second, we don't know what it said. Nannie Lee Fenner said she glimpsed it. Oswald was threatening to blow up the FBI and the Police Department if his wife continued to be interviewed by them. Hosty said he recalled the note saying:

> If you have anything you want to learn about me, come talk to me directly. If you don't cease bothering my wife, I will take appropriate action and report this to the proper authorities.

There are sound reasons for disbelieving both of the accounts given, quite apart from the fact that they are extremely different one from another. If Nancy Fenner's account had been accurate, it would have been seized upon by the FBI as an 'example' of how violent Oswald was, and we would quickly have heard about the note on the front pages of the newspapers. Hosty doubted Fenner had seen much of what was in the folded note, in any case, but in spite of the fact there is some evidence Marina Oswald had, as a foreign national, been bothered by Hosty, his greatly modified version did not make much sense in the context of things either.

Within hours of the assassination taking place, and presumably after Oswald's arrest, Hosty was called into J. Gordon Shanklin's office. Shanklin, the agent-in-charge of the office, was 'agitated and upset' said Hosty, and he wanted to know about the Oswald note. This was hardly the reaction one would expect to a note of complaint, which suggests it was about something quite different. When Oswald was killed by Jack Ruby, Gordon Shanklin called Hosty into his office and, pulling the Oswald note from his desk drawer, handed it to Hosty, telling him: 'Oswald's dead now. There can be no trial. Here, get rid of this.' When Hosty tore it up, Shanklin remonstrated: 'No! Get it out of here. I don't even want it in this office. Get rid of it.' Hosty then flushed the pieces down the toilet.

Gordon Shanklin later denied any knowledge of the Oswald note, which only serves to to suggest that the note was of great importance. Another agent at the Dallas office, Kenneth Howe, saw the note in Hosty's tray, where it lay until the time of the assassination. Howe asked Shanklin about it. 'He said . . . he didn't want to discuss it with me.' But if this was such a trifling note, why did William Sullivan, Hoover's second-in-command, no less, know about it and refer to it as a note concerning an 'internal problem' at the Dallas office? It was said that instructions to destroy the note came from 'above', from headquarters level '. . . in order to avoid embarrassment to the bureau'.

In 1996 Hosty wrote a book, *Assignment: Oswald* and it was hoped the agent might have been more forthcoming about the contents of the note. He was extremely forthcoming about many things, especially the consequences of destroying the note. He recounted how Gordon Shanklin, when he was about to be put on the spot, asked for 'emergency' retirement – and was granted it – and how he himself believed he might, as easily as not, have been criminally prosecuted for destroying the note. Criminal prosecution did not involve 'retirement' or loss of a job. Being found guilty on a criminal prosecution charge meant the state penitentiary. Hosty considered himself extremely lucky not to be sent down this road. But of all Agent Hosty had to tell us, the contents of the note did not come into it. A small indication that it was considered dynamite was obtained from one reference he made to it, however. He was telling how one third of the Dallas office staff disclaimed any knowledge of the note, and declared this impossible. 'Agents shared everything with one another,' he wrote, **'especially something as juicy as this**.'

It has been suggested that FBI man and CIA agent Oswald may have pulled a loose thread in respect of those he had been involved with in New Orleans, and found he had evidence of the conspiracy to kill President Kennedy. If this were the case, who would he tell? Not the CIA. He would have passed the word to the FBI.

Our second note also turned up shortly before the Assassination Committee came into being. It was a note apparently in Oswald's hand and bearing the pertinent date, 'Nov 8 1963'. It ran as follows:

> Nov 8 1963
>
> Dear Mr Hunt
> I would like information codcerding [sic] my position.
> I am asking only for information. I am suggesting that we discuss the matter fully before any steps are taken by me or anyone else.
> Thank you.
> Lee Harvey Oswald

Since this letter appeared in 1975 it has been the subject of controversy and suspicion. Not all researchers are prepared to accept it as genuine. It was posted anonymously, bearing a Mexico City postmark, and addressed to esteemed

FIGURE 37

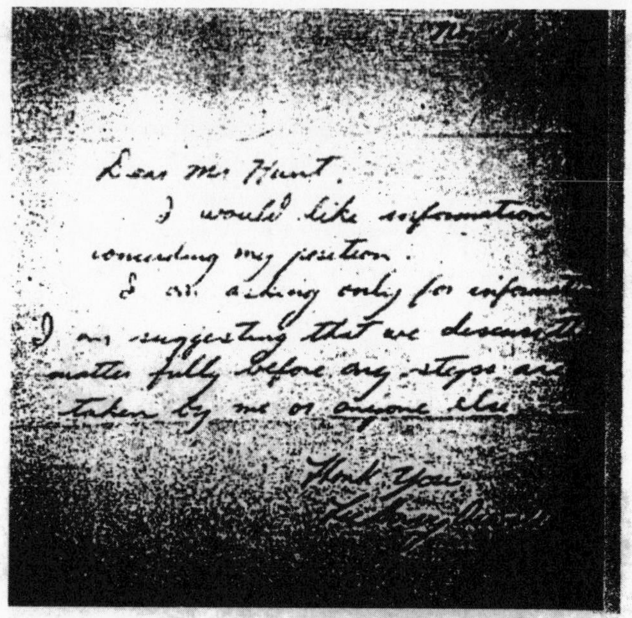

Dear Mr Hunt,
I would like information
concerning my position.
I am asking only for informa
I am suggesting that we discuss th
matter fully before any steps ar
taken by me or anyone else.
Thank You

The Dear Mr Hunt note. But which Mr Hunt?

Warren critic and researcher, Penn Jones Jnr. The prime reason for suspicion must be that it had just 'turned up'. no one knew of it and therefore, no one had sought it. Another source of suspicion may be the timing of its 'turning up', just at a point where there was an upsurge of interest in the assassination of President Kennedy in Congress, prior to the commencement of the work of the House Assassinations Committee.

On balance, however, most of the researchers accept that the note was written by Oswald. Having accepted it as genuine, the next problem is to identify the 'Mr Hunt', to whom it was addressed. There are two 'Hunts' who spring to mind. One is H.L. Hunt, the oil billionaire, and E. Howard Hunt, the CIA agent later to be involved in the Watergate scandal. Of the two, E. Howard Hunt is considered the front-runner. There is the obvious CIA connection, Hunt was believed to be in Mexico City at the time the letter was written, which would account for it being found there, and he was also said to be in Dallas at the time of the assassination.

But then it is my belief that Oswald, as I have said before, was not involved in the plot to kill the President. He was waiting to be sent on what he believed was the next mission the CIA had for him, to fly to Cuba and then to make his way back to Russia. He had been pressing Marina to return to Russia, and she could have returned by conventional means. The note, in this case, would suggest he was unhappy with the arrangements for his flight to Cuba which, it seems, was to be by a tiny Piper aircraft. Whatever the case, there is still mystery here, and we should be reminded there are more than two 'Mr Hunts' in the world.

CHAPTER THIRTY-TWO

Say Goodbye to America

WHEN JOHN F. KENNEDY launched himself into the Presidency in 1961 it appeared that the dawn of a new era had begun in American politics. He was young, vigorous and generally attractive, and his appearance on the scene seemed to herald a turnaround in political thought and action, the likes of which had never before been seen. But such a statement did not merely represent what JFK set out to achieve; it represented rather more the hopes and aspirations thrust upon him by a new generation tired of the old politicians and their ways; it represented the feeling which existed in strong minority groups tired of the racism and oppression they believed was sustained by government, and it represented the hopes of the sick and the poor, who found their country had little by way of priority for dealing with sickness and poverty.

Joe Kennedy, father of JFK, was responsible for his son reaching the White House. This is not to say, by any means, that Jack would not have made it without his father's help. Joe Kane, hired to tutor Jack in political matters when he ran for Congress, said 'Jack could have gone to Congress like everyone else for ten cents.' It is a statement of fact, however, that Joe lavished money on his son's campaigns and worked tirelessly behind the scenes to obtain his success. It had been Joe's intention to promote his eldest son, Joe Junior, for the Presidency, but Joe Jnr. was killed on a heroic flying mission during the Second World War, and father Joe turned his attention to Jack, his second son. Jack, who had had no political ambitions, accepted the role his father bestowed on him without complaint. His intensive campaigns which took him to Congress and to the Senate were very much family affairs, though with huge financial backing from

Joe, which created a powerful election machine. His record in Congress was uneventful and undistinguished, though he served his electorate well, but by the time he went to the Senate he was beginning to acquire a taste for politics. It was not long before he began to be seen as an emerging high-flier.

In spite of the enormous bandwagon of a campaign which Joe created, and which reached out to all parts of the United States, Jack was not, by any means, swept into the White House. He crept in with a majority of less than 20,000 votes over his opponent, Richard Nixon, from a total of 69 million votes cast. But it was enough. The breath of fresh air which accompanied the introduction of a new, youthful and tenacious administration was felt throughout the United States. But he was also endowed with an opposition, however. Among those who made up his opposing camp were many who knew and did not trust Joe Kennedy, who was seen as the power behind the throne.

Lying on the new President's desk when he took office was a plan for a Cuban invasion which had been hatched by the CIA and approved by the outgoing President, Dwight D. Eisenhower, and by the Chiefs of Staff. The Bay of Pigs disaster has been dealt with in some detail in an earlier chapter. Suffice to say that its approval by JFK constituted probably the biggest blunder he was to make in his time in office. There is little doubt it resulted in the creation of a new opposition which played a critical role in his assassination. President Kennedy would make many friends during his thirty-eight months in office but he would also make enemies. And many of these enemies would be people in high places.

At home, Jack Kennedy was not afraid to face up to unpopular issues. The unfair burdens shouldered by the American black population claimed his attention and he made genuine efforts to address this problem. Rooted in segregationalism and racial inequality, the hardships of unemployment and poverty were morally indefensible and socially intolerable. Kennedy realised that the time for action was now and he was not slow to introduce needed legislation. He abolished the poll taxes in Federal elections which extended the franchise to huge numbers of poorer blacks, not to mention poorer whites also. He introduced a Civil Rights Bill which sought to bring an end to discrimination in stores, hotels and restaurants and provided the authority for the Attorney General to effect the desegregation of public education where it had not already been achieved.

The President was not averse to using his personal powers of persuasion, either. He said:

> The Negro baby born in America today, regardless of the section of the nation in which he is born, has about one-half as much chance of

> completing high school as a white baby born in the same place on the same day, one-third as much chance of completing college, one-third as much chance of becoming a professional man, twice as much chance of becoming unemployed, about one-seventh as much chance of earning $10,000 a year, a life expectancy which is seven years shorter, and the prospects of earning only half as much.

Kennedy involved himself in efforts to restore the dignity of black people. He made sure they were as honoured with his presence as any other branch of society. He fought in the universities at Mississippi and Alabama for their right to equal opportunities in education at all levels and he appointed five Federal judges from their ranks. 'I am not sure that I am the most popular figure today . . . in the South,' he said, 'but that is all right.'

Problems in the farming industry did not escape Kennedy's notice, nor his actions. The efforts of his administration did not produce instant answers, but the impact made was positive and measurable. The President was able to say:

> In the last twenty one months we have not, by any means, solved the farm problem. But we have achieved the best two-year advance in farm income of any two years since the depression . . .

On all fronts at home and abroad, JFK engaged himself in forward-looking policies which broke the mould and projected a fresh approach to old as well as new problems. He was preoccupied by the problems created by the closing of the borders to East Germany and the raising of the Berlin Wall, and he kept a constant eye on the development of nuclear arms. It was in this arena that he achieved an enormous success. He negotiated East–West agreement with the Soviets in a treaty banning nuclear testing in the environment. This was a success not exclusively for the United States but for the whole world. It was the first of its kind and there was no doubt that it was the foundation upon which the control of nuclear development was based. He spoke on the subject to the American nation:

> I speak to you tonight in a spirit of hope . . . [Since] the advent of nuclear weapons, all mankind has been struggling to escape from the darkening prospect of mass destruction on earth.
>
> Yesterday a shaft of light cut into the darkness.
>
> This treaty is not the millennium . . . But it is an important first step – a step toward peace, a step toward reason, a step away from war . . . This

> treaty is for all of us. It is particularly for our children and our grandchildren, and they have no lobby here in Washington.
>
> According to the ancient Chinese proverb, 'A journey of a thousand miles must begin with a single step' . . . Let us take that first step.

But for all his efforts and the progress he made domestically and internationally, and in spite of his rapidly growing popularity, there were those who passionately believed John F. Kennedy was leading the United States in the wrong direction, those who could not wait until the White House was rid of him and all the Kennedys. To them the prospect of a second term for this 'brash upstart' was cause for dismay. It is my belief there were members of the Establishment – those who ruled America through their wealth and the vast power which came from their multinational business 'clout' – perhaps including some uncomfortably close to the young President – who were prepared to override democratic government and the will of the people to overthrow the Kennedy regime by force. There were those whose whispered thoughts were assuming shape and form. And there were those who already had the sickly smell of death in their nostrils in the months before Kennedy's visit to Dallas . . .

By and through his new vision, his forthrightness and his vigorous approach to the affairs of the nation, John F. Kennedy was taking government in a new direction. In the past the needs of the Establishment had enjoyed a considerable priority on the part of the elected government. The politicians and the mechanisms of government were there to serve the best interests of those bankers, businessmen, oil giants, industrialists and media moguls before anything – or anybody – else. Even the armed forces might be said to have been held in readiness to protect the interests of the Establishment in other lands, should the need arise. Kennedy had new priorities, however, and the Establishment blanched at the prospect of a government which did not place its interests first. Kennedy's priorities lay in the direction of a government for the people, first and foremost. Whatever was best for the people was best for the government. But what was best for the people often flew in the face of what was best for the Establishment.

After John F. Kennedy was killed, many of his policies were, over a period of about eighteen months, dismantled. But in the case of his Vietnam policy to withdraw US personnel, this was reversed with unseemly haste. A meeting in Honolulu two days before the assassination between Dean Rusk, Robert McNamara, McGeorge Bundy, Admiral Felt and Henry Cabot Lodge, US Ambassador to South Vietnam, discussed JFK's decision to withdraw one

FIGURE 38

THE WHITE HOUSE

WASHINGTON

~~TOP SECRET~~ - EYES ONLY

October 11, 1963

NATIONAL SECURITY ACTION MEMORANDUM NO. 263

TO: Secretary of State
Secretary of Defense
Chairman of the Joint Chiefs of Staff

SUBJECT: South Vietnam

At a meeting on October 5, 1963, the President considered the recommendations contained in the report of Secretary McNamara and General Taylor on their mission to South Vietnam.

The President approved the military recommendations contained in Section I B (1-3) of the report, but directed that no formal announcement be made of the implementation of plans to withdraw 1,000 U.S. miltitary personnel by the end of 1963.

After discussion of the remaining recommendations of the report, the President approved an instruction to Ambassador Lodge which is set forth in State Department telegram No. 534 to Saigon.

McGeorge Bundy

McGeorge Bundy

Copy furnished:
Director of Central Intelligence
Administrator, Agency for International Development

cc:
Mr. Bundy ✓
Mr. Forrestal
Mr. Johnson
NSC Files

~~TOP SECRET - EYES ONLY~~

Committee Print of Pentagon Papers
BY MSZ 7/15/77

White House letter showing President Kennedy approved returning 1,000 military personnel from Vietnam. This was believed to be the first instalment which would result in complete withdrawal from Vietnam.
The lucky 1,000 arrived home before Christmas 1963.

FIGURE 39

THE WHITE HOUSE

WASHINGTON

~~TOP SECRET~~ November 26, 1963

NATIONAL SECURITY ACTION MEMORANDUM NO. 273

TO: The Secretary of State
The Secretary of Defense
The Director of Central Intelligence
The Administrator, AID
The Director, USIA

The President has reviewed the discussions of South Vietnam which occurred in Honolulu, and has discussed the matter further with Ambassador Lodge. He directs that the following guidance be issued to all concerned:

1. It remains the central object of the United States in South Vietnam to assist the people and Government of that country to win their contest against the externally directed and supported Communist conspiracy. The test of all U. S. decisions and actions in this area should be the effectiveness of their contribution to this purpose.

2. The objectives of the United States with respect to the withdrawal of U. S. military personnel remain as stated in the White House statement of October 2, 1963.

3. It is a major interest of the United States Government that the present provisional government of South Vietnam should be assisted in consolidating itself and in holding and developing increased public support. All U. S. officers should conduct themselves with this objective in view.

4. The President expects that all senior officers of the Government will move energetically to insure the full unity of support for established U. S. policy in South Vietnam. Both in Washington and in the field, it is essential that the Government be unified. It is of particular importance that express or implied criticism of officers of other branches be scrupulously avoided in all contacts with the Vietnamese Government and with the press. More specifically, the President approves the following lines of action developed in the discussions of the Honolulu meeting of November 20. The offices of the Government to which central responsibility is assigned are indicated in each case.

~~TOP SECRET~~ (page 1 of 3 pages)

White House letter issued a few days after Kennedy's death. JFK's policy for withdrawal was reversed.

thousand personnel from Vietnam, and plans were made accordingly. Two days after the assassination – Sunday – an emergency meeting was held in Washington between Lyndon B. Johnson, most of those who were at the Honolulu conference, and CIA Director John McCone, at which Kennedy's withdrawal policy – which is believed to have had as its ultimate aim complete withdrawal before the end of 1965 – was quickly reversed. John F. Kennedy was not even buried when this happened. He was buried only three days after his murder.

The hurried Sunday meeting signalled a policy of escalation of involvement in Vietnam. The war in Vietnam generated business, the value of which was estimated as being in excess of two hundred billion dollars. This went mainly to those who provided arms, armaments and oil. In other words, the Establishment. But in the conflict America lost 50,000 of its sons and Vietnam numbered its losses in millions.

A few years after the assassination, in 1968, when there was a groundswell of popular support to put Senator Robert F. Kennedy in the White House, he too was shot and killed. The following year Edward Kennedy, the third brother, was mysteriously involved in an incident in which a young woman died. Cleared of any responsibility for that, the whiff of scandal was enough to keep this Kennedy out of the White House forever. Are we to believe these were separate events? Are we to believe there is no link between these events and the assassination of President Kennedy? Or would it not be reasonable to say that those who had killed JFK to get rid of him from government were not about to let another Kennedy take his place? I refer you to the words of the Cuban pilot in Chapter Twenty-four.

When President Kennedy died on 22 November, and Lee Harvey Oswald was disposed of two days later, the scene was set for an enormous cover-up. This, however, would have been to no avail if a competent investigation had exposed the truth. What was the problem with the Warren Commission? The problem came in the shape of ex-CIA Director Allen Dulles and Representative John J. McCloy. It has been known for many years that Dulles and McCloy dominated procedures in the Commission. Veteran researcher Harold Weisberg was the first to reveal this, although others have underlined the fact. Earl Warren was chairman in name only – a figurehead. He did not control what went on, nor the conclusions drawn. The other members of the Commission knew it was being railroaded and, with the exception of Gerald Ford, they voiced their unhappiness and lack of support for the resultant report. It would seem that the final conclusion – that Lee Harvey Oswald, alone, was responsible for the assassination of the President – was reached before the Commission began its work.

Dulles and McCloy were mainly responsible for the appointment of J. Lee

Rankin as General Counsel, and between the three of them, they played the decisive role in running the show. Dulles had been fired by Kennedy following the Bay of Pigs débâcle and should never have been considered for membership of the Warren Commission. But then both Dulles and McCloy were Establishment figures. Dulles had been a director of the Jiteny Schroder Banking Corporation and was a member of Washington's exclusive Metropolitan Club, whilst McCloy had been president of the World Bank and chairman of the Board of Chase-Manhattan Bank. He was also a trustee of the Rockefeller Foundation and held directorships in the Union Pacific Railroad, the powerful United Fruit organisation, AT&T, Allied Chemicals and Metropolitan Life, among others. While there is no doubt that the government and government agencies appear to have been determined to conceal the truth of how and why John F. Kennedy was murdered, the so-called presidential investigation was, incredibly, largely in the hands of the Establishment, it seems. Did the Establishment have it all in hand at all levels and all stages?

Since the death of President Kennedy in 1963 the American people have honoured his memory and held it in the highest esteem, much to the frustration of the Establishment and also members of successive governments. To them, the affection and esteem bestowed upon the slain Kennedy is an embarrassment. They want this man to disappear, to be buried and forgotten, once for all. They hope that the passage of time and the numerous attacks made on his memory will have that effect, and that the Warren version of affairs, if left in place long enough, will be the only account of his demise to survive in the history books.

Those interested – or involved – members of the Establishment must find it hard to understand why the memory of John F. Kennedy survives as it does. After all, there was the full-scale attack made on his reputation when the lurid details of his womanising were revealed. The people of the United States acknowledged Kennedy's weaknesses, however, and were magnanimous in not allowing them to sully their affection for the man. Also, without entering into dispute that Kennedy had weaknesses, it was, of course, realised that the truth may have differed considerably from what the muckrakers wrote about him, and he was not around to argue his corner.

Nor was this the only attempt to blight the people's perception of their lost President. I was in the United States at the time of the 30-year remembrance of his death and randomly bought one or two newspapers. I was shocked to read the attacks made, not so much on his personal life, but on what he stood for, his presidency and his achievements. In the *Dallas Morning News* dated 17 November 1993, columnist David Broder, whose work was distributed by the *Washington Post* Writers' Group, no less, said:

> Thirty years after his death, John F. Kennedy has left the realms of mythology and become a figure in history. It's a good thing for him – and for his country The mythologized Mr Kennedy was the architect of a political and generational revolution bold in breaking from the weary policies of the past. Had he not been untimely murdered, the myth goes, he would have spared the young people of America the agony of Vietnam, supplied them with a thriving economy, and a sense of public service.

He got it right, but what Kennedy was, and what he achieved, is now consigned to mythology, which, to me, smacks of wishful thinking. Broder continues, spending a large part of his column quoting Richard Reeves (*President Kennedy: Profile of Power*):

> [He was] a capable but seriously flawed politician and person, often uncertain and overly cautious. [He reacted] to events he often neither foresaw nor understood. He had little ideology beyond anti-communism and faith in active pragmatic government.

But this jaundiced view from Broder/Reeves did not get into the contest of knocking Kennedy compared to Jon Carroll of the *The Atlanta Journal* in their 23 November 1993 issue, however. Under the headline, 'Thirty years after JFK's assassination, fraudulent Kennedy mystique persists', he wades in with:

> Kennedy was the first great fraud of the post-modern era. He was the surprised and grateful object of a mass delusion . . . John F. Kennedy was a bit-player, insignificant historically, unimpressive intellectually, unappetising morally. **And it matters not at all who shot him.** [Author's empasis.] LBJ was a fraud too, but he was a fraud who liked to pass good laws. The Kennedy mystique changed the way America thought about its presidents, and it changed it for the worse . . . Camelot.. Why the hell did we need that?

This requires no comment from me, though I should add that Jon Carroll was also a columnist for the *San Francisco Chronicle*. Returning to the *Dallas Morning News*, this time their 21 November 1993 Sunday edition, an article quotes author G. Paterson saying that Americans today must

> . . . reckon with a past that has not always matched [their image] of

> Kennedy as their young, fallen hero who never had a chance. Actually, he had his chance and he failed.

This, then, was the press in 1993. It is, at best, all myth, mythology and mystique. At worst the accomplishments of President Kennedy are swept aside and I cannot help feeling that the Establishment was well pleased with its journalists who attacked the memory of President Kennedy. Unhappily for them it appears not to have dented the feelings of the people towards their fallen President.

The book, *Case Closed* by Gerald Posner came out about the time of the 30th anniversary, coinciding with the anti-Kennedy press we have described above. I find it hard to believe this was not part of an overall strategy on the part of the Establishment to discredit the memory of John F. Kennedy. It would appear that never in the history of publishing has a book obtained the volume of publicity – worth millions of dollars, if purchased – accorded to this book, and I find that suspicious by itself. The publicity was not reserved exclusively for America; it appears it stretched across the world. It certainly was featured in a big way in Britain and in British newspapers. But this was no ordinary book on the assassination. This was a forceful re-assertion of the Warren position. It railed against Oswald, who was painted an all-out villain, and even presented the findings of a three-dimensional computer study which entirely supported the Warren case against Oswald. What Mr Posner failed to tell his readers, however, was that the makers of the computer study, Failure Analysis of California, made a twin study which defended Oswald and opposed the Warren findings, therefore producing a totally different result. There were many shortcomings in Mr Posner's book, and his attack on the respected researchers who have contributed so much to our understanding of what really happened was beneath contempt. Mr Posner has never been an accredited 'Kennedy researcher': he is a lawyer, and he behaved as a lawyer prosecuting an accused who had no benefit of defence counsel and was, therefore, totally at his mercy.

Make no mistake, the United States suffered nothing less than a coup d'etat when President Kennedy was killed. This was a powerful force asserting itself over the will and best interests of the people. Kennedy was to be removed at all costs. Asked privately who was responsible for President Kennedy's murder, I have it from a first-hand source that President Lyndon B. Johnson replied, 'It was the oil men and the CIA.' Translating 'oil men' to the wider Establishment and accepting 'CIA' to refer to 'renegades' to whom we have alluded before (and not to the CIA as a whole), I can agree with this. In the past I have called the perpetrators men from 'big business' with the CIA 'renegades' who might easily, in turn, have sought help in finding the marksmen from Mafia figures. In my book *Vendetta: the Kennedys* I bestowed the name of Consortium upon those representatives of the Establishment who met together to plan the murder of their President. That will do. I am clear in my own mind this was the work of that other 'government', the Establishment, and that the reason for their determination to kill Kennedy was the erosion of their power and influence, which the President had soundly undertaken as the policy of his government in favour of the improvement in quality of life for all Americans and those in other lands.

It would seem there has been an unhappy legacy from the way the government reacted to the assassination of its President. I have learned from my many friends in the United States that it was from the time of Kennedy's death and the Warren Report cover-up that attitudes towards government began to change in America. People began to realise that those who held power had other agendas – higher priorities – than holding faith with them. And if those in power could be party to the great deception of the Warren Report then they could be party to other deceptions. For many Americans, whatever confidence in government remained was to be further undermined by the Watergate scandal which hit the Nixon administration but a few years later. What happened to the noble Constitution of the United States established by the founding fathers? What happened to the Great American Dream? Where do we look for American idealism?

The suggestion may well be true that the situation will not be remedied until there is a return by government to investigate the Kennedy assassination truly and thoroughly, allocating to the investigation all the funds it requires and all the time it needs. In the period which has elapsed since the Kennedy tragedy, there is no denying that the country has done well economically and the people have enjoyed a rising prosperity. No one can argue with this, nor fail to appreciate the important benefits which have been obtained from this affluence. Many Americans have begun to ask, however, what has happened to the soul of the nation: what is happening to the fabric of society and where, also, do we look for the lost innocence of this great nation? President George W. Bush, in a campaign speech on television in the autumn of 2000, said:

> Our wallets are full but our hearts are empty. It's time we put the heart back in America.

A nation graphically represented by the triumphant eagle, the United States is well equipped to revitalise itself in future generations, but instead of the politicians – who have lost the people's trust – controlling the nation, cannot the nation contrive to control the politicians? Isn't that the way it was intended to be? And is there not the means of keeping government out of the hands of big business? Must the people really say goodbye to the America they knew?

I am convinced the people of the United States will never forget John F. Kennedy. He is truly their tragic hero. But will they allow those who represent them in government to forget him, what he stood for, and why and how he died? And will the history books finally record the truth about what happened on 22 November 1963?

Bibliography

Bishop, Jim. *The Day Kennedy Was Shot*. Funk & Wagnalls, New York 1968

Blair, Joan and Clay, Jr. *The Search for J.F.K.* Berkley Pub. Corp., New York 1976

Blumenthal, Sid (Ed). *Government By Gunplay*. Signet, New York 1976

Brennan, Howard L. with Cherryholmes, J. Edward . *Eyewitness to History*. Texian Press, Waco Tx. 1987

Buchanan, Thomas G. *Who Killed Kennedy?* Secker and Warburg, London 1964

Crenshaw, Charles A. MD. *JFK Conspiracy of Silence*. Penguin Books USA Inc., New York 1992

DiEugenio, James. *Destiny Betrayed*. Sheridan Square Press, New York 1992

Epstein, Edward Jay. *Legend: The Secret World of Lee Harvey Oswald*. Hutchinson & Co. (Pubs) Ltd, London 1978

Fox, Sylvan. *The Unanswered Questions About President Kennedy's Assassination*. Award Books, New York 1965

Galanor, Stewart. *Cover-up*. Kestrel Books, New York 1998

Garrison, Jim. *On the Trail of the Assassins*. Sheridan Square Press, New York 1988

Gibson, Donald. *Battling Wall Street*. Sheridan Square Press, New York 1994

Gibson, Donald. *The Kennedy Assassination Cover-up*. Nova Science Pubs. Inc., New York 2000

Groden, Robert J. *The Killing of a President*. Viking Penguin, New York 1993

Groden, Robert J. and Livingstone, Harrison E. *High Treason*. The Conservatory Press, Baltimore, Maryland 1989

Hoffman, Ed and Friedrich, Ron. *Eye Witness. JFK* Lancer Prods. and Pubs., Grand Prairie, Tx. 1997

Hosty, James P. Jr. *Assignment: Oswald.* Arcade Publishing Inc., New York 1996

Hepburn, James. *Farewell America.* Frontiers Pub. Co., Vaduz, Liechtenstein 1968

Keith, Jim (Ed). *The Gemstone File.* IllumiNet Press, Atlanta Ga. 1992

La Fontaine, Ray and Mary. *Oswald Talked.* Pelican Pub. Co. Inc., Gretna, Louisiana 1996

Lane, Mark. *Rush to Judgement.* Thunder's Mouth Press, New York 1966, 1992

Lane, Mark. *Plausible Denial.* Thunder's Mouth Press, New York 1991

Lasky, Victor. *J.F.K. The Man and the Myth.* The Macmillan Co., New York 1963

Lifton, David S. *Best Evidence.* Macmillan Pub. Co. Inc., New York 1980

Lorenz, Marita with Schwarz, Ted. *Marita.* Thunder's Mouth Press, New York 1993

Manchester, William. *Death of a President.* Michael Joseph Ltd., London 1967

Manchester, William. *One Brief Shining Moment.* Little, Brown & Co., New York 1983

Marrs, Jim. *Crossfire.* Carroll and Graf, New York, 1989

Marrs, Jim. *Rule By Secrecy.* Harper Collins Pubs. Inc., New York 2000

Meagher, Sylvia. *Accessories After the Fact.* Bobbs-Merrill Inc., New York 1967

Morrow, Robert D. *First Hand Knowledge: How I Participated in the CIA-Mafia Murder of President Kennedy.* S.P.I. Books, New York 1992

Newman, John. *Oswald and the CIA.* Carroll and Graf, New York, 1995

North, Mark. *Act of Treason.* Carroll and Graf, New York 1991

Prouty, L. Fletcher. *The Secret Team.* Inst. For Historical Review. Costa Mesa, Ca. 1973 & 1992

Scheim, David E. *Contract on America: The Mafia Murder of President John F. Kennedy.* Shapolsky Publishers Inc., New York 1988. Published in Britain as *The Mafia Killed President Kennedy.* W.H. Allen, London 1988

Shaw, J. Gary with Harris, Larry Ray . *Cover-up.* Thomas Pubs. Inc., Austin, Tx. 1976, 1992

Sorenson, Theodore C. *Kennedy.* Harper & Row, New York 1965

Summers, Anthony. *The Kennedy Conspiracy.* McGraw-Hill Book Co. New York 1980; Revised Warner Books, New York 1992

Thompson, Josiah. *Six Seconds in Dallas.* Berkley Medallion Books, New York 1967

Twyman, Noel. *Bloody Treason.* Laurel Publishing, Rancho Santa Fe, Ca. 1997

Weberman, Alan J. and Canfield, Michael. *Coup d'etat in America.* Quick American Archives, San Francisco, Ca. 1975

Wecht, Cyril, MD, JD. *Cause of Death.* The Penguin Group, New York 1993

Weisberg Harold. *Post Mortem.* Harold Weisberg, Publisher, Frederick, Md., 21701, 1969

Zirbel, Craig I. *The Texas Connection: The Assassination of John F. Kennedy.* TCC Publishers, Scottsdale, Arizona 1991

Name Index

Subject Index